The Church Says Amen

The Church Says Amen

An Exposition of the Belgic Confession

by

J. VAN BRUGGEN

INHERITANCE PUBLICATIONS
NEERLANDIA, ALBERTA, CANADA
PELLA, IOWA, U.S.A.

National Library of Canada Cataloguing in Publication Data
Bruggen, J. van (Jan van), 1909-1965
  The church says amen : an exposition of the Belgic Confession / J. Van Bruggen.

Translation of: Amen der kerk.
Includes bibliographical references.
ISBN 0-921100-17-5

1. Belgic Confession. 2. Reformed Church—Creeds. 3. Reformed Church—Doctrines. I. Title.
BX9429.B4B7813 2003   238'.42   C2003-910223-8

Library of Congress Cataloging-in-Publication Data
Bruggen, J. van (Jan van), 1909-1965.
  [Amen der kerk. English]
  The church says amen : an exposition of the Belgic Confession / by J. van Bruggen.
      p. cm.
Includes index.
  ISBN 0-921100-17-5 (pbk.)
  1. Belgic Confession. 2. Reformed Church—Creeds. 3. Reformed Church—Doctrines. I. Title.
BX9429.B4B7813 2003
238'.42—dc21
                                                                                                2002156701

Originally published as *Het amen der kerk: De Nederlandse Geloofsbelijdenis toegelicht* by Oosterbaan & Le Cointre, Goes, 1964 (seventh printing, 1977), The Netherlands.

Translated by Johanna VanderPlas
The translator expresses her great appreciation to Rev. G. VanRongen and Mr. J. Numan for their willingness to edit the translation as thoroughly as they did. A heartfelt thankyou to you both for so ably answering my questions and providing corrections.

The Scripture quotations in this publication are from The Holy Bible, New King James Version, copyright 1982, and are used with permission from Thomas Nelson Inc., Publishers.

Cover Photo: *Grote Kerk, Oudewater* by Carel van Gestel
Oldenhof 14, 6665 DP Driel, The Netherlands

All rights reserved © 2003 by Inheritance Publications
Box 154, Neerlandia, Alberta Canada T0G 1R0
Tel. (780) 674 3949
Web site: http://www.telusplanet.net/public/inhpubl/webip/ip.htm
E-Mail inhpubl@telusplanet.net

Published simultaneously in U.S.A. by Inheritance Publications
Box 366, Pella, Iowa 50219

Available in Australia from Inheritance Publications
Box 1122, Kelmscott, W.A. 6111 Tel. & Fax (089) 390 4940

Contents

Chapter / Article   *Page*

Preface by C. Bouwman 7

Chapter I: The Confessions 9
Chapter II: The Belgic Confession 15

The Articles of the Belgic Confession

1. There Is Only One God 21
2. How God Makes Himself Known to Us 26
3. The Word of God 30
4. The Canonical Books of Holy Scripture 33
5. The Authority of Holy Scripture 37
6. The Difference Between the Canonical
 and Apocryphal Books 41
7. The Sufficiency of Holy Scripture 43
8. God Is One in Essence, Yet Distinguished
 in Three Persons 49
9. Scripture Proof of this Doctrine 55
10. Jesus Christ True and Eternal God 59
11. The Holy Spirit True and Eternal God 62
12. The Creation of All Things, Especially the Angels 67
13. The Providence of God 77
14. The Creation and Fall of Man and His Incapability
 of Doing What Is Truly Good 81
15. Original Sin 89

16. Divine Election	95
17. The Rescue of Fallen Man	101
18. The Incarnation of the Son of God	104
19. The Two Natures in the One Person of Christ	108
20. The Justice and Mercy of God in Christ	112
21. The Satisfaction of Christ Our High Priest	116
22. Our Justification Through Faith in Jesus Christ	122
23. Our Righteousness Before God	129
24. Man's Sanctification and Good Works	133
25. Christ, the Fulfilment of the Law	140
26. Christ's Intercession	144
27. The Catholic or Universal Church	148
28. Everyone's Duty to Join the Church	161
29. The Marks of the True and the False Church	163
30 and 31. The Government of the Church	171
The Officers of the Church	172
32. The Order and Discipline of the Church	178
33. The Sacraments	183
34. The Sacrament of Baptism	189
35. The Sacrament of the Lord's Supper	202
36. The Civil Government	214
37. The Last Judgment	220
Index	228

Preface

Getting doctrine right is the first step to getting life right. The truth of that reality may not be widely accepted today, but it remains reality nevertheless. "Your Word is a lamp to my feet," sang the psalmist, "and a light to my path," and no passage of time or change in culture will alter that truth for the child of God. In no way, therefore, can anyone serious in the service of the Lord consider doctrine to be so much unnecessary lumber burdening us as we walk the road of life.

But what does God say in His Word? What is correct doctrine? Over the centuries of church history, God's people have repeatedly read the Scriptures and sought to apply their promises and obligations in the dust and dirt of daily life. That required people to come to grips with what God said about the origins of man and the cause of our brokenness, about His gracious gift in Jesus Christ and His sacrifice on the cross, about the work of the Holy Spirit and the regeneration of man, and so very much more. As they studied and meditated on God's revelation, Christians over the centuries repeated after God in their own words what they heard God say in the Bible. Through processes of debate and conflict the Holy Spirit gave God's people greater and clearer insight into His Word, and so enabled His people to echo with greater accuracy His promises to sinners. This effort to say in their own words what they heard God say in the Bible has produced those documents known as Confessions — of which there are numerous, of greater or lesser clarity and accuracy.

One confession that has become universally known as a clear and accurate summary of God's revelation is the well-known *Belgic Confession*, penned by Guido de Brés in 1561. This confession was soon treasured by the Reformed Churches of The Netherlands and over the years followed Dutch emigrants around the world wherever the Lord gave a place to faithful offspring of the Dutch Reformation. Its impact in the societies and cultures where these emigrants settled has been enormous, and indeed continues to be enormous simply because it echoes so plainly and faithfully what God has revealed in Scripture.

Throughout the English-speaking western world, today's generation is taught to give more credence to one's personal experiences and thoughts than to the wisdom our fathers accumulated over their years of being busy with God's revelation. That can only mean an impoverishment for the future, simply because the human heart is depraved and therefore by nature not tuned in to God's revelation. To act as if we are the first to read God's word is folly to the extreme. We need to stand on the shoulders of those who have gone before us, to learn how they applied God's promises in the grit and grime of life's struggles, and repeat for ourselves (be it with words learned from them) what God has promised also to us — for His promises do not change. That need makes a good commentary on a treasured confession invaluable for today's English-speaking Christians.

Over the years the best English commentary available on the *Belgic Confession* was P.Y. de Jong's *The Church's Witness to the World*. This commentary, however, laboured under the shared burdens of wordiness and scholasticism. Various popular commentaries have appeared over the years to fill the gap (including my *Notes on the Belgic Confession*), but none sufficiently provided the solid and learned exposition this confession required. For that reason an effort was undertaken to make available to the English world the commentary by Rev. J. van Bruggen — a work that has stood the test of time and been a great blessing to many.

May the Lord grant that this work be received in the English-speaking world as readily as it was in the Dutch-speaking world where it first appeared, and so be of service in equipping today's generation of modern Christians to echo whole-heartedly the glorious promises God has given in Jesus Christ.

Kelmscott, Western Australia					C. Bouwman

CHAPTER I

THE CONFESSIONS

1. Definition

A confession is a document in which the Church expresses what it considers to be the truth according to the Word of God. It is thus not a private document, but a document which the Church has compiled or accepted as an expression of its common faith. "Considers to be the truth" does not imply a lack of absolute certainty, but rather means to "accept" and "treat" something as the truth. It has the same meaning as the word "count" in the Form for the Lord's Supper: "that God will count us worthy to partake of the supper of our Lord Jesus Christ."

2. The Church's right and obligation

In 1 Timothy 3:15 the Church is called the "pillar and ground of the truth." The Church, therefore, has the task of making the truth known (pillar = bulletin board) and upholding it (ground) in the world. This does not mean that the truth as such is dependent on the Church, for the truth rests in God, but in the world, the community which bears and upholds the truth is the Church.

In order to fulfil this calling, the Church has been promised the guidance of the Holy Spirit. It must perform this calling as a "communion of saints." This is essential because God, in Scripture, repeatedly speaks in relation to specific times, circumstances, and people. Scripture does not contain precisely formulated answers to our questions. Those answers lie buried in it like gold in ore. Scripture is not, therefore, merely to be listened to, but rather, to be searched out. To understand God's Word for us and for all times from the always concrete speech of God, which is bound to time and place, is not a task that one person alone can accomplish. After all, Ephesians 3:17-19 says, "that you, being rooted and grounded in love, may be able to comprehend with all the saints what is the width and length and depth and height — to know the love of Christ which passes knowledge; that you may be filled with all the fullness of God."

Now the Church must not only proclaim the truth but must also uphold it against the thoughts of unbelief which seek to obscure and push aside God's Word. Scripture itself is clear, but "those who are untaught and unstable twist [it] to their own destruction" (2 Peter 3:16). It will not suffice, therefore, for the Church simply to point to Scripture, as is the tendency of Biblicism. The Church must also say *what* it reads in Scripture.

For all these reasons it is necessary for the Church to confess the Word of God (confess = repeat, to say the same as). The Church has both the right and the obligation to do so.

3. Authority of the Confessions

The Confessions are not above or alongside Holy Scripture but below it. They have a derivative authority. Scripture has its own authority. But when the Confessions are faithful to Scripture and repeat it, they really do have authority. Within the Church, where this authority is acknowledged, one may appeal to them as to a decisive authority, and everyone must recognize their authority.

4. Purpose of the Confessions

The Confessions serve:
- A. to give public testimony to the truth of the faith and the doctrine of the Church (presentation of the Belgic Confession to Philip II)
- B. to preserve the truth for future generations (Heidelberg Catechism)
- C. to uphold the truth in opposition to error (Canons of Dort)
- D. to bring to expression, preserve, and promote the unity of all believers (Three Forms of Unity)

5. The Confessions of the Reformed Churches

A. The Ecumenical Creeds (listed in Article 9 of the Belgic Confession)

1. *The Apostles' Creed*, which developed from the confession of faith at baptism and has been known in its present form since approximately A.D. 500.

2. *The Nicene Creed*. This title is incorrect. Its correct title is the *Nicaeno-Constantinopolitan Creed*. This creed presents a summary of the decisions made by the councils of Nicea and Constantinople concerning Christ's divinity and the Trinity.

3. *The Athanasian Creed*. This title too is definitely incorrect because the wording of this creed is not to be found in any of the writings of Athanasius. It should be called *Quicumque*, which is the creed's Latin opening word. "Whosoever (Lat. *Quicumque*) will be saved . . ." Its origin is unknown. It presents the Augustinian development of the doctrine concerning God and Christ.

B. The Three Forms of Unity

1. *The Belgic Confession*. Thirty-seven articles drafted by Guido de Brés and made public in 1561.

2. *The Heidelberg Catechism*. Divided into fifty-two Lord's Days and drafted by Zacharius Ursinus and Caspar Olevianus in 1563.

3. *The Canons of Dort*, also called the Five Articles Against the Remonstrants.[1] They were drafted by the Synod of Dort in 1618-1619 and deal with:

   I. Divine election and reprobation
   II. Christ's death and the redemption of man by it
   III/IV. Man's corruption and his conversion to God and the manner in which these things come about
   V. The perseverance of the saints

Each chapter is followed by a "Rejection of Errors" concerning the doctrine confessed in that chapter.

In order to understand the Church's doctrine, the liturgical forms are also important. The word "form" comes from the Latin word *forma* (fixed form). A form is a document which gives a fixed form to the Church's unity or to its practice in connection with the administration of the sacraments, the exercise of discipline, and so forth.

---

[1] The Remonstrants (Arminians) were the followers of Jacob Arminius. — TRANS.

6. Appreciation and disputation

The Roman Catholic Church considers its doctrinal decisions to be infallible. When the Pope speaks from his chair (*ex cathedra*) and fulfils his office of Shepherd and Teacher of all Christians, he possesses infallibility by the divine assistance promised to him in Saint Peter. All papal rulings concerning faith and morality, therefore, are infallible in their own right and not in virtue of the consent of the universal Church. How much this view clashes with what Holy Scripture teaches us should be clear from Article 7 of the Belgic Confession.

The value we ascribe to the Confessions is explained in paragraphs 2, 3, and 4 of this chapter. But this appreciation for the Confessions as a repetition of Scripture and therefore as a measuring-line has been disputed from of old, even within the Protestant camp.

The Anabaptists, who, as fanatics, rejected all external authority, did not want to acknowledge the authority of Scripture and accused Luther of having freed us from the Roman Pope only to replace him with a paper Pope (the Bible). It is understandable, then, that they did not want any confessional authority either.

Later on, Biblicism did not want to acknowledge any confessions either. It was of the opinion that Holy Scripture was sufficient for us and that the recognition of a confession conflicted with the sufficiency and clarity of Scripture. Moreover, a confession would not do justice to the majesty of the Word.

The Arminians and all adherents to Liberal Theology were strongly opposed to confessions. They wanted to recognize them, at most, as a declaration which would tell people our subjective opinions. They did not want to hear of the Confessions having any authority. That would conflict with the majesty of God's Word, enslave the conscience, and cause divisions.

Today, the authority of the Confessions is especially disputed by dialectical theology. Karl Barth is the father of this theology. Barth's starting point is always his philosophical speculation about God as "the wholly Other." Between Him, the Exalted One, and us, insignificant inhabitants of the earth, no communion is possible. He is always transcendent, and above and beyond us. His absolute freedom, in which He is not limited in any respect, does make it possible for Him to speak to us. But we cannot capture and reproduce His divine Word, which splits open the rocks, in our human words. When He speaks to us, it is like lightning tearing through a sheet of paper. There is contact, but the paper cannot hold the lightning. At best, a tiny hole may have been scorched into the paper, a "sign" indicating where the lightning struck. In the same way, what we call "God's Word" is no more than a sign that He has spoken, not His true Word itself. At best it is a footprint in the snow, but that is merely a reminder of the foot, not the foot itself. According to Barth, therefore, our talk about God must always be dialectical (dialogue; word and response). It must be yes and no at the same time. We can never speak about Him in a single affirmation (confirmatory pronouncement) as if we "had" Him. Every affirmation must at the same time also be a negation. We never have the truth about God cut and dried and at our disposal. Barth therefore fulminates against Roman Catholics and Calvinists who suppose that they have the truth at their disposal and have it recorded in their formulas. A pronouncement about God is at best a horizon within which we move, a signpost pointing the way to the truth, but never the truth itself.

This is the theological construction which presently dominates the whole spirit of the Dutch Reformed (State) Church. It thinks that the renewal that has taken place there has taken the Confessions out of the safe, where formerly it lay safely hidden without exercising any influence. Nevertheless, the people do not want to be bound to any confession. They desire not a confessional Church but a confessing Church. (This is a false contrast: in order to be a confessing Church, a confession is required.) Article 10 of the new Church Order of the Dutch Reformed (State) Church, which was adopted in 1951, states, "The Church confesses the self-revelation of the Triune God in harmony with the confession of the fathers." That may sound beautiful. But it raises questions. What is the confession of the fathers? What is the content of that confession? Furthermore, what does "in harmony with" mean? Thus they want to confess but leave the content of the confession undecided. It isn't surprising, then, that people do not want to hear anything about a Reformed respect for the authority of the Confessions as a repetition of God's Word.

In synodical Reformed circles[2] it is increasingly argued that the Confessions have authority only in the sphere of the church. In science, politics, and social organizations a person must arrive at his own formulation of what the Word of God requires for those spheres (the famous "Christian principles"). The desire to bind education and politics to the Church's confession is regarded as ecclesiasticizing life, and this is railed against as churchism and a Roman Catholic practice. Christian life, however, is undivided. The faith confessed and preached in the Church must be preserved and put into practice in education, politics, and everything.

In these circles, one also hears people pleading constantly for "reducing the Confession." People want to go back to the twelve articles of the Apostles' Creed, and on that basis unite Christians who are presently divided on a wide variety of issues. But the Three Forms of Unity simply confess what is already contained in the Apostles' Creed. To put aside this more elaborate formulation of faith, which came about as a result of later conflicts, would only re-open the way to all of those errors condemned in the past.

Over against all this false prophecy we do well within the communion of saints to recognize with joy the authority of the Confessions because they enable us to understand what the Church, on the basis of Scripture, believes with the heart and confesses with the mouth.

---

[2] "Synodical Reformed circles" refers to the Reformed Churches in The Netherlands (syn.) after they deposed Dr. Klaas Schilder (and many other faithful office bearers) in 1944. These actions caused the Liberation of 1944. — Editor.

CHAPTER II

THE BELGIC CONFESSION

1. Guido de Brés

Guido de Brés, the author of our Confession, was born in 1522 in Bergen, Henegouwen (in today's Belgium). He received a Roman Catholic upbringing and as a result of personal Bible study made a resolute break with the Roman Catholic Church and joined the Reformation. He was less than twenty-five years old at the time.

He had to flee to England, and later, when he became a minister, had to flee again to France. At that time he also visited Switzerland. On these journeys he met a number of prominent figures of the Reformation: Johannes a Lasco, Martin Micron, Utenhove, and others, including John Calvin. From 1552 to 1556 he was a travelling minister in Rijssel and its surrounding areas. After that he had to flee to France.

On his return he took up the position of minister in Doornik. There he lived in a shabby house, while a small summer-house near the city walls served as his study. He compiled the Confession in this summer-house, and on the night of the 1st to the 2nd of November, 1561, it was thrown over the walls of the castle of Doornik in a sealed parcel so that in this way it might reach the king of Spain. It was accompanied by a letter addressed to His Majesty.

De Brés fled from his summer-house and the Inquisition seized his library. From official reports we know that it was of considerable size and included works of Calvin, Luther, Melanchthon, Zwingli, Oecolampadius, and others. The official records also report numerous notes which De Brés had made from Scripture and from the works of these reformers. Having been imprisoned in Valenciennes, he was hanged there on the gallows on May 31, 1567. In cheerful confidence of faith he sealed his confession with martyrdom.

2. *Le Baston de la Foy*

In 1555 De Brés published a booklet which appeared in an expanded reprint in 1562. In translation, the title is, *The Staff of Faith, Able to Shut the Mouths of Faith's Enemies*. The title page adds, "Hereby one can also learn about the antiquity of our faith and of the true Church. Compiled from Holy Scripture, books of the old Church leaders, councils, and many other writers." The smaller edition consisted of 570 pages. It was an attack on *Le Bouclier de la Foy (Shield of Faith)*, written by Nicole Grenier, regular canon of St. Victor, and published in Paris in 1547. In his *Baston* De Brés presents the works listed on the title page as an antidote to Grenier's Roman Catholic propaganda.

3. *La Racine*

In 1565 De Brés put out another booklet which was translated into Dutch as early as 1570 under the title, *The Root, the Origin, and the Foundation of the Anabaptists or Rebaptizers of Our Time*. The title page adds, "With abundant refutations of the most peculiar arguments with which they are accustomed to disturb the Church of our Lord Jesus Christ and to deceive the simple." This booklet is a defence against the Anabaptist errors concerning Christ's incarnation, the baptism of infants, and so forth. Anabaptist fanaticism was a grave danger for the Church of the Reformation, and this error was being propagated by clever men.

It is obvious that these two books are of great significance for an understanding of what De Brés meant in various passages in his confession. Although we are not to explain the Confession on the basis of all kinds of theological writings but rather on the basis of Holy Scripture, that does not negate the fact that in order to understand its original meaning these books by De Brés are of immense value.[3]

4. The Church's acceptance

Already in 1561 the congregation at Antwerp accepted Guido de Brés' *Confession de Foy* and in 1563 the provincial Synod of

---

[3] Much of the content of these books can be found in C. Vonk, *De Voorzeide Leer*, vols. IIIa, b (Barendrecht: Drukkerij Barendrecht, 1956).

Armentieres accepted it. Office-bearers already had to subscribe to it at that time as a testimony to their doctrinal unity. Likewise at the Convention of Wesel, 1568, and at the Synod of Emden, 1571, our Confession functioned "to demonstrate the unanimity in doctrine among the Churches of The Netherlands," and Emden, 1571, decided "to subscribe to the Confession of faith of the Churches of The Netherlands." The National Synod of Dort, 1618-19, pronounced "that this Confession did not contain any teaching in conflict with the truth expressed in Holy Scripture, but on the contrary, everything in it conformed to that truth and to the Confessions of the other Reformed Churches." In this way the Confession was quickly accepted as a document of the Church.

The Synod of Dort drew up a form for subscription to the confession by the ministers, in which they declared that they felt and believed from the heart that the doctrine contained in the Confessions was in full agreement with God's Word and that they "consequently" promised to preach this doctrine and not to oppose it.

This Form of Subscription was used until King William established his State Church in 1816. From then on ministers had to declare that they would "accept in good faith the doctrine which, in conformity to God's Word, is contained in the accepted forms of the Church of The Netherlands . . ." This change opened the way for the view that one had to teach the doctrine of the Confessions not *because*, but *insofar* as it conformed to Scripture. In this way Liberalism was given a legal place in the Church.

5. Text

Guido de Brés wrote the Confession in 1561 in French. A Dutch translation of it was already available in 1562. In 1583, Rev. Arent Cornelissen, minister at Delft, produced a Dutch translation of the modified Confession of the Synod of Antwerp, 1566. In the first edition there were no headings for the various articles. Articles were merely numbered. Rev. Cornelissen assigned headings to all the articles. In his edition he also included the texts which had already been printed in the margin of the first edition. In 1611 the Synod of Veere produced a new translation of the text of Antwerp, 1566.

The Inquisition was in hot pursuit of this booklet and eradicated it as much as possible. As a result, copies were often scarce. And naturally the confusion at that time did not help in producing an accurate edition. There were some differences between the various editions due to printing errors and inaccuracies on the part of the publishers. The Synod of Dort put an end to this confusing state of affairs. It gave the mandate to establish a French, Dutch, and Latin text. Due to time constraints, however, a decision on a Latin text was not made in its sessions. The Synod of Dort omitted the headings above the articles to which the Remonstrants had remarked. These headings do reappear in modern editions, but they are not to be taken as official. The Synod of Dort also omitted the texts in connection with the articles.

6. The polemical character

Our Confession was born out of the struggle of the Church. In this struggle two main fronts can be identified.

A. The Roman Catholic front.

In the Middle Ages, the Church of the Lord was extremely corrupt. Its doctrine had virtually become total error. It taught the free will of man and the merit of good works. It transformed the Lord's supper into an idolatrous mass. It imposed celibacy upon the shepherds, who had been transformed into priests. It believed it could grant absolution by means of confession. There were many other errors as well. Our Confession fights against all the errors of this deformed communion. Think of Guido de Brés' *Le Baston*.

B. The Anabaptist front.

The fanaticism of the Anabaptists, of which we have already spoken, was an extremely dangerous threat to the faith, and De Brés wrote his *La Racine* against this error. Throughout the Confession, too, it is precisely this fanaticism which is rejected. Our Confession is thus truly a document born out of the struggle of the spirits of the sixteenth century. But it is not, for that reason, outdated. An error may manifest itself in different forms in different times, but in essence it never changes. How could it be otherwise, after all, since the truth which it opposes is always the same? The Confession continues to present the weapons we require in the struggle today.

7. Division

The Confession deals in principle consecutively with the following:

A. God and the means by which He is known (1-11)
B. Creation, providence, the fall and its consequences (12-15)
C. Election, Christ, and the benefits of salvation (16-26)
D. The Church and its sacraments (27-35) and its protectors (36, 37)

The Articles of the Belgic Confession
A Commentary and Explanation

ARTICLE 1
THERE IS ONLY ONE GOD

> *We all believe with the heart and confess with the mouth that there is only one God, who is a simple and spiritual Being; He is eternal, incomprehensible, invisible, immutable, infinite, almighty, perfectly wise, just, good, and the overflowing fountain of all good.*

1. "We ... believe with the heart and confess with the mouth"

Only the first article begins with these words, derived from Romans 10:9, 10. Most of the articles that follow start with "We believe." These two words, however, imply the lengthier introductory clause of Article 1, "We ... believe with the heart and confess with the mouth." This opening indicates that what is expressed in the articles is not a matter of personal insight or consideration, but rather has been learned from the Word of God by accepting that Word in faith. These words indicate that this confession is not merely a matter of intellectual understanding, but a matter of wholehearted and total acceptance. We believe with the heart!

In the tense days of the Reformation there were many who said, "Precisely because faith is a matter of the heart, it need not be discussed" (Nicodemites).[4] Others considered it superfluous to have

---

[4] The Nicodemites were French Protestants who inwardly agreed with the Reformation, but for fear of persecution did not terminate their membership and participation in the Roman Catholic Church. They excused their failure to stand up for their convictions by claiming that they were following the example of Nicodemus the Pharisee who was afraid to come to Jesus by day. For that reason Calvin called them "Nicodemites." Calvin condemned the attitude of these Protestants and encouraged them to be honest in their convictions, even if persecution would result (Philip Schaff, *History of the Christian Church*, 3rd ed., vol. 8 [Peabody, Massachusetts: Hendrickson Publishers, 1996] pp. 610-614). — TRANS.

to express faith in words since Word, Church, and sacraments were merely external matters and one could say what one wished concerning them (Libertines). Scripture, however, closely connects believing and confessing (see the texts with which Guido de Brés prefaced his Confession: Matthew 10:32, 33; Romans 10:10; 2 Timothy 2:12; 1 Peter 3:15). Calvin asks: Is there ever a fire where flame and heat are lacking? The misconceptions mentioned here continue to be temptations, even today.

2. All

In our discussion of the opening line of this article (see paragraph 1 above), we skipped the little word "all" because it really does deserve special attention. The superbly Reformed significance of this word becomes apparent when we compare the way this article commences with the words of the Roman Catholic Confession of the Vatican Council (1870): "The holy Catholic Roman Church believes and confesses, that there is one true, living God, Creator and Lord of heaven and earth, almighty, eternal, infinite, incomprehensible . . ." and so forth. The content of this article appears quite similar to that of our article. But notice its beginning! Our confession says, "We *all* believe"! The Vatican says, "The . . . church (= the clergy) believes." For the members of the church, it is sufficient if they merely agree with "the church." The Roman church is very indulgent toward their remaining pagan and idolatrous practices so long as its authority is acknowledged. But what kind of faith is that which exists only in the minds of the clergy and, even then, is still nothing more than a system of abstract ideas?

3. No "proof"

God's existence cannot be "proven." If it were possible to "prove" Him, He would not be true God since what we can prove is subject to our insight and thinking. We can only believe in God and know Him because and in so far as He has made Himself known to us by His Word and has caused us to accept that Word in faith. As a result, we are not less certain of God's existence, but our certainty comes in a different manner.

Nevertheless, man has repeatedly attempted to "prove" God's existence. The following examples are just some of the numerous "proofs of God's existence":

A. The religious proof: No one has ever discovered a people entirely without religion. Such a universal notion of God's existence cannot be a product of imagination.

B. The teleological proof: The whole of creation and life is suited to its purpose. This could not have happened if a higher Power had not designed everything in this way.

C. The moral proof: Every person has the idea that he is subject to laws and norms and is accountable to a Higher Power. That indicates that there is indeed such a Higher Power.

All these "proofs," however, could be refuted and they are not convincing.

4. Being

This word of our Confession has given rise to fierce opposition.

It has been said to demonstrate the scholastic design of our Confession and to show clearly that our Confession deviates greatly from the original Reformation. To be sure, this word is not derived from Scripture. The question, however, is whether its meaning is Scriptural. This word too can be misunderstood, especially because it has become loaded with the philosophical speculations concerning "the existence of things." But which word cannot be misinterpreted? De Brés certainly did not hesitate to use this word in order thereby to link up with the early church. The early church did not use it in a philosophical way and neither does our Confession. The purpose of this word is to indicate that God actually *is*.

5. The purpose of the list

This article lists a number of God's attributes (virtues or perfections). It does not intend to be thorough — as if such a thing were possible! It was childish of the Arminians, therefore, to remark that the word "almighty" — inserted by Dort, 1618-19 — was not included in the original Dutch text. Nor is it at all the intention to offer a "definition" (excuse the term) of God. What is offered here is a description of the God we believe in and confess, a description which is glory, praise, and adoration. With each of the words used here we must avoid all philosophical speculation and learn their content from Scripture. Our meditation on God's virtues must be a meditation on Scripture. Then it will not be barren and fruitless, but "a competent teacher of Godliness" (Calvin), by which we learn to expect and desire all things from "the overflowing fountain of all good" and learn to thank Him for all that we receive.

6. One, simple, spiritual

"One" means that there is one God. There is not a single person or thing that bears the slightest resemblance to Him. All the other things that are considered "gods" are idols or non-gods.

"Simple" is not the opposite of "plural" but of "complex." This word stands in opposition to the Arminians — among others — who disconnected God's existence and God's will from each other. It is also opposed to the absolutizing of God's love (in the nineteenth century) and to the present-day theology of solidarity, which speaks of the "struggling" and "suffering" God. The Confession chose this word from the difficult necessity of opposing heresy. In defining this term, however, it is hard to say anything more than the negative: no composition, no contradiction, no tension, no process.

"Spiritual" means "not material." The Barthians claim that in Scripture spiritual is in contrast to fleshly (sinful). According to them, all it says here is that God is far from sin but nothing definite is said about whether or not He has a physical body. But regardless of how Scriptural the contrast between flesh and spirit might be, Scripture also recognizes the distinction between matter and spirit. The angels are also spirits, but not like God. They are created spirits.

7. Eternal

Dogmatics distinguishes between *aeternus* and *aeviternus*.[5] Angels and people are *aeviternus*. They have a beginning. God gave them that beginning so that they might exist "eternally." God alone is *aeternus*. He is without beginning or end, and He is not

---

[5] *Aeternus* means without beginning or end; *aeviternus* means eternal but with a beginning. — TRANS.

bound to the succession of moments as is the case in our mode of existence; He transcends time.

8. No semicolon

In his book on the Belgic Confession, Abraham Kuyper put a semicolon after the word "almighty." In so doing he wished to introduce into the text of the Confession the distinction between God's "incommunicable" attributes (before the semicolon) and His "communicable" attributes (after the semicolon). By "communicable attributes" people mean those divine attributes of which God has imparted something to man, as well. God is wise and good, and so is man. "Incommunicable attributes," then, are those attributes which God does not share with man, for example, His invisibility. Our Confession, however, does not recognize such a division and it is unacceptable. We do not share in any of God's attributes. His wisdom is entirely different from ours.

9. Controversy

The confession of Article 1 rejects:

A. Atheism: the claim that there is no God. Materialism is also atheistic.

B. Polytheism: the opinion that there are many gods, an opinion which is found in paganism everywhere.

C. Henotheism, which thinks that each nation has its own God.

D. Agnosticism, which says that we cannot know God and know nothing of Him, so that we can neither confirm nor deny His existence.

E. Scepticism: the philosophical trend which thinks it can arrive at the truth and consequently at the knowledge of God through doubt.

F. Deism: the notion that God and the world are absolutely separate from each other and that God very rarely concerns Himself with the world.

G. Pantheism, which identifies God and the world and denies God His own personal existence outside of the creation.

H. Barthianism with its speculations concerning God's transcendence, which make it impossible for us to say one word of truth about Him, the "wholly Other."

ARTICLE 2
HOW GOD MAKES HIMSELF KNOWN TO US

We know Him by two means: First, by the creation, preservation, and government of the universe; which is before our eyes as a most beautiful book, wherein all creatures, great and small, are as so many letters leading us to perceive clearly the invisible qualities of God namely His eternal power and deity, as the apostle Paul says in Rom 1:20. All these things are sufficient to convict men and leave them without excuse. Second, He makes Himself more clearly and fully known to us by His holy and divine Word as far as is necessary for us in this life, to His glory and our salvation.

1. We know Him.

From various sides it is alleged that we cannot know God. Yet, through His revelation, by which He makes Himself known, we may know Him. Our knowledge of Him is inadequate; it does not equate with who He is. It is, however, correct and sufficient for us (see the conclusion of this article).

2. Two means

It is important to refer to the French and Latin texts here. They speak about *deux moyens* (two ways) and *duobus modis* (*modis* is the ablative plural of *modus*, "way"). That should warn us, at least, not to take "means" to mean "source." The source of our knowledge of God is God Himself. From that source the knowledge of Him comes to us in two ways, by two means. The word "means" implies too that there are no such things as innate ideas or inborn knowledge of God. Nor do we come to know God in a mystical way, simply by becoming absorbed in ourselves.

Neither may we regard creation and Scripture as "sources" from which we can draw our knowledge and which we can do without once we have drawn all our knowledge from them (Rome). God makes Himself known to us by these means and so we are always bound to these means. By the use of these means we ought to listen to Him.

3. The "first means"

The first means is His "creation, preservation, and government of the universe." By this work of God one knows the Worker. Through it He displays His virtues (Psalm 19:1) and the course of history demonstrates His power and government (Psalm 33:10, 11a).

In all of this God makes Himself so clearly perceivable that through these works of God everyone comes to the realization that God exists. Since this revelation through His works comes to all people, it is also known as "general revelation." Since our understanding is darkened, however, of ourselves we misunderstand this revelation. It is as if we are cross-eyed and can read the "book" of general revelation only through the glasses of special revelation, through the Word. Only in the light of the revelation through the Word do God's greatness, power, and wisdom, His goodness and justice in His creation, preservation, and government of all things, become clearly evident to us.

By this "first means" we are not taught what God is and wishes to be for us. It does not teach us about His covenant and His grace in Christ Jesus. "General revelation," then, does not lead to salvation.

4. No "natural" knowledge of God

It did not take long for Reformed theology to take the old scholastic detour, which spoke of two sources of knowledge of God. The Roman Catholic Church has canonized this error in the pronouncement of the Vatican Council (1870): "The holy mother Church maintains and teaches that God, principle and ultimate object of all things, can be known with certainty from creation by the natural light of human reason." There could thus be a natural knowledge of God apart from the Bible. One person judged this more favourably than another, but according to some, one could actually learn everything about God from the "source of creation." In the end it led to people (e.g. German Christians) regarding creation as the real source of the knowledge of God and rejecting Scripture as Jewish speculation.

People have claimed that in the Canons of Dort III/IV, the Reformed Churches confess a natural knowledge of God, but that is not what is meant by the expression "light of nature" found there. It points to the knowledge and insight of creation arrived at through intelligent perception and contemplation and deems it to be very limited.

It must also be noted that this article does not say that all people know God, but that *we* — believers — know God. By faith we know God and we do so by two means, in two ways. In order of existence, the creation may precede the *Word*, but in the order of knowledge the *Word* has priority over the creation. Without the glasses of the *Word* no one can read the book of creation. The unbeliever is unable and unwilling to know God by means of this book. Even though God is revealed in His works, the unbeliever hates God's evidence. He turns off the light that God kindled and replaces it with his smoking candle. His depravity prevents him from knowing God by means of His works.

The non-biblical religions, whose "knowledge of God" consists of an incorrect understanding and a wrong explanation of God's revelation through the works of His hands, are therefore not less completely developed forms of the true religion but are false religions. The difference between heathendom and the faith is not a matter of the one being more or less true than the other but of the lie versus the truth, of falsehood versus truth.

Karl Barth strongly opposed the teaching of the "natural knowledge of God." And rightly so. He was mistaken, however, when he also lashed out at this article for it does not even come close to acknowledging a "natural theology." Barth posited that no one knows God other than Christ alone. We know Him only "in Christ," but that never becomes a knowledge which is ours. But since God has expressed His Name in *our* language, we are able to repeat it and know Him.

5. No excuse

This article says that the effect of the knowledge obtained by God's self-revelation by means of His works is sufficient to leave every man without excuse (see Romans 1:18-31). Once summoned before God's judgment seat, no one shall be able to say that he did not know that God existed or else he would certainly have worshipped Him. "Because, although they knew God, they did not glorify Him as God, nor were thankful" (Romans 1:21; see also 1:22, 23). By His revelation, by the work of His hands, God maintains mankind's responsibility.

There is more that could be said here. "General revelation" also restrains much evil. Furthermore, the notion of the existence of God which all receive in this way opens the way for preaching to people about the God who is still unknown to them.

6. The "second means"

The second means is "His holy and divine Word." We must not immediately think in this connection of the Bible. God's Word already came to man before the slightest beginning of the Bible. This Word, which God first spoke Himself in Paradise and continued to deliver to us "in different ways" (Hebrews 1:1) went through a long history (the history of revelation). As a wise and sensible Teacher, God has followed a long course in order to unveil His secret counsel to us (Q&A 19 of the Heidelberg Catechism).

Adam's knowledge of God before the fall into sin may have been purer than ours because his heart was pure, but our knowledge is richer. Before the fall Adam did not yet know the depth of God's gracious forgiveness of sin, and after the fall he knew of God's love only from the promise about the seed of the woman, but we have the privilege of knowing it through the completed work of the crucified and risen Christ.

Nevertheless, our knowledge too is still incomplete. God's omnipotence is more marvellous and His wisdom greater than we can understand. But we know enough. All that we need to know in this life to God's honour and our salvation the Lord wants to teach us by His Word.

The Bible is certainly not a handbook of all kinds of knowledge. Nevertheless, in that realm too we are safely guided only by the Bible which is a lamp to our feet (Psalm 119:105).

ARTICLE 3
THE WORD OF GOD

We confess that this Word of God did not come by the impulse of man, but that men moved by the Holy Spirit spoke from God, as the apostle Peter says. Thereafter, in His special care for us and our salvation, God commanded His servants, the prophets and apostles, to commit His revealed word to writing and He Himself wrote with His own finger the two tables of the law. Therefore we call such writings holy and divine Scriptures.

1. **Context**

    Articles 3 through 7 all discuss Scripture:
    - Art. 3: the inspiration of Scripture;
    - Art. 4: the canonicity (= genuineness) of Scripture;
    - Art. 5: the authority of Scripture;
    - Art. 6: the difference between canonical and apocryphal books;
    - Art. 7: the perfection of Scripture.

2. **Division**

    This article can be divided into two sections:
    A. concerning the spoken Word of God
    B. concerning the written Word of God

3. **The spoken Word**

    In the past, God spoke at many times and in various ways to the fathers by the prophets (Hebrews 1:1). These prophets did not speak "from their own hearts" but were driven by the Holy Spirit (2 Peter 1:21). In order to instil in their human consciousness what He wanted to make known to them, the Holy Spirit utilized many means: direct address (Genesis 1:28; 2:16), an inner voice (Numbers 24:3-4, 15, 16), visions (Revelation 1:10), dreams (Genesis 28:12), miracles (Exodus 4:1-9), the lot (1 Samuel 14:36-42), and the Urim and Thummim (Exodus 28:30).

4. The written Word

The spoken Word was followed by the written Word. This article uses the word "thereafter." God caused what had first been spoken to be recorded in order to prevent distortion and to make it possible to spread it abroad. The writing was "commanded" by God — sometimes by direct command (Jeremiah 30:2) and sometimes through the course of events (1 Corinthians 2:10, 11).

5. Inspiration

We may say that the written Word is the record of the spoken Word, as long as we understand that it is not a faulty human record, but an inspired one. "All Scripture is given by inspiration of God" (2 Timothy 3:16).[6] The Greek word *theopneustos* used here must be understood as a passive word. Christ acknowledged the Old Testament as the Word of God (Matthew 5:17-18; Luke 24:27; John 5:39; etc.). The apostles demanded that their words be acknowledged as God's Word (Galatians 1:8, 9; 1 Thessalonians 2:13).

The special work of the Holy Spirit by which He brought Holy Scripture into existence (inspiration) must not be confused with His work in all believers, by which He enables them to understand the Word of the Lord (illumination). There are many errors concerning this work of inspiration. Here, we mention only the fundamental view (only the primary matters are inspired), the gradual view (the Bible is *more* inspired than other books by believers; it is thus the most beautiful religious book), the mechanical view (the Holy Spirit used the authors like typewriters, so that there is none of their own personal involvement in their writings).

Inspiration certainly did not stifle the personal involvement of the authors. The authors worked by personal volition and in accordance with the gifts they were given (see Luke 1:3). In this connection we must note the differences in language and style between the various writers. For this reason we maintain the organic view of inspiration. It is a great work of God, in connection with which we can speak of:

---

[6] The author notes here that the translation found in the Statenvertaling (a translation authorized by the States General of the United Netherlands) of 1637 is preferable to that of the *Nieuwe Vertaling* (a new translation) of 1951). — TRANS.

A. the preparation: through upbringing, education, experience, and many other factors God made the writers of the Bible into the kinds of people He wanted them to be
B. the instigation: God motivated them to write (see also paragraph 4)
C. the direction: God guided their investigations so that they arrived at the truth without any mistakes
D. the instilling: God instilled in them those thoughts which would best achieve His intention

This divine inspiration of Scripture has been confessed by the Church up until the Reformation. It was not a matter of dispute during the Reformation of the sixteenth century. Today it is generally denied on the basis of what are called "scientific grounds." Many times in history, however, God has put these "wise men" to shame!

The personal involvement of the authors in the act of writing means that they wrote as "children of their time." In order to arrive at a clear understanding of their words, we must therefore pay attention to the environment in which they lived and to the time, the dispensation of revelation, in which they worked (human factors). A knowledge of archaeology and ancient history can be valuable for a good understanding of the various books.

6. The relationship between the spoken and the written Word

Although they are not identical in volume (John 21:25), they are in authority. The fanatics of every age, however, have subordinated the written Word to the spoken Word. From what was said in paragraph 5, it should already be clear that they were wrong in doing so. People have also disconnected the two by saying that God's Word is contained in the Bible, but the Bible is not God's Word. Dialectical theology makes that claim, too. According to these theologians, God never relinquishes His hold upon His Word. We cannot place our hands on the Bible and say, "This is God's Word," because God's Word never comes down to our level. It sometimes touches our level, and the Bible is a sign of that. And if it pleases God He can speak to us again by that Scripture — in the preaching, for example. On this view, we would never be able to appeal to Scripture with an "It is written," as the Saviour did (Matthew 4:4, 6, 10). How completely this theology is in conflict with our Confession is clear from the words of this article.

7. Biblical criticism[7]

The divine character of Scripture forbids us to subject it to the criticism of our reason. The Barthians do so quite frankly and boldly, of course, which suits them most conveniently. "Textual criticism" is entirely different. That is the scholarly activity of establishing the correct text from the numerous manuscripts that have been preserved and which differ among themselves to some degree.

8. "In His special care"

Note the gratitude for Scripture which is expressed in these words. How ought we to respond to such a special care?

ARTICLE 4
THE CANONICAL BOOKS OF HOLY SCRIPTURE

We believe that the Holy Scriptures consist of two parts, namely, the Old and the New Testament, which are canonical, against which nothing can be alleged. These books are listed in the Church of God as follows.
The books of the Old Testament: the five books of Moses, namely, Genesis, Exodus, Leviticus, Numbers, Deuteronomy; Joshua, Judges, Ruth, 1 and 2 Samuel, 1 and 2 Kings, 1 and 2 Chronicles, Ezra, Nehemiah, Esther; Job, Psalms, Proverbs, Ecclesiastes, the Song of Songs; Isaiah, Jeremiah, Lamentations, Ezekiel, Daniel, Hosea, Joel, Amos, Obadiah, Jonah, Micah, Nahum, Habakkuk, Zephaniah, Haggai, Zechariah, and Malachi.

---

[7] Biblical criticism, also known as "higher criticism," aims "... *to determine upon its own subjective basis what is to be accepted and what is to be rejected after the best text has been established.*" Textual criticism, or "lower criticism," aims to determine "... *what the best biblical text really is*" (Francis A. Schaeffer, *The Complete Works of Francis A. Schaeffer*, 2nd ed., vol. 4. [Wheaton, IL: Crossway Books, 1982] pp. 117, 118). — TRANS.

The books of the New Testament: the four gospels, namely, Matthew, Mark, Luke, and John; the Acts of the Apostles; the fourteen letters of the apostle Paul, namely, Romans, 1 and 2 Corinthians, Galatians, Ephesians, Philippians, Colossians, 1 and 2 Thessalonians, 1 and 2 Timothy, Titus, Philemon, Hebrews; the seven other letters, namely, James, 1 and 2 Peter, 1, 2 and 3 John, Jude; and the Revelation to the apostle John.

1. Division
A. Holy Scripture consists of two parts (against the Anabaptists)
B. Its books are canonical and there are sixty-six of them (against the Roman Catholics)

2. The unity of the Old and New Testaments

Already in the first century Marcion rejected the Old Testament. He deemed it a bad work of the vengeful God of the Jews, far below the level of the New Testament which preaches a God of love. At the time of the Reformation the Anabaptists rejected the Old Testament. They claimed that God had only an earthly covenant with Israel and therefore the Old Testament speaks only of earthly blessings. As proof, they appealed to 2 Corinthians 3:6 "for the letter kills, but the Spirit gives life." But it does not say there that the letter (law) is dead, but that it *kills*. It is thus very much alive! In the nineteenth century the Old Testament was largely ignored and most Church books included only the New Testament, and the Psalms in the metrical version. Adolf von Harnack wrote: "Rejecting the Old Testament in the second century was a mistake which the ancient Church did not accept; preserving it in the sixteenth century was a lot which the Reformation could not shirk; maintaining it as a canonical record in Protestantism in the nineteenth century is the result of ecclesiastical and religious impotence." According to Harnack, most objections to Church and faith originate from wrongly maintaining the Old Testament. Even in our century the German Christians regarded the Old Testament as pornography fit for the dunghill. In opposition to these views, Article 4 confesses the unity of the Old and New

Testaments. We are taught this unity in Holy Scripture (see paragraph 5 of the previous article for Christ's evaluation of the Old Testament). Did He not declare that He had not come to abolish but to fulfil? The relation between the Old and New Testaments is discussed further in Article 25. In summary we can define that relationship as follows: the Old Testament speaks of the coming Christ and the New Testament of the Christ who has come and will come again.

3. Canonical

The word "canonical" is derived from the Greek word *kanon*, which means yardstick or guide. It is used to designate the list of Bible books. "Canonical" then means "belonging to that list." But it is also used to mean "the standard for faith and life." It is in this sense that it appears in this article. It says there that one may not contradict these books. That they are termed "canonical" indicates that they are perfect, sufficient, and authoritative and that they offer us guidance for our faith and life. Here the Confession takes a stand against the Roman Catholic error which makes the Church the canon. According to Rome, the Church is above Scripture. For this reason the Roman Catholics have, from of old, forbidden the laity to read Scripture. Today they are more lenient in this respect. Still, only those translations approved by the Church may be read, for example, the Jerusalem Bible.

In the Roman Catholic Church there is a "progressive trend" which encourages the reading of Holy Scripture, but the official Church of Rome invariably claims that although the reading of the approved translation of the Bible can be beneficial, it is far from necessary.

4. Numbered

We reject the idea of an "open canon" which implies that a new book could yet be added to the Bible, whether by ongoing inspiration or by finding something which to date has remained hidden. The canon is closed; its books are numbered. There have been more inspired writings, or at least books by which God made His Word known. Think of "The Book of the Wars of the LORD" (Numbers 21:14), "The Book of Jasher" (Joshua 10:13), "The

Annals of the Prophet Iddo" (2 Chronicles 13:22), and, to mention just one more, an epistle of Paul to Laodicea (Colossians 4:16).

Not all the flowers on a tree develop into fruit. Many are blown off. But no gardener attempts to reattach them to the tree. It is possible that in the sands of Egypt or in the ruins of Imperial Rome an epistle of Peter will one day be found. But it will not have to be added to the canon.

The apocryphal books, which the Septuagint (the Greek translation of the Old Testament, said to have been the work of seventy [= *septuaginta*] elders) added to the Old Testament and which Jerome included in the four hundred copies of the translation he produced (the Vulgate), do not belong to Holy Scripture. The Church of Rome does accept them. How the Church arrived at this division between canonical and apocryphal books will be discussed in the following article.

In the list of books in the official publication of the Confession in 1619 the book of Habakkuk was omitted by mistake. The list speaks of "the first book of Ezra" because Nehemiah is sometimes called "2 Ezra." Hebrews is attributed to Paul, but that is incorrect (see Hebrews 2:3).[8] To say this is not to deviate from the Confession, because the issue here is not the authorship of this book but its canonicity, and that we do not dispute.

The Jews have other names for these books and have also put them in a different order.

5. Hebrew and Greek

The books of the Old and New Testaments have been given to us in Hebrew and Greek. We may certainly make and use translations, but we may never do so in order to replace the original languages. A translation is nothing more than an always imperfect aid. If we could translate perfectly, we could also preach perfectly. Translating is always a matter of interpreting. There are many translations, and it is good to be familiar with them.

---

[8] Rev. Van Bruggen indeed states this strongly; however, since it is not certain who wrote the letter to the Hebrews, it should not be ruled out that Paul could have written it. The annotation to this verse in the Dutch Staten Bijbel makes a strong argument in favour of Paul's authorship. — Editor.

ARTICLE 5
THE AUTHORITY OF HOLY SCRIPTURE

We receive all these books, and these only, as holy and canonical, for the regulation, foundation, and confirmation of our faith. We believe without any doubt all things contained in them, not so much because the Church receives and approves them as such, but especially because the Holy Spirit witnesses in our hearts that they are from God, and also because they contain the evidence thereof in themselves; for, even the blind are able to perceive that the things foretold in them are being fulfilled.

1. **Division**
   This article deals with:
   A. the authority of Holy Scripture
   B. how this authority is recognized

2. **Canonical**
   Here the Confession appears to use the word "canonical" in the sense of "standard or rule for faith and life." It is stated here that the canonicity of Scripture means that we regulate our life according to it. Scripture determines what we should or should not believe. All human opinions must be tested on the basis of it. It silences all contradictions. Whenever faith does not abide by this rule and estranges itself from Scripture, it becomes confused, loses its power and becomes unfruitful. It is also worthwhile to take note here of the fact that our Confessions always emphasize that we believe without question or criticism *all* that is contained in Scripture (see also Q&A 21 of the Heidelberg Catechism). Furthermore, our faith is *based* or founded on Scripture. Our faith has no other "proof" than Scripture. Therefore we should never attempt to win the ignorant and unbelievers over to faith and try to convince others of the validity of our faith by means of all kinds of reasoning and "argumentation." All our self-conceived proofs only encourage contradictions and can also be contradicted. Therefore we can only, and must repeatedly, demonstrate that what we believe

is taught in Scripture. Scripture is the only basis for our faith. It is also the only means by which we *uphold* our faith. The better we are acquainted with Scripture, the stronger our faith will be. Therefore we should constantly busy ourselves with studying it and learning to understand it (1 Peter 2:2).

3. "Receive"

This is a well chosen word. We receive, accept, Scripture as holy and canonical (1 Corinthians 15:1; 1 Thessalonians 2:13). It is not because we have elevated it as such and interpreted and declared it to be so. It *is* holy and canonical. We do not need to make it so (which we could never do anyway, just as we cannot rob it of its holiness). We can only accept it for what it is and we do that through faith. The Church has not made or established the canon (the entire collection of books), but found it. The canon came to the fore on its own. God took care of that. First He gave the books and then He also let them be found. All that the Church did was simply receive, accept.

Man has often tried to explain, by means of external criteria, why the Church accepted *these* particular books. Such criteria is not to be found. The authority of Scripture does not permit its certainty to be mathematically proven by external proofs. People have pointed to the agreement among the various authors, who lived in a period of time spanning no less than sixteen centuries, as evidence of the unity of Scripture. However, this is not a binding proof either, although it is a point worth noting.

4. Three grounds?

People have wanted to accept Scripture as the Word of God by pointing to several grounds. Moreover, it has been claimed that this article mentions three of these grounds. If that were so, the Reformed (complete) confession of the truth would have to be a synthesis (combination) of what Roman Catholics, Baptists, and liberals believe. However, this suggests that these three merely have a somewhat biassed view of Scripture. The "grounds" referred to are:

A. *The Church*

Not that the Church's acceptance of the canonical books as the Word of God would be classed as the principal ground, but nevertheless it was a ground. For Rome this is the only ground. Rome says: the Church existed first, before Scripture, and because the Church accepted Scripture as God's Word, we do so too. Underlying this idea is the distinction between clergy and laity. Rome claims that the laity would not be able to discern what God's Word is; that only the clergy can do so by means of the Spirit's special gifts. This way the word "receive" in reality comes to mean declare, point out.

B. *The witness of the Holy Spirit*

This witness is considered to work in us totally independent of Scripture. The Ethicals saw in this the ground for the acceptance of Scripture. They argued that since the life worked in us by the Holy Spirit is also to be found in Scripture, we recognize it as the Word of God. However, in this way it is the experience of the congregation which decides.

C. *Scripture*

The Arminians considered that we ourselves can discern whether or not something is divine Scripture. They said that we could accept something as the Word of God if what was prophesied actually happened. Although such reasoning claims to base the acceptance of Scripture in Scripture itself, in actual fact it is based on human understanding.

5. Whereby?

This article does not give "grounds" for the authority of Holy Scripture, but brings to light how we come to acknowledge this authority. Here the word "because" does not indicate a reason, but points out a cause, a causal connection. That this is possible can be illustrated by means of an example. In the following sentence it takes on one meaning the one time and another meaning the next. "The train travelled at 100 km per hour because (causal connection) the engine-driver increased the speed; he did so because (reason) the track was safe and the area was level." Hence, this article does not say "why," but "how" (by what means) we recognize the authority of Scripture. First of all, although it is not the principal means, there is the work of the Church, which instructs us in Scripture and teaches us to bow before its authority. Although the Church is not the most significant means by which the authority of Scripture is pointed out, in reality the Church usually does come first. In actual fact it is by the witness of the Holy Spirit in our hearts that we recognize the authority of Scripture. This witness may never be considered to be independent of Scripture (John 16:14). It does not have a content or message of its own; it is not a whisper: "those books are true." The Spirit Himself testifies in Scripture that it is the Word of God. How often doesn't Scripture declare this concerning itself? Consider Hosea 1:1; Matthew 1:22; 5:17, 18; Luke 24:27. The Spirit (by means of faith) lets this witness within Scripture sound forth in our hearts. He opens our eyes for the splendour and truth of Scripture and makes us bow down before its authority. This is because the divinity and truth of Scripture can be perceived. Just as chocolate has its own flavour, by which it can be distinguished from coffee, so Scripture has its own power and effect by which it can be distinguished also from the books of great spiritual writers. Read Plato or Cicero; that can certainly impress. Read Scripture though: it is a two-edged sword! "Even the blind are able to perceive that the things foretold in them are being fulfilled" (see also Isaiah 42:7). The prophecies, often spoken centuries before, were fulfilled, and the course of the history and life of the Church unfolds along the specific paths already determined by Scripture centuries before. It is this majesty of Scripture that we are made to acknowledge through the Holy Spirit.

This inner certainty that Scripture is indeed God's Word is something we have greater need of than bread. Otherwise, how could we possibly hold onto the Word of Scripture at times when it would not suit us, or when it would demand self-denial, yes, even cost us our life? Nothing or no one other than the Holy Spirit is able to give us this certainty. He provides us with this certainty by His witness so that it becomes our own by means of accepting and searching Scripture in faith. Let certainty be sought this way in order for it to be strong!

ARTICLE 6
THE DIFFERENCE BETWEEN THE CANONICAL AND APOCRYPHAL BOOKS

We distinguish these holy books from the apocryphal, namely, 3 and 4 Esdras, Tobit, Judith, Wisdom, Ecclesiasticus, Baruch, additions to Esther, the Prayer of Azariah and the Song of the Three Young Men in the Furnace, Susannah, Bel and the Dragon, the Prayer of Manasseh, and 1 and 2 Maccabees. The Church may read and take instruction from these so far as they agree with the canonical books. They are, however, far from having such power and authority that we may confirm from their testimony any point of faith or of the Christian religion; much less may they be used to detract from the authority of the holy books.

1. Apocryphal

Usage of this word varies. Its literal meaning is "hidden." It was used in order to indicate hidden (i.e. buried) books. The Jews had the habit not to annul holy books that had become useless but to store them away or bury them in caves. It could also mean that a particular book was of secret, obscure or unsure origin, or that authorship was incorrectly ascribed. Moreover, it was used to point out which books were not to be used when reading to the congregation. Today the term apocryphal applies to a number of writings which originated toward the end of the Old Testament era and during the first centuries of the Christian era. In addition to these we also know of the New Testament pseudepigrapha (*pseudo* = lie; *graphein* = writing; hence, untruthful, false writings) such as the Gospel of the Twelve, the Gospel of Peter, the Gospel of Thomas, the Acts of Paul, the Letter of Peter to Jacob, the Revelation of Paul, etc.

2. Church usage

In the translation of the Septuagint (approximately two hundred years before Christ) ten books were added to the Old Testament. The Jews had never included these in the canon and

Christ and His apostles never quoted from them. Athanasius and Jerome did not recognize them as divine. However, because Hebrew was not known and the Septuagint was used for the Old Testament, its apocryphal additions found their way into the Churches. The Roman Catholic Church has included them in the Vulgate (approved translation), among the books of the Old Testament, and regards them as semi-canonical, which means canonical but to a second degree. The reformers did not recognize them as divine, but did not completely break from using them. At the Synod of Dort the question arose whether or not the apocryphal books should be included in the translation of the Bible. The Dutch were strongly opposed to it, but because no other Church outside their country had previously excluded them, and for fear of embarrassing the foreign delegates, it was decided to include them. However, they were to be inserted after the books of the New Testament so that it would be clear to all that they did not belong to the Bible but were merely an appendix. Besides, they were prefaced, warning the reader along the lines of this article. The apocryphal books were also printed in smaller print and were not accompanied by annotations.

3. Characterization

The unreliability of some of the books is apparent from the historical errors which they contain. According to the book Judith, Nebuchadnezzar was king of the Assyrians, resided in Nineveh and fought against Israel after the exile. On the other hand the books of the Maccabees do offer an accurate historical supplement to our knowledge of history between the Old and New Testaments. Some of the apocryphal books contain beautiful proverbs, but they are mostly wonderful tales of fantasy which aim to glorify the excellence of Israel and her great heroes (especially Daniel), and the advantage of a life of obedience to the Law. In addition to this they promote the merit of good works. In a few of the books a strong influence of Greek philosophy is evident.

Jerome rightly observed that because God's Word was entrusted to Israel (Psalm 147:19, 20) it should be written in their language, but there is no Hebrew version of any of the apocryphal books. Apparently they were written in Greek.

ARTICLE 7
THE SUFFICIENCY OF HOLY SCRIPTURE

We believe that this Holy Scripture fully contains the will of God and that all that man must believe in order to be saved is sufficiently taught therein. The whole manner of worship which God requires of us is written in it at length. It is therefore unlawful for any one, even for an apostle, to teach otherwise than we are now taught in Holy Scripture: yes, even if it be an angel from heaven, as the apostle Paul says. Since it is forbidden to add to or take away anything from the Word of God, it is evident that the doctrine thereof is most perfect and complete in all respects.

We may not consider any writings of men, however holy these men may have been, of equal value with the divine Scriptures; nor ought we to consider custom, or the great multitude, or antiquity, or succession of times and persons, or councils, decrees or statutes, as of equal value with the truth of God, since the truth is above all; for all men are of themselves liars, and lighter than a breath. We therefore reject with all our heart whatever does not agree with this infallible rule, as the apostles have taught us: Test the spirits to see whether they are of God. Likewise: If any one comes to you and does not bring this doctrine, do not receive him into your house or give him any greeting.

1. **Division**
   The following three parts can be identified in this article:
   A. Scripture is sufficient for our faith and for salvation
   B. the foundation of this confession
   C. the meaning of this confession as revealed by Scriptural argumentation

2. **No "*lumen internum*"**
   Anabaptists and other fanatics repeatedly scorn God's Word. According to them it is no more than a dead letter. It is the Spirit who makes alive, they say. This Spirit will guide by means of direct

works of revelation to the conscience, an "inner light" (*lumen internum*).

To a lesser extent one also detected such fanaticism in all kinds of conventicles (meetings) where the pious, in times of Church deformation, attempted to edify one another. It was often the case that in such circles more value was ascribed to what "enlightened" believers had to say than to what Scripture said. In those circles too the writings of pious ancient writers were highly respected.

At the beginning of its third part this article rejects all this as being a denial of the sufficiency of Scripture.

3. No "tradition"

Tradition = passed on. Traditions are those things which earlier generations have passed on to us as truth, or customs that ought to be maintained. Of course, the significance of these traditions should not be underestimated. The results of the efforts of previous generations can help us to arrive at a correct understanding of Scripture. However, traditions can never be a source on par with Scripture. They too must constantly be tested in the light of Scripture. This is the way in which the ancient Christian Church honoured tradition. It never turned to tradition as a foundation for any dogma, although it did draw from tradition's teachings. In the ancient Church there existed no tension between Scripture and tradition. Tension concerning tradition only surfaced when the value ascribed to the tradition of the Church of Rome took a turn for the worse, first through the Council of Trent, and later through the Vatican Council of 1870. By this apostate development tradition became a second source of revelation, first alongside, but later above Holy Scripture. According to this error God's revelation comes to us not only via Scripture, but also, and especially, via tradition.

The Church of Rome is of the opinion that this tradition, taught by Christ and the apostles, is handed to us via the writings of the early Church fathers. Furthermore, it is handed to us via the insights and customs believers formed in response to what was taught by Christ and the apostles. Rome also considers the doctrine of the Church as a source for tradition, and no less as a means of arriving at a consensus among believers.

The Church of Rome supports this with the following "arguments:"

A. "The Church existed long before Scripture, and throughout that time lived by the spoken Word."

No one can deny this. Yet "thereafter" (see Article 3 and 4) God took a different direction. He saw to it that from whatever was first handed down to us, those things He considered necessary and beneficial to us were recorded in writing. This is what we must now abide by. Besides, who today is able to discern between truth and falsehood in the degenerate traditions?

The Roman Catholic remedy for this is the infallible declaration of the Pope, a remedy which is worse than the problem!

B. "Much of what was taught by the prophets, spoken by Christ, and preached by the apostles has not been recorded; and what was recorded was determined entirely by the circumstances. This frequently led to 'insignificant' things being written, for example, the command to take a coat for travelling. The main points were spoken, and what was written merely served to clarify these."

In this way Rome lets the Bible be disintegrated into a collection of coincidental and often insignificant messages. However, the Reformed rightly repudiated this, proclaiming instead a "predestined Bible." God brought Scripture into being according to His eternal decrees. Christ also accepted the Old Testament as a decisive unity and often referred to it by saying: "the Scripture [singular!] says . . ."

C. "Many issues of our faith are only known by tradition, for example, purgatory, the independent administration of the holy supper by the priests, etc. After all, these things have surely been established [!]; they are generally taught by the Church."

The foolishness of this assertion is so obvious, that it is unnecessary to disprove it.

D. "Scripture itself points to an authoritative tradition. For example, John 20:30 and 21:25 state that Jesus performed more signs than those which have been recorded [there it speaks of more!] and in 2 John 1:12 and 3 John 1:13 the apostle says he does not wish to pass on everything by means of paper and ink. [As if this suggests that only the essentials were spoken!] See also 2 Thessalonians 2:15: 'hold the traditions which you were taught, whether by word or our epistle.' "

However, all these texts apply to the situation in the early days. "Thereafter" God followed the way of the written Word to which we are bound (see Deuteronomy 12:32; Acts 18:28; 26:22; Revelation 22:18).

Hence according to Rome we receive the exact knowledge of God by way of traditions. Rome certainly depends on these traditions to substantiate its errors concerning the immaculate conception of Mary, her ascension into heaven, and many others.

4. "No doctrinal authority"

Further development of the accepted tradition led to Rome's doctrinal authority of the Church which focuses on the infallible declarations of the Pope (see paragraph 6 of Chapter I). Rome equates Church and Scripture and ultimately places the Church above Scripture. Here Roman Catholic teaching proceeds from the "inner mystery" of the Church. This teaching is as follows. The Church is the Bride of Christ, His body. In it He continues His human nature on earth. The Church is the comprehensive incarnation. In this way Christ still speaks on earth through the Church. Therefore the Church is not bound to the Word, but only to Christ. Scripture is a comprehensive witness to all this, a written document to accompany it. The Church is not born from the Word, but of Christ, who lives in it, speaks through it, and never leaves it. Out of the Church's fullness of life, Scripture is born, the truth of which is proven by the Church.

It will no doubt be clear to all how flagrantly this conflicts with Scripture. Here man, appealing to the guidance of God's Spirit, absolutely lords it over the Word of the Spirit.

5. The sufficiency of Holy Scripture

Scripture itself clearly teaches its own sufficiency as is apparent from the texts pointed out by this article. That it is "sufficient" does not mean that we can learn everything from it, for example carpentry and astrology. However, this does not negate the fact that Scripture is relevant to all that man does. It has been given to man with a view to his salvation so that man would know God. This article expresses this very clearly.

It has been said that Scripture is not enough for us, for each person chooses what he wishes to read from it. The Roman Catholics, in particular, argue from this angle repeatedly. They say that on its own Scripture gives no certainty. No one will deny that every heretic defends his heresy with Scripture. However, that does not mean that Scripture, when taken in its entirety and compared with Scripture, defends each heresy. Even though the "ignorant and foolish" twist its words, that does not necessarily mean that it is obscure or contradictory in what it says. Would God be less than Plato or Epicurus, who were very capable at conveying to students what it was they wished to convey to them?

Relativism, too, which also appeals to today's fanatics, plays down the need to acknowledge that Scripture is sufficient. It argues that Scripture is sufficient, but we merely know it in part. Therefore one can never say: thus says the Lord. We only hear a bit of what He says; others hear something else. In this manner one arrives at a "pluriform" truth, which is nonsense. In this way man also loses all certainty and conviction. However, this is only because man will not truly acknowledge the clarity of Scripture, which is a part of Scripture's sufficiency.

6. Unity and purpose of Scripture

To arrive at a correct understanding of Scripture, each word must be read in the context of the whole of Scripture. By isolating words from the whole context of Scripture one is able to claim and "prove" whatever one wishes.

In the "Remonstrance" he drafted and delivered to the emperor and his courts together with the Confession and a Petition at the Diet of Worms (1578), Marnix of St. Aldegonde beautifully declared "that only they do justice to Scripture who connect what follows with whatever precedes, and who explain the obscurities by what is clear, carefully considering time, persons, and circumstances."

Scripture has been given to us so that we would "believe that Jesus is the Christ, the Son of God, and that believing (we) may have life in His Name" (John 20:31); that we "may be thoroughly equipped for every good work" (2 Timothy 3:17). It teaches us the way to salvation; a way which follows its course through *this* life. Therefore Holy Scripture teaches us how we are to live and make decisions in *this* life. It is *always* a light on our path, also when it comes to appropriating knowledge.

7. Attributes

All that we believe concerning Scripture is summarized in the confession of its following four attributes:

A. *Its divine authority*: (see Articles 3 and 5).

B. *Its clarity*: That it is unclear to us in many places is the result of the dimness of our minds and the wrong inclinations of our will. No matter how bright the light may shine, one cannot see it without an eye. Our eyes must be opened for the light of Scripture, which is the equivalent of being given faith.

C. *Its sufficiency*: In order to know God and the way of salvation in Christ, nothing needs to be added to Scripture. We know the Lord from Scripture, not from "Scripture and reason" or from "Scripture and experience" or from "Scripture and nature" or, as some Christian Scientists maintain, from "The key to Scripture" or, like the Mormons, from "Scripture and the book of Mormon" or, as the Jehovah's Witnesses maintain, from "Scripture and their own publications."

D. *Its necessity*: Apart from Scripture no one can come to a correct knowledge of God.

The Church of Rome contradicts the Reformation's whole emphasis on *"Sola Scriptura"* (Scripture *alone*). Rome places the Church in authority over Scripture, maintains that only the clergy can understand it, wants to supplement it with tradition and by no means considers it necessary in order to know God, since, according to Rome, God can only be known by means of the doctrine of the Church.

By virtue of its attributes, we ought to honour Scripture in our whole walk of life, to which it has a lawful claim!

ARTICLE 8
GOD IS ONE IN ESSENCE,
YET DISTINGUISHED IN THREE PERSONS

According to this truth and this Word of God, we believe in one only God, who is one single essence, in which are three persons, really, truly, and eternally distinct according to their incommunicable properties; namely, the Father, the Son, and the Holy Spirit. The Father is the cause, origin, and beginning of all things visible and invisible. The Son is the Word, the wisdom, and the image of the Father. The Holy Spirit is the eternal power and might who proceeds from the Father and the Son. Nevertheless, God is not by this distinction divided into three, since the Holy Scriptures teach us that the Father, the Son, and the Holy Spirit each has His personal existence, distinguished by Their properties; but in such a way that these three persons are but one only God.

It is therefore evident that the Father is not the Son, nor the Son the Father, and likewise the Holy Spirit is neither the Father nor the Son. Nevertheless, these persons thus distinguished are not divided, nor intermixed; for the Father has not assumed our flesh and blood, neither has the Holy Spirit, but the Son only. The Father has never been without His Son, or without His Holy Spirit. For They are all three co-eternal and co-essential. There is neither first nor last; for They are all three one, in truth, in power, in goodness, and in mercy.

1. **Context**

    Articles 2-7 discuss God's self-revelation and how this is communicated to us in Holy Scripture.

    Articles 8-11 confess what God has revealed to us concerning Himself. This is discussed sequentially as follows:

    Article 8 deals with the Trinity;

    Article 9 deals with the Scriptural proof of this;

    Article 10 deals with the divinity of Jesus Christ;

    Article 11 deals with the divinity of the Holy Spirit.

2. Division

In opposition to the ancient error of the Arians this article confesses God's Unity, and in opposition to the error of the Sabellians it confesses a Triune God. Therefore it can be divided into two sections, but within each section both God's Unity and Trinity will be confessed, and rightly so:

A. The three Persons must be distinguished from one another, but they are not three gods

B. The three Persons must be distinguished from one another, but they may not be separated from one another

3. Terminology

In the following articles we come across a number of terms not found in Scripture: essence, person, incommunicable attributes and, in Article 9, Trinity. The way in which scholastics played around with these terms bore more resemblance to mental gymnastics than dealing with a confession of faith. In their discussions they irreverently reduced God to a mere mathematical formula. The reformers refused to take part in this. Some reacted by saying that in order to be freed from such barbaric, scholastic distinctions it was best to resolutely do away with these terms. The reformers would not have objected, if doing so did not simultaneously discard the Scriptural content of the confession concerning God. Yet, that is exactly what happened. At the time of the Reformation there was also a revival of all the old errors, as though Satan was plotting to rob the Gospel of its power. Socinus and Servetus denied the Trinity. Servetus referred to the Athanasian Creed (symbolum athanasia-num) as a *symbolum satanasianum*. He accused all those who confessed the Trinity of denying God. For the sake of safeguarding the Scriptural inheritance of the Church against the re-emergence of these errors, the above mentioned terms, as a brief summary of the contents of Scripture, could not be done away with.

In addition to this, the Roman Catholics, who lumped all heresies together, called the reformers Arians and Anti-Trinitarians (i.e. denying the Trinity = the three Persons of God). In order to refute these insinuations about their work the reformers were bound to hold on to these terms. Despite our wish to replace these terms with better ones, we cannot do without them today either. We remain ever conscious of the fact that with these terms we merely stammer about something which is beyond human comprehension.

4. Ancient errors

Article 9 lists an extensive list of those who propagated a variety of opinions, but whose views were rejected by the Church: Jews, Muslims, Marcion, Mani, Praxeas, Sabellius, Paul of Samosata, Arius. We wish to pay some attention to these for in so doing we will better understand why our Confession expresses what it does concerning the Trinity.

In the first few centuries the Church had to fight a fierce battle in order to safeguard the confession of God's self-revelation against all kinds of errors. When the Gospel first went out into the world it had to engage in a battle against Judaism (which is antitrinitarian and knows of only one Divine Person) as well as against heathendom with its many gods. Later it had to fight against Islam, which agrees with Judaism with respect to the essence of God. In the "civilized world" Hellenism prevailed. Greek philosophy, with its many schools, dominated the way people thought. Hellenism was very syncretic (combining, joining), selecting elements from a variety of religions and combining them into one all-encompassing whole. This gave rise to the danger of the Gospel being incorporated as a new element into the prevailing philosophy of the day with the result that the Gospel was merely seen as another philosophy and robbed of its power. Gnosticism made this a terrible reality. Hence in the early days, when the Gospel first went out, all kinds of strange and absurd teachings concerning God were preached. If the Church had not recognized and banished this, the Gospel would have faltered when taking its first steps and the Church would have collapsed at the beginning of its history.

These errors experienced a revival during the time of the Reformation. Consequently the Church of the Reformation clung tenaciously to the truth, denouncing the errors already exposed by the early Church in the first centuries. We must continue to do so today too, for the old heresies continue to exist in new forms. In opposition to the hollowing out and falsifying of faith by the liberals who only know of the Father, and the Methodists, who only preach the Son, and the Mystics who only honour the Holy Spirit, the complete confession concerning the Trinity must continue to be propagated with power. (Mystics = Greek *mu-ein*, i.e. to close the eyes. By closing the eyes and looking within oneself, man believed he was able to learn about the deity, a spark of which, he thought, lay within each person. By the name *Mystics* we refer to those people who do not wish to obtain their knowledge of God through reading Scripture, but seek it in the work of the Holy Spirit in the hearts of man.)

The main point in the struggle of the ancient Christian Church was the resistance to two basic errors:

A. *The denial of God's Trinity*

Sabellius claimed that the names Father, Son, and Holy Spirit were three names for one person. He said that, just as the very same person can be a husband, doctor, and taxpayer, so the one and the same Divine Person in one instance acts as Father and Creator, in another as Son and Redeemer, and in another as Spirit and Sanctifier.

Praxeas regarded the three Persons as modalities (modes, forms of revelation) of the Father. According to him it was the Father who suffered (*Patripassians*).

Paul of Samosata considered the three Persons as just three attributes of the one Person. According to him Jesus was not God.

Mani, a Persian, maintained some strange views on the subject. According to him Christ was a "being of light" sent to earth by the good God in the resemblance of a body in order to deliver us from the power of the evil god. However, the apostles, he said, had not understood Christ. That was a bonus for Mani, the so-called "comforter." Manicheism was very influential and spread over Asia, Africa, and Europe. Augustine was a member of the Manicheans for nine years.

Marcion hated the "god of the Old Testament," which together with some portions of the New Testament, was rejected by him. He did not recognize Christ as God.

Over against this, Article 8 confesses that the Father did not assume the flesh, and that in the one essence there are three Persons, in deed and truth, and who are and have been distinguishable from eternity.

B. *The denial of God's Unity*

Arius denied the divinity of Christ. According to him He was God's first and most significant creation. In opposition to this Article 8 confesses that the Father has never been without the Son and that all three are equal in eternity, and are in one and the same essence.

The result of the struggle against all these errors is reflected in the ancient creeds. The Apostles' Creed does not confess the Trinity as a separate article beside the other articles, but confesses it in all its articles. The whole design of the Apostles' Creed is trinitarian. Furthermore, the Nicene Creed and the Athanasian Creed also confess the Trinity (see paragraph 5, A of Chapter I).

Hence we can regard the term "Trinity" as a shield against errors. "Three" opposes Sabellius and "one" opposes Arius.

5. Trinity

This term is not to be found in Scripture. However, this one word clearly and briefly denotes what we mean by it. The whole of Scripture teaches us that there is one God and that this God is one. Yet it speaks of the Father, the Son, and the Holy Spirit and presents each of them as God. The one and indivisible God is so wonderful that He exists in three Persons (not: made up of three Persons!). This does not mean that the essence of God is divided. All three Persons have one and the same essence. With each of them we do not interact with a part of God, but with God Himself. With regard to us the Father is the same God as the Son or the Holy Spirit. However, with regard to one another each of them has in that essence His own independent existence. With regard to the Father the Son is Son, and the Holy Spirit is Spirit, the One who was Sent. In the essence of God each has His own attributes by which He is distinguished from the others. Here the term "incommunicable attributes," which we rejected in the context of Article 1, *does* apply.

Concerning the Holy Spirit, Article 11 says that "in order He is the third Person of the Holy Trinity." By this distinction between the Persons as first, second, and third, one may not in the least consider a hierarchy. Rank or succession are out of the question.

All three Persons are equally and eternally God. However, in God there is this order of existence, that the Son is begotten of the Father. He receives His life from the Father (John 5:26). The Son is the "brightness of God's glory and the express image of His person" (Hebrews 1:3). He is the Word in whom the Father reveals Himself (John 1:1ff.). The Holy Spirit proceeds (like a breath) from the Father and the Son.

Scripture also reveals this sequence in God's works, that the Father first created, after which the Son redeemed, and the Holy Spirit completed all God's works through sanctification.

It is better for us to worship God's glory than to attempt to express it. However, in order to keep our worship pure it is essential for the sake of keeping heresies at bay that we carefully weigh our words.

6. Significance

The confession of the Trinity is not irrational, as it is ridiculed to be by Moslems and liberals. We do not say that three Beings are one Being, and that three Persons are one Person, but that in the one essence of God there are three Persons. This confession surpasses human understanding. Therefore one speaks of the "mystery" (i.e. the secret) of the Trinity. There can be no objection to this, being mindful of the fact that all that is revealed to us in Scripture about God and His works is a "mystery," a secret, which we only know by means of revelation and even then contains impenetrable depths. It is no easier to discuss creation and providence than it is to discuss God's Trinity.

This confession is not just some dry, abstract theory. Our fathers lived by it. Note too the trinitarian design of the Form for Baptism and all the prayers. If we let go of this confession or set it aside, our faith will wither and threaten to degenerate. This confession opens our eyes to God's greatness. He is so great that He does not need anything from us. When He was on His own before creation, He was not lonely. Company and conversation are available to Him within Himself. He is complete in Himself and is independent of anything and anyone outside of Himself. Yet He, who is so magnificent that He does not need anything from us, can provide us with all we need. Our complete salvation is from Him, the Father, who provided payment by His Son and sanctifies us by His Spirit. By means of this confession we are also protected from Pantheistic errors (the idea that everything is God; He is in all things) and Deistic errors (the idea that God is distant, separated from all things), and we learn to understand that God is transcendent, elevated above creation, *and* immanent, inherent in all things.

ARTICLE 9
SCRIPTURE PROOF OF THIS DOCTRINE

All this we know both from the testimonies of Holy Scripture and from the respective works of the three Persons, and especially those we perceive in ourselves. The testimonies of Scripture which lead us to believe this Holy Trinity are written in many places of the Old Testament. It is not necessary to mention them all; it is sufficient to select some with discretion.

In the book of Genesis God says: Let Us make man in our image after our likeness . . . So God created man in His own image . . .; male and female He created them. Also: Behold, the man has become like one of Us. From God's saying, Let Us make man in Our image, it appears that there are more divine persons than one; and when He says, God created, He indicates that there is one God. It is true, He does not say how many persons there are, but what seems to be somewhat obscure in the Old Testament is very plain in the New Testament. For when our Lord was baptized in the river Jordan, the voice of the Father was heard, who said, This is My beloved Son; the Son was seen in the water, and the Holy Spirit descended upon Him in bodily form as a dove. For the baptism of all believers Christ prescribed this formula: Baptize all nations into the Name of the Father, and of the Son, and of the Holy Spirit. In the gospel according to Luke the angel Gabriel thus addressed Mary, the mother of our Lord: The Holy Spirit will come upon you, and the power of the Most High will overshadow you;

therefore the child to be born will be called holy, the Son of God. Likewise: The grace of the Lord Jesus Christ and the love of God and the fellowship of the Holy Spirit be with you all. In all these places we are fully taught that there are three persons in one only divine essence.

Although this doctrine far surpasses all human understanding, nevertheless in this life we believe it on the ground of the Word of God, and we expect to enjoy its perfect knowledge and fruit hereafter in heaven. Moreover, we must observe the distinct offices and works of these three Persons toward us. The Father is called our Creator by His power; the Son is our Saviour and Redeemer by His blood; the Holy Spirit is our Sanctifier by His dwelling in our hearts. The doctrine of the Holy Trinity has always been maintained and preserved in the true Church since the time of the apostles to this very day, over against Jews, Muslims, and against false Christians and heretics such as Marcion, Mani, Praxeas, Sabellius, Paul of Samosata, Arius, and such like, who have been justly condemned by the orthodox fathers. In this doctrine, therefore, we willingly receive the three creeds, of the Apostles, of Nicea, and of Athanasius; likewise that which in accordance with them is agreed upon by the early fathers.

1. Division

This article commences with an introductory sentence, not written by Guido de Brés but inserted by Dort, which serves to connect this article to Article 8. The remainder of the article can be divided as follows:

    A. A list of texts on which the confession about the Trinity is based

    B. References to what Scripture says concerning God's works on which this confession is based

    C. An appeal to history

2. List of texts

As stated by the Heidelberg Catechism in Q&A 25, we speak of God the Father, Son, and Holy Spirit "because God has so revealed Himself in His Word that these three distinct persons are the one true and eternal God." Indeed, Scripture is our only proof of the Trinity. It is our only source through which we know God in the glory of His Trinity. Man has at one stage attempted to prove "*vestigia Trinitatis*" (traces of the Trinity) in creation. To this end man pointed to the three dimensions of space: length, breadth, and height; the three elements of time: past, present, and future; the three persons in language: I, you, and he; and the three parts of living organisms: root, trunk, and crown; head, torso, and limbs, etc. However, this is creative fantasy.

This article certainly does not give an exhaustive list of texts but — as it admits — has selected some with discretion. The explanation of these texts is clear. We merely add the following:

A. In Genesis 1:26 "Our" is not a plural of majesty (like "We," spoken by a monarch). This is not found in the languages of the east.

B. In Matthew 28, the baptismal command teaches both the Unity of God (Name, not names) and the Trinity of God ("and the Son . . . and the Holy Spirit;" not: "or the Son . . . or the Holy Spirit," which it should say if the modalists were right).

C. 1 John 5:7. This text is claimed by many to have been incorrectly inserted in late manuscripts and hence disregarded. The *Statenvertaling* (= [Dutch] States Translation) has included it. There is a difference of opinion about this within Reformed circles. However, even if this text were to be deleted, this would not, contrary to what Jehovah's Witnesses assert, nullify the doctrine of the Trinity. There remains ample proof.

3. Further Scriptural evidence

There has been much ado about the opening words of this article: "from the respective works of the three Persons, and especially those we perceive in ourselves." People claim that here the Confession suggests a second source of knowledge alongside Scripture, a source within man at that. People have even used these words to justify a "*lumen internum*" (see paragraph 2 of the chapter on Article 7). However, if that were really the case, the Confession would contradict itself. Take note of Article 7!

Some consider that this first sentence was later inserted as an introductory summary above this article. The first part of this sentence, "the testimonies of Holy Scripture," clearly refers to the first part of this article, the list of texts. The second part, their "respective works ... and especially those we perceive *in* ourselves," refers to the second part of this article, where "the distinct offices and works of these three Persons toward us" is discussed. However, it is argued, doesn't it say "those we perceive in ourselves?" Yes, it does indeed say that, but the word "in" used to have a much broader meaning.

The second part of this article does not just enumerate a list of individual texts, but summarizes what Scripture tells us about God's works. "Offices" means the same as "works." It refers to task or activity. It is in this way that the *Statenvertaling* speaks of the office of song in 1 Chronicles 6:31, 32 and of the person who had the office over the things that were baked in pans in 1 Chronicles 9:31. Each of the Persons has His own specific activity, His own office. The Father is our Creator by His power, the Son is our Redeemer by His blood, and the Holy Spirit is our Sanctifier by His dwelling in our hearts. Yet creation, redemption and sanctification are the work of the one and the same God, for the Father created by the Word and by the breath of His mouth (Psalm 33:6).

4. Appeal to history

This appeal is an ineffective proof if it is detached from Scripture. Nevertheless, it may support the Church's unfailing confession concerning this mystery. De Brés undoubtedly included this section in such detail in order to prove that the Reformation, contrary to the accusations of the Roman Catholics, was not introducing a "new doctrine" but aligned itself with the Church of old. By "the early fathers" is meant the faithful synods. Here De Brés had written: the holy synods. The word "holy" was used not to imply that a synod is always holy, but as a way of distinguishing faithful synods from those which were false and unfaithful. We do not want to maintain what was taught by every synod, but only that which was taught by synods in faithfulness to Scripture.

ARTICLE 10
JESUS CHRIST TRUE AND ETERNAL GOD

We believe that Jesus Christ according to His divine nature is the only begotten Son of God, begotten from eternity, not made, nor created — for then He would be a creature — but of the same essence with the Father, equally-eternal, who reflects the glory of God and bears the very stamp of His nature, and is equal to Him in all things. He is the Son of God, not only from the time that He assumed our nature but from all eternity, as these testimonies, when compared with each other, teach us: Moses says that God created the world; the apostle John says that all things were made by the Word which he calls God. The letter to the Hebrews says that God made the world through His Son; likewise the apostle Paul says that God created all things through Jesus Christ. Therefore it must necessarily follow that He who is called God, the Word, the Son, and Jesus Christ, did exist at that time when all things were created by Him. Therefore He could say, Truly, I say to you, before Abraham was, I am, and He prayed, Glorify Thou Me in Thy own presence with the glory which I had with Thee before the world was made. And so He is true, eternal God, the Almighty, whom we invoke, worship, and serve.

1. **Division**
   A. That Jesus according to His divine nature is of the same essence with the Father
   B. Scriptural proof of this

2. **Arianism**
   Arius (256-336), who became a priest in Alexandria in 313, denied that Jesus is God. He was probably not the first to do so, but due to his popularity this error gained wide acceptance among the people. According to him Jesus was the first and most significant creation of the Father, created with a view to the subsequent creation of all things. However, there would have been a time when He did not exist.

This article, which to the very last word passes on the inheritance of the ancient Christian Church, places itself in opposition to these claims of Arius. His greatest opponent was Athanasius, the *pater orthodoxiae* (the father of orthodoxy). A decision against Arius was made at the Council of Nicea (325). Yet his heresy continues to exist in a variety of forms. The liberals still deny the divinity of Christ. They do call Him the Son of God, but this merely serves to describe the position He holds, a position which reveals His outstanding qualities. In this way they also accept the foundation of the World Council of Churches which speaks of "Jesus, God and Saviour." In the nineteenth century people began to distinguish between the "historical Jesus" and the views of Him as presented by the Bible. The latter is doctrinal history. Such an attitude of course allows each and everyone to extract from the Bible a "Jesus" which best suits him! That is how we derived a "liberal Jesus-image," a "social Jesus-image," and an "apocalyptic Jesus-image." The number of paintings depicting "images of Jesus" increased abundantly, none of which would have been recognized as depictions of Him save for the accompanying captions which stated that they represented "images" of Him.

Here lies a dividing line. Whoever denies that Jesus is God is a liar and is not of the truth. How emphatically the apostle John emphasizes this in his letters!

3. Fourfold evidence

The divinity of Jesus can be proven from Scripture in four ways. It ascribes to Him, firstly, divine names (John 1:1; Romans 9:5); secondly, divine attributes, such as "eternal" (John 8:58); and thirdly, Godly honour: we must be baptized into His Name (Matthew 28:19), believe in Him (John 14:1), and bow before Him in worship (Philippians 2:10). Finally, in the fourth place, Scripture ascribes to Him divine works: "all things were made through Him" (John 1:3).

4. Only-begotten and firstborn Son of God

John calls Jesus "the only begotten of the Father" (1:14), and "His only begotten Son" (3:16, 18). The Heidelberg Catechism says that He is called this because He is "the eternal, natural Son of

God." Since the Father expresses through Him, His only Son, the total "brightness of His glory" (Hebrews 1:3) there is no room beside Him for another, someone supplementary. To have only one Son is no deficiency for God, but it is *everything*, because this one Son is God. Yes, we have been "adopted" as children in Him and through Him (Lord's Day 13 of the Heidelberg Catechism). The Form for Baptism (prayer of thanksgiving) says, "That Thou hast received us through Thy Holy Spirit as members of Thy only Son and so adopted us to be Thy children" (John 1:12).

Christ is also called God's firstborn, not in relation to God, as if He had more "sons," but in relation to us. In Romans 8:29 we read "the firstborn among many brethren" and in Colossians 1:15 "the firstborn over all creation."

The attempts of Arius and the Jehovah's Witnesses to conclude from this that Christ, though before us, is no more God's Son than we are and like us was created, are futile. Such a "conclusion" would bring us in opposition to what Scripture clearly teaches. "Firstborn" in Scripture is a reference to one's legal status. Concerning Israel's great King, Psalm 89:27 says, "I will make Him My firstborn, the highest of the kings of the earth."

5. "To be or not to be"

The confession of the divinity of Christ was more than just an afterthought for Athanasius and the ancient Christian Church. Indeed, by it the Church stands or falls. If Jesus is not *God*, one may no longer call Christianity the universal and only true religion. Then mission work has no authority. Then we lack certainty in our knowledge of God. It may well be so that Jesus has spoken more beautifully about God than any other teacher of religion, but if He is not God, who can then be sure that He has accurately revealed God to us? Furthermore, if Jesus is not God, and did not descend from the Father, but is a man who came up from below, then our worship of Christ is directed at ourselves, creatures, rather than at God. Therefore the Confession is so elaborate on this point: Jesus is God! We will deal with His human nature and the unity of His two natures when we discuss Articles 18 and 19. De Brés, by means of his positive elaboration in this article, wished to oppose the slander of Rome that the "new doctrine" was nothing but Arianism.

ARTICLE 11
THE HOLY SPIRIT TRUE AND ETERNAL GOD

We believe and confess also that the Holy Spirit from eternity proceeds from the Father and the Son. He is neither made, created, nor begotten, but He can only be said to proceed from both. In order He is the third Person of the Holy Trinity, of one and the same essence, majesty, and glory with the Father and the Son, true and eternal God, as the Holy Scriptures teach us.

1. Limitation

The Holy Spirit is confessed more elaborately in Lord's Day 20 of the Heidelberg Catechism than it is in this article. Concerning the Holy Spirit, in Lord's Day 20 we confess, "First, He is together with the Father and the Son, true and eternal God." This is the extent of this article's confession, whereas Lord's Day 20 continues, "Second, He is also given to me, to make me by true faith share in Christ and all His benefits, to comfort me, and to remain with me forever."

Hence the Holy Spirit fulfils the work of Christ. He completes this work in us. He works our sanctification. He kindles faith in us through the preaching of the Gospel, and by it makes us share in Christ and all His benefits. He renews us, and strengthens us in our battle against sin. He "comforts" us, constantly directing our eyes to the promises of the Lord in times of doubt and temptation. He will remain with us that way forever. He will not leave His work unfinished, but will continue it "till we shall finally be presented without blemish among the assembly of God's elect in life eternal" (Form for Baptism).

In the Apostle's Creed the article "I believe in the Holy Spirit" is followed by a confession concerning the Church, the forgiveness of sins, the resurrection of the body and the life everlasting. The Holy Spirit is active in all these things (see for example Romans 8:11).

Yet even by reporting all this work of the Holy Spirit, the Heidelberg Catechism has not yet covered all that the Spirit does. No mention is made of the great and divine work of the Holy Spirit in the creation and sustenance of all things, concerning which Scripture is not silent. See Psalm 104:30: "You send forth Your Spirit, they are created; and You renew the face of the earth;" and Genesis 1:2: "And the Spirit of God was hovering over the face of the waters;" and Exodus 31:3, where it says concerning Bezaleel, that he was "filled . . . with the Spirit of God, in wisdom, in understanding, in knowledge, and in all manner of workmanship, to design artistic works, to work in gold, in silver, in bronze . . ." etc.

2. Divine Person

The only point the Confession wishes to make here is that the Holy Spirit is eternal God. Right from the beginning the Church has acknowledged this in practice. For example, in the administration of baptism the Spirit is honoured as God. However, theoretical reflection on God's revelation created problems so that a lack of clarity on this point prevailed among the early Church fathers. These problems arose because Scripture says relatively little about the Holy Spirit. After all, the Holy Spirit did not come to speak concerning Himself, but to glorify Christ (John 16:14). In addition to this, the Greek word for the Holy Spirit (*pneuma*) is neutral and refers to Him vaguely as a "gift." This suggests that the Holy Spirit (neutral) is a "thing," a "gift." On the other hand, Scripture does speak of Him as God and as an independent Person. The problem was reduced when people began to see that sometimes Christ is also spoken of as a "gift" and that the neutral word *pneuma* is often followed by a masculine relative pronoun.

Arius had said: the Father alone is God. All things are made by Him. The Son is no exception. He too is a creation of God. His followers said the same concerning the Holy Spirit. In the year 381, at the Council of Constantinople, the Church rejected this error (see our Nicene Creed). This rejection is echoed in this article by the words "neither made, created, nor begotten."

Scripture also offers fourfold proof concerning the divinity of the Holy Spirit. It ascribes to the Holy Spirit:

    A. *divine names*: In Acts 5:3, 4 He is called God
    B. *divine virtues*: He is omnipresent (Psalm 139:7)
    C. *divine works*: He was involved in creation (Psalm 33:6)

D. *divine honour*: We are also baptized into His name (Matthew 28:19)

That the Holy Spirit is a Person and not merely a power or gift is also evident from the fact that it is said of Him that He "searches all things, yes, the deep things of God" (1 Corinthians 2:10), and that we can grieve Him (Ephesians 4:30).

3. "Proceeding from both"

Concerning the Holy Spirit, this article does not merely say that He is not made, nor created, as was also said concerning the Son in Article 10; it also adds that He is not begotten. The Son is born from the Father (begotten), but the Spirit "proceeds" from the Father and the Son. The Church has always maintained that there is a distinction between the generation of the Son and the proceeding forth of the Holy Spirit. This distinction is derived from Scripture. Concerning the Spirit it is never said that He is born. However, the Church has been equally careful to refrain from defining this distinction or trying to clarify it further, for nothing has been revealed to us about that.

This article says that the Spirit "proceeds from the Father *and the Son*" and, further, that he proceeds "from both." The italicised words have given rise to much contention. These words originally did not appear in the Nicaeno-Constantinopolitan Creed. They were first inserted by the Synod of Toledo, A.D. 589. However, the Eastern Church never accepted this. This "filioque" ("and the Son") became one of the reasons for the split between the Eastern and Western Churches in 1054. It still marks the split between the two. The Eastern Church does not want to accept it and maintains that the Spirit does not proceed from the Father and the Son, but only proceeds from the Father.

This difference has far reaching consequences for life. If what the Greek Church declares is correct, namely that the Son and the Spirit both proceed from the Father independently, then God lays claim to us along two ways that run parallel to each other. That would mean that God lays claim to us by way of revelation through the Son in the historical process of the Church with its administration of the Word and sacraments, but also by way of revelation through the Spirit, independent of that historical process, independent of Word and sacraments, direct and immediate within our inner being. It is clear that this opens the floodgates to all kinds of mystical fanaticism. Hence sects flourish in the East. The worst part of it is that it meets little resistance.

4. Comfort

In the Holy Spirit we have received God Himself as our "Guide on the way to eternal, blessed life." He is no Gift at our disposal, but we are at His. He prays for us (Romans 8:26).

5. Blasphemy against the Spirit

Scripture warns us not to "grieve" the Spirit (Ephesians 4:30); not to "quench" Him (1 Thessalonians 5:19) i.e. not to despise His gifts or to oppose His works, not to "insult" Him (Hebrews 10:29), and not to blaspheme against Him (Matthew 12:31, 32; Hebrews 6:4-6; 1 John 5:16). Scripture calls blasphemy against the Spirit the "sin leading to death" (1 John 5:16), and declares it to be unforgivable. Christ referred to this sin when His enemies blasphemed, "This fellow does not cast out demons except by Beelzebub, the ruler of the demons" (Matthew 12:22-32). Jesus replied that blasphemy against the Son of Man would be forgiven, on the condition of repentance and conversion, but that blasphemy against the Holy Spirit will never be forgiven. Of course, this is not because the Son is less than the Spirit. Here we must pay attention to the point in time this was spoken by Christ. Christ still had to die and was not yet glorified. He was still the suffering servant. Therefore it was not without reason that just at that point in time He announced Himself as "the Son of Man." His glory was still hidden. Soon He was to receive the Holy Spirit as His Spirit and pour Him out upon all flesh at Pentecost, so that He would reveal Christ, and to witness of His work, especially through the fulfilment of the Old Testament by the New.

In John 7:38 we read that Christ said, "He who believes in Me . . . out of his heart will flow rivers of living water." John then adds, "But this He spoke concerning the Spirit, whom those believing in Him would receive; for the Holy Spirit was not yet given, because Jesus was not yet glorified" (John 7:39). This does not mean of course that the Holy Spirit did not exist as yet. That "the Holy Spirit was not yet given" meant that He was not yet poured out and had not as yet appeared as the Spirit of Christ, as would only take place at Pentecost. Since then the Holy Spirit has spoken the Gospel of Christ so clearly, that no one needs to have any doubt or uncertainty concerning Christ. Now no one can excuse himself that he does not know Christ and His works.

Whoever has received the wondrously radiant Gospel, and has known the way, yet willingly and knowingly rejects all the benefits, promised through baptism into the Name of the Triune God, and who becomes apostate, blasphemes the Spirit and crucifies again the Son of Man (Hebrews 6:4-6). There is no forgiveness for such outright rejection of the Gospel whereby the sinner hardens himself. Whoever rejected Jesus in the days He walked on earth could still expect a subsequent pardon, namely, the arrival and work of the Spirit, but whoever opposes that too, and hardens himself, can expect nothing more. He remains in sin. For him repentance will no more be possible.

Hence this terrible sin can only be committed by those who have received the Gospel.

In the life of believers it sometimes happens that a person considers himself guilty of this sin. Sometimes that becomes an obsession (a delusion) which can lead to serious psychic disturbances, or can even cause incurable depression; it has even led to suicide.

One does well to realize that those who are guilty of this sin are not worried or concerned about it. Their heart is hardened to such an extent that they delight in blaspheming the Mediator and the way of salvation. Therefore, whoever fears he has committed this sin, has not yet committed it. Difficulties with the Gospel, a struggle to accept it, occasions of aversions to it, or the inclination to reject it during such a struggle, is not an act of blaspheming the Spirit. That occurs when there is an outright and conscious rejection. Nevertheless, the knowledge that man can arrive at such a horrendous and unforgivable sin makes us careful not to reject the Gospel; it makes us careful to subject our thoughts to the obedience of Christ.

6. Present-day fanaticism

The growing "Pentecostal Movement" of our day accuses the Church of no longer possessing, let alone seeking, the "gifts of the Spirit," which this movement seeks through speaking in tongues, healing, and revelations. It seeks to resume these extraordinary works of the Spirit. In so doing it aims once again to bring "the complete Gospel" as opposed to the "emaciated and crippled Gospel, preached by the Church." This is not at all in agreement with Scripture. Scripture demonstrates that God progresses from the extraordinary to the "ordinary." The special gifts were the festive signs by which the Spirit came to live in the congregation, but which are not permanent. "But earnestly desire the best gifts. And yet I show you a more excellent way" (1 Corinthians 12:31). Paul then describes that "way" in 1 Corinthians 13 and it is evident that this is the way of love. This is what we must seek (see also 1 Corinthians 14:19).

ARTICLE 12
THE CREATION OF ALL THINGS, ESPECIALLY THE ANGELS

We believe that the Father through the Word, that is, through His Son, has created out of nothing heaven and earth and all creatures, when it seemed good to Him, and that He has given to every creature its being, shape, and form, and to each its specific task and function to serve its Creator. We believe that He also continues to sustain and govern them according to His eternal providence and by His infinite power in order to serve man, to the end that man may serve his God.

He also created the angels good, to be His messengers and to serve His elect. Some of these have fallen from the exalted position in which God created them into everlasting perdition, but the others have by the grace of God remained steadfast and continued in their first state. The devils and evil spirits are so depraved that they are enemies of God and of all that is good. With all their might, they lie in wait like murderers to ruin the Church and all its members and to destroy everything by their wicked devices. They are therefore by their own wickedness sentenced to eternal damnation and daily expect their horrible torments. Therefore we detest and reject the error of the Sadducees, who deny that there are any spirits and angels; and also the error of the Manichees, who say that the devils were not created, but have their origin of themselves, and that without having become corrupted, they are wicked by their own nature.

1. Context

Article 1 immediately made clear that the 37 articles, of which it is the first, all wish to confess faith in God. Articles 2-7 subsequently discussed the means by which we know Him; and Articles 8-11 discussed God Himself and His works of personal or internal generation and the sending forth of the Holy Spirit. Articles 12 and 13 immediately move on to confess His external works of creation and providence. Neither our Confession nor the Heidelberg Catechism make a sharp distinction between the two. Article 12 already speaks of God's providence. God's preservation of all things began immediately after His first act of creation.

Having discussed God's self-revelation, our Confession does not first deal with His counsel and election. It does that further on. By first speaking of God's great works our Confession prepares us for reflection upon His eternal decrees. God's eternal decrees are not discussed in isolation from the created reality but, so to speak, from the perspective of this reality. A method worthy of consideration! Whoever ventures to speak of God's counsel, sometimes foolishly called "His point of view from eternity," risks engaging in unlawful speculation.

2. Division

    A. God's creation of all things, and His purpose in doing so
    B. God's creation of the angels and their work
    C. The fall of some angels, their destruction and punishment
    D. Rejection of the errors of the Sadducees and the Manicheans

3. *Ex nihilo*

The confession of God's creation of all things is something the Church of all ages has in common. It was not a point of contention in the sixteenth century, but became so much later, through apostasy, in the nineteenth century.

This article says that the Father has created all things "through the Word, that is, through His Son" (Genesis 1:2b; Psalm 33:6; John 1:3; Hebrews 11:3). Creation was the work of the Triune God. The Holy Spirit was also involved in it. This article certainly does not deny this. When the first sentence of this article was expanded, (De Brés had only written: "We believe, that this one [unique] God created heaven, earth . . ." etc.) a reference should also have been made to the Holy Spirit.

Creation is the act of God's almighty will, by which He called into being, out of nothing, all things. That God created "out of nothing" (*ex nihilo*) are not words quoted from Scripture. Perhaps it is derived from 2 Maccabees 7:28, "Know that God has brought forth from nothing." One could turn to Hebrews 11:3, but there it is not stated quite so explicitly. Gnostics knew of the notion "*me-on*," non-existent, and thereby wished to convey the notion of an eternal, unformed substance, lacking quality. This is the "nothingness," they say, which God used to create everything. Well now, it has been claimed that one can find this Gnostic element in our Confession. But that is nonsense. *Ex nihilo* = *post nihilum*, there was nothing before.

God commenced His creation "when it seemed good to Him." There is nothing more to say. This is enough. God did not proceed to create in order to relieve Himself of His abundance (emanation), nor to overcome His "loneliness," nor from any other necessity, but because He considered it good, and *when* He considered it good (Revelation 4:11). "In the beginning" is when time commenced. Since time did not exist *prior* to that, one cannot really ask: "what existed *before* creation?"

God did not merely create a prehistoric matter from which everything else just developed, but gave each creature its own being, shape, form, and specific function (task).

Each creature has its own purpose, including those purposes we have never seen nor shall see. God created everything "for Himself" (Proverbs 16:4). Creation is there to praise Him.

Yet in His covenant God gave His creation to mankind. Now all of creation must serve man, so that man may in turn use it to serve God!

Do not overlook the fact that this article also commences with the words "we believe." The creation of all things by God is no less an element of faith than receiving the Holy Spirit through Christ! Whoever meddles with this "element," damages faith and diminishes the comfort. It is for our comfort that we are told that God is the Father almighty, Creator of heaven and earth (see Lord's Day 9 of the Heidelberg Catechism).

We believe *in* this God. That is different than believing something about God, believing that He exists. The demons believe that too (James 2:19). Just read there how little such belief is worth! We believe in, that means to say, we put our trust in, and entrust ourselves to this God.

4. First and second creation

Man wants to regard Genesis 1:1 "In the beginning God created the heavens and the earth" as a general heading for the Creation story. This story would then begin with verse 2. However, it is clear that verse 2, "the earth . . ." refers to verse 1 and is a continuation of what was stated there. Therefore one cannot regard Genesis 1:1 as a general heading for it is the beginning of the story itself.

What we read in Genesis 1:1 is what we call "the first creation." By it God called all "matter" into existence. Initially we do not read anything else about the heavens mentioned there. Verse 2 only relates how the "earth," called into being by God's act of creation, existed. It was still "without form, and void; and darkness was on the face of the deep." One cannot call this situation "chaos." "Chaos" is the result of a collapse; it is a ruin. The fantasy of cyclic evolution asserts that the cosmos is renewed every seven thousand years. At the end of that period it collapses and its remnants are the foundations for a new evolution. The phrase "In the beginning" of Genesis 1 would therefore mark the beginning of the present-day evolution, which commenced with the chaos of the previous one. Yet Scripture teaches us a linear development: from God's first world to His last world.

The "second creation" is the six days of preparation as recorded for us in Genesis 1:2ff. There we have demonstrated how God proceeded and progressed in His work of creation.

5. Creation Mediator

Following the teachings of Dr. A. Kuyper it has often been said, and is still being said, that Christ, as the Word, is Mediator of Creation. But this is wrong. A mediator mediates between two conflicting parties in order to bring the two to reconciliation. However, between God and His cosmos there is no contrast, no conflict. Not God and His created world, but God and sin are each other's opponents.

6. Faith and knowledge

Naturally, secular science started to concern itself with the question of the origin of all things. It claimed that everything came into existence through an autonomous evolutionary development (Greek: *auto* = self; *nomos* = law; autonomous means: according to a self contained and self activated law).

According to this way of thinking, causality (where the one thing causes the other in an unbreakable chain) is said to be responsible for everything. Through this autonomous development, that which was higher arose from the lower, and more developed forms of life proceeded from simpler forms. From dead material, which arose from mist and sediment, the living cell would have evolved after a long process. Over the course of millions of years and long series of changes in form, man would eventually have developed from this living organism. This development would have followed the course of "the survival of the fittest." In "the struggle for life" those specimens which couldn't adapt themselves to changes in climatic circumstances, or survive transfer to other climates, died off. Only the strongest, which could adapt themselves, survived. In these acquired adaptations new characteristics were passed on to future generations. In this way new and improved forms of life came into being. At the end of it all, man would have come into existence from one or another extinct and as yet undiscovered (missing link!) species of the apes. In order to explain the millions, or even billions, of years required for this whole process, people turn to paleontology (the study of fossils).

People have also applied this process of evolution to the explanation of the origin of "culture," including religion and morality. It has developed into a world view, an ideology, which relativizes everything.

Impressive schools of thought have developed in this way. However, each was superseded by another. They were all fads. They could not last, for they were not the truth. They were built upon hypotheses (suppositions and mere assertions). Hence there has been no success in demonstrating the transition from dead to living matter. Furthermore, all the evidence points to one source of man's origin. As far as the bold, repeatedly overthrown assertions of paleontology are concerned, one does well to distinguish between *facts* and things found (which no one denies), and the observations and conclusions based on them. Neither can they prove that the world is millions of years old by measuring the age of objects on the basis of the laws of nature. God created objects which, if analyzed by evolutionists on the day of creation, would already appear aged when in fact they had only just come into existence. For example, Adam may well have appeared to be in his twenties when created. Likewise, trees would, if cut down soon after creation, have all the rings of many years while being only a few days old.

The materialistic theory of evolution, which even attempted to trace the origin of life to physical-chemical processes, is not adhered to by anyone any longer. Nevertheless mankind holds on to the principle of autonomous evolution. People still always prefer to submit themselves to the speculations of an ever-deficient understanding rather than to the sure Word of God. Yet the fear of the Lord is the beginning of wisdom and knowledge. There can be no contrast between that which is taught by Scripture and true knowledge. Whenever there is a contrast between what appears to us as "knowledge" and Scripture, then we are dealing with a "false," deceptive knowledge. This is one of the most successful tools Satan uses to pervert souls. Herman Bavinck was correct in writing, "The first page of the Bible is more significant than all the folios of the naturalists and philosophers."

Scripture gives us the sure comfort that all things lie in the hand of our heavenly Father. It gives us a view to the fulfilment of all things. However, evolution begins and ends with a question mark. Where did "the beginning," "the prehistoric matter," come from? What got "causality" going? In what direction are we driven by it? He who rejects the Word, deprives himself of answers!

7. Six days

Since the time of Origin various views have been held concerning the "six days" spoken of in Genesis 1. They can be divided into three groups:
  A. Scripture gives a visual representation of the origin of things in six scenes
  B. the "days" were periods of time
  C. one must maintain that the days were of 24 hour duration

re: A. This view was adopted by Athanasius and Augustine and by scholastic theology of the Middle Ages. The reformers rightly rejected it, for Genesis 1 serves as a description of God's works in time in history. In the fourth commandment God establishes His six day working week as a foundation for maintaining the practice of working six days and resting on the seventh.

Karl Barth is of the opinion that in the beginning of Genesis we are not dealing with history, but with super-history. "History," he says, "is always an interplay between man and circumstances. So where man is not involved, one cannot speak of history. History only commences with man's arrival. We therefore cannot," he claims, "discuss what took place before that. That is super-history which cannot be expressed in human vocabulary. Hence the beginning of Genesis is 'saga.' It proclaims that God is above everything, and it points out that God does His work 'in Christ.' The fact that Eve was taken out of Adam's side, indicates that the congregation originates from the death (wound in the side) of Christ." However, in this way one can make anything out of anything! In this way too one can assert whatever one wants concerning creation.

Hence the "Framework Theory"[9] is popular. According to this theory Genesis 1 does not offer a description of history that really took place. It merely concerns itself with the fact that God is Creator, from whom everything has originated. This is explained within the framework (setting) of the Jewish Sabbath-week. It is in connection with this increasingly popular view that the decisions of the Synod of Assen, 1926 (the matter of Geelkerken), are in the process of being reversed within synodical circles.[10] Yet the "Framework Theory" poses the matter in exact opposition to Scripture. Scripture says in the fourth commandment that the Jewish Sabbath week is modelled upon God's creation week. The Framework Theory turns this around.

Hence in a variety of ways it is claimed that the Bible begins with "visions" concerning the beginning and concludes with "visions" concerning the end (Revelation). However, the last Bible book also presents itself as a written account of visions, while Genesis presents itself as a written account of historical events! The deciding factor here is whether or not we want to believe the Word.

re: B. By trying to explain the days of Genesis 1 as eras, man has tried to incorporate into Genesis 1 the "results" of "the" science which speaks of millions of years when speaking of the origin of things; this is an unprofitable interference. In that context a period is a succession of days and nights. However, in Genesis 1 every day is the time span between two nights. Each day is one day.

re: C. Whether the days of creation were really of twenty-four hours duration is difficult to determine. The lengths of the first days were not determined by the rotation of the earth around its axis in regard to the sun (which was only created on the fourth

---

[9] It should be noted that this was written in the 1950s. "Framework Theory" is to be distinguished from "Framework Hypothesis," although they may be related. — Editor.

[10] "Synodical circles" refers to the Reformed Churches in The Netherlands (syn.) after they deposed Dr. Klaas Schilder (and many other faithful office bearers) in 1944. These actions caused the Liberation of 1944. — Editor.

day). Yet these first days are described in the same way as the days after the creation of the sun. We do well not to go beyond the description that they were "days of creation."

8. Heaven

Concerning the creation of the heavens, Genesis 1 does not report anything other than the fact itself. It immediately goes on to speak about the creation of the earth and the creatures that lived on it. Scripture is not a complete chronicle of all God's works, but it is His Word for fallen mankind, to whom in His grace He grants Christ for re-creation, so that God would still progress from His world of the beginning to His world of the end. The heaven of Genesis 1:1 cannot be the firmament (sometimes called the first heaven). God created that on the second day. Nor can it be the starry sky (also called the second heaven). God created that on the fourth day. Therefore it must be the heaven of heavens (the third heaven), the dwelling place of God and His holy angels. That is a place, not a state of things. Jesus went there. We cannot say where that place is. We say, as Scripture does, that heaven is above. However, "above" is relative, indicating one direction for people in the northern hemisphere, but an opposite direction for those living in the southern hemisphere. Therefore "above" does not refer to a locality which can be understood in terms of distance or height — the measures we use to determine the position of a locality — but it is to be understood in terms of value. That is, it is a state to be valued above the present life. Since the creation of heaven, God has "lived" there. That is, it is there He reveals Himself most clearly and most gloriously. Heaven has been included in the historical process of creation and progresses through its own history (no "super-history").

9. Angels

Angels are spirits (Hebrews 1:14). They are not ethereal (of delicate substance) but immortal beings. They are not powers, but powerful persons. Scripture depicts them for us as self-aware (Luke 1:19), having desires (1 Peter 1:12), worshipping (Hebrews 1:6), able to rejoice (Luke 15:10), and able to speak (1 Corinthians 13:1).

God created thousands and ten thousands of them. They were not generated from one, but were created simultaneously and therefore have no family relationships. There are cherubim and seraphims, dominions, principalities, and powers (Isaiah 6:2; Colossians 1:16; Hebrews 9:5). Hence there are differences in their world, but we cannot clarify it any further. Their work is to praise God. They also serve Him as messengers in the work of revelation. They are sent to serve those who shall inherit salvation, and shall assist Christ in the final separation of the righteous from the unrighteous. This article deals particularly with the help they offer the believers. They do not contend with flesh and blood, but against the powers of hell. What a comfort it is to know that they who are on our side in Christ, are greater than those who are against us (Psalm 34; 91)! The Roman Catholic Church promulgates that every believer has a personal guardian angel, but one finds no basis for this in Scripture.

10. Devils

With the words "some of these have fallen" this article refers to the fall of many angels. This must have taken place after the seventh day (Genesis 2:4), and before the fall of mankind. One division of the angels (*Legion*, Luke 8:30) rebelled against God; and another division chose to be on His side. The New Testament gives only a sober account of this fall in 1 Timothy 3:6 and Jude 1:6. From the first text it can be concluded that the sin of the angels consisted of pride; from the second text it can be concluded that they no longer wanted to take up the positions they were appointed to by God. Hence, it was an insubordination to the hierarchical order. The head of the fallen angels is called Satan, which means adversary (of God). Together with his many evil spirits he fights against the Church as a whole, but he also attacks each member personally (Ephesians 6:12; 1 Peter 5:8), and he does so by means of lying and deceit (Lord's Day 43 of the Heidelberg Catechism). God was not pleased to save any of these angels. Eternal damnation alone awaits them. At Christ's ascension into heaven Satan was bound, so that he could no longer go his own way unimpeded, and could no longer deceive the nations. Shortly before Christ's return he shall once more be released (Revelation 20:1-6; 11:7-14). God conquers him, not according to the rule that justice lies with the strongest but according to the strength of justice!

This article says that the good angels have "by the grace of God remained steadfast and continued in their first state," but it does not indicate what kind of "grace" this was. In this, God's election was seen to be at work (1 Timothy 5:21). However, "grace" speaks of mercy toward the guilty. Perhaps De Brés' original intention would have been better rendered with "thanks be to God" in recognition here of God's work and as an expression of thankfulness that now there remain for us powerful helpers in dangers and battles. In the present-day text one must understand the word "grace" in a broader sense.

11. Sadducees and Manicheans

The former denied the existence of the angels. They regarded them as powers which proceeded from God. The teaching of some Jews and of Marcion is equally opposed to Scripture, as if the angels would be semi-gods, who assisted in creation. Concerning the words, "let us make men" (Genesis 1:26), Philo says they were spoken between God (*not* Triune according to him) and these semi-gods. Mani, under the influence of ancient (dualistic) Persian religion, taught that the powers of good and evil are created by a good god and an evil god respectively. Hence the evil spirits are evil "without having *become* depraved." Evil would then forever stand beside God, not under Him.

ARTICLE 13
THE PROVIDENCE OF GOD

We believe that this good God, after He had created all things, did not abandon them or give them up to fortune or chance, but that according to His holy will He so rules and governs them that in this world nothing happens without His direction. Yet God is not the Author of the sins which are committed nor can He be charged with them. For His power and goodness are so great and beyond understanding that He ordains and executes His work in the most excellent and just manner, even when devils and wicked men act unjustly. And as to His actions surpassing human understanding, we will not curiously inquire farther than our capacity allows us. But with the greatest humility and reverence we adore the just judgments of God, which are hidden from us, and we content ourselves that we are pupils of Christ, who have only to learn those things which He teaches us in His Word, without transgressing these limits.

This doctrine gives us unspeakable consolation, for we learn thereby that nothing can happen to us by chance, but only by the direction of our gracious heavenly Father. He watches over us with fatherly care, keeping all creatures so under His power that not one hair of our head — for they are all numbered — nor one sparrow can fall to the ground without the will of our Father. In this we trust, because we know that He holds in check the devil and all our enemies so that they cannot hurt us without His permission and will. We therefore reject the damnable error of the Epicureans, who say that God does not concern Himself with anything but leaves all things to chance.

1. Division

A. Our good God rules all things
B. He is not the author of sin although He has dominion over it
C. His inscrutable ordinances surpass our understanding
D. God's government of all things offers us unspeakable consolation
E. Rejection of the error of the Epicureans

2. Providence

The word "providence," found in the heading of this article, is not actually used in the article itself. It can be found in Article 12. It is not found in Scripture, but summarizes in one term what Scripture teaches us concerning God's relationship with His created cosmos. Concerning this relationship it has been claimed on the one hand that it was one of complete separation. God would, according to this view, have brought everything into being, but after that He no longer concerned Himself with it (Epicurus, Deism). Everything would then occur according to the nature of the things created. On the other hand, it has been claimed that God and His creation are one (Pantheism).

With the deistic separation of God from His cosmos, some came to the conclusion that everything happens "by chance;" others concluded that creation contained compelling powers which ruled everything. That led to the attempt to trace these powers and then to regulate oneself according to them (astrology and other "occult sciences"). The teaching of fate (destiny) as a power which dictates the course of our lives was also promoted. Islam is absolutely fatalistic. It claims that whatever Allah has once decreed, will happen. He cannot change that either. During the Middle Ages scholars in their cloisters philosophised about the "problem of God's government," but in practice astrology and all other kinds of idolatrous practices flourished. Even popes let themselves be guided by them. Things haven't improved today. "Magic and fortune-telling" have a hold on many. The craving for gambling is also a recognition of "fortune." The reformers have battled against all of this. Using the detailed treatises of Augustine on this issue, they again pointed out from Scripture that God governs the world.

With the term "providence" then, we mean:

A. *God's maintenance*: He preserves what has been created; He brought everything into existence and ensures the continuation of such existence. Sometimes He does so directly and immediately (angels), sometimes indirectly, by the mediation of other actions (people, animals). Some objects He maintains in their created form (sun and earth), others in their generations (trees and animals);

B. *God's government*: He leads every creature and every situation according to His purpose. That purpose is His glorification in heaven and hell. Nothing hinders Him in this. He is great. The rage of the demons and the sins of mankind are no obstacles to Him either. They do sin against His will, but not independent of His will. He is above every creature and rules over it, while the creature does as it pleases.

3. Character

Concerning all this, Article 13 speaks in a practical, believing manner. Lord's Day 10 of the Heidelberg Catechism does so too. What is said is clear without any need of further clarification. Full emphasis is laid on the comfort of God's government. Included in that is our calling not to live our lives independent of the confession of this divine government. Rather, we are to look to it in all that befalls us, as described by Q&A 28 of the Heidelberg Catechism. On closer theoretical reflection, questions arise which surpass our understanding.

This article has a beautiful solution to what we should do with such questions. Of course, mankind has wanted to explain God's "rational" (!) government. Optimistic Humanism and also Roman Catholic teaching under the influence of Neo-Platonism declared all adversity reasonable, as prerequisites for prosperity, like a dark background against which the light would show up better. The appalling experiences of our century have swept away these inventions of the mind. Modern philosophy and literature consider our lives to be governed by destiny. We have been cast into a horrible existence. What other option do we then have but to adapt ourselves and to accept our fate? Who still has hope? The world is absurd! Over against Roman Catholic and Humanist theodicy (justification of God's actions) and in opposition to the fatalism of modern philosophy (existentialism) which lacks outlook, we gladly hold on to the good advice of this article!

4. God and evil

Man sins (James 1:13). Under God's government he is not a robot without a will. After the fall man retained his own (depraved) will, by means of which he himself chooses and acts, and so remains responsible for his actions (more concerning this in Article 14). However, if man sins, it does not occur independent of God. God "allows" it and therein works (active permission) good (see Genesis 45:8; 50:20). God is not the author of sin and is not guilty of it. He inclined the hearts of Joseph's brothers but only to what they themselves wanted to do. So, by the manipulation of the evil of these brothers, God saw to it that there would be grain for Jacob's house in Egypt. In this instance the LORD's action has been revealed to us. In most cases, what God does with evil remains hidden from us.

5. Natural law and miracles

Since God in His providence continues to work according to a fixed order, we can observe it and describe it. We call its formulation "natural law." Yet "nature" does not establish a "law."

Sometimes God works by a method which we cannot see beforehand or afterward. Then we say, "It's a miracle!" However, Scripture calls all God's works miracles.

6. Common grace?

By His providential order God leads the beginning of His world to its end wherein His mercy and His righteousness will shine forth in heaven and hell. It is incorrect therefore to speak of "common grace" when God, in His sustenance of all things, permits, by means of sinful developments, the unfolding of those things which He laid down in creation. His sustenance of all things serves both justice and mercy. His sustenance causes both the wheat and the weeds to ripen. Surely one cannot speak of grace applying to weeds which are allowed to grow only to be thrown into the fire!

ARTICLE 14
THE CREATION AND FALL OF MAN AND HIS INCAPABILITY OF DOING WHAT IS TRULY GOOD

We believe that God created man of dust from the ground and He made and formed him after His own image and likeness, good, righteous, and holy. His will could conform to the will of God in every respect. But, when man was in this high position, he did not appreciate it nor did he value his excellency. He gave ear to the words of the devil and wilfully subjected himself to sin and consequently to death and the curse. For he transgressed the commandment of life which he had received; by his sin he broke away from God, who was his true life; he corrupted his whole nature. By all this he made himself liable to physical and spiritual death. Since man became wicked and perverse, corrupt in all his ways, he has lost all his excellent gifts which he had once received from God. He has nothing left but some small traces, which are sufficient to make man inexcusable. For whatever light is in us has changed into darkness, as Scripture teaches us, The light shines in the darkness, and the darkness has not overcome it; where the apostle John calls mankind darkness.

Therefore we reject all teaching contrary to this concerning the free will of man, since man is but a slave to sin and no one can receive anything except what is given him from heaven. For who dares to boast that he of himself can do any good, when Christ says: No one can come to Me unless the Father who sent Me draws him? Who will glory in his own will, when he understands that the mind that is set on the flesh is hostile to God? Who can speak of his knowledge, since the unspiritual man does not receive the gifts of the Spirit of God? In short, who dares to claim anything, when he realizes that we are not competent of ourselves to claim anything as coming from us, but that our competence is from God? Therefore what the apostle says must justly remain sure and firm: God is at work in you both to will and to work for His good pleasure. For there is no understanding nor will conformable to the understanding and will of God unless Christ has brought it about; as He teaches us: Apart from Me you can do nothing.

1. Division

This article gradually leads up to the rejection of "all teaching ... concerning the free will of man." This is the main point of the article. All that precedes this statement of rejection serves as a preamble to it. For that reason the comprehensive subject of the "creation and fall of man" is not dealt with exhaustively here.

We can divide the article as follows:
A. the creation of man in God's image (first sentence)
B. the fall into sin ("But, when man was in this high position . . . by his sin he broke away from God")
C. what became of man as a result of sin ("he corrupted his whole nature" . . . "calls mankind darkness")
D. rejection of the error concerning the "free will" (commencing with "Therefore we reject" to the end of the article)

2. Historical background and actual significance

This article strikes a blow on the anti-Roman Catholic front. There the error concerning the "free will" was, and still is, one of the focal points, according to which man is "free" to choose between good and evil. He can do the one as easily as the other, and is therefore inclined to do good. This error was occasionally heard during the first centuries, but it didn't come to the fore with force until Pelagius propagated it and John of Eclanum defended it in opposition to Augustine, its greatest opponent. The Church rejected this error at the Synod of Orange, A.D. 529. Yet this did not eradicate it. During the century in which the Great Reformation took place, it became a point of contention between Erasmus and Luther, Pighi and Calvin, Father Grenier (monk of St. Victor) with his book *Le bouclier de la Foy* (= *Shield of Faith*) and Guido de Brés with his *Baston de la Foy* (= *Staff of Faith*). At the beginning of the seventeenth century it was once again defended by Arminius and his followers (the Arminians or Remonstrants) who were opposed by Gomarus and the Counter-Remonstrants. At the beginning of the nineteenth century, Hendrik de Cock and the Secessionists (1834) had to engage in battle on this point with Hofstede de Groot and the men of the Groningen school. It is still the subject of controversy between the Reformed and all kinds of liberal theologians and Humanists.

The tenacity of this error's existence is not to be attributed to error or ignorance, but rather to the haughty independence of the sinner who refuses to surrender to God's grace.

This error forms the basis of many other errors: denial of the Scriptural teaching of election and the attack on the redeeming work of Christ. Each of them prevents an understanding of the Scriptural teaching concerning the conversion and deliverance of the sinner.

The Church of Rome tenaciously holds on to this error. However, it has done so somewhat more moderately through Semi- or Neo-Pelagianism. Concerning the decree on justification the Council of Trent (1545-1563) declared that "the free will in fallen man is not in the least extinguished, but is weakened and reduced in power." Further, this Council declared in Canon 5: Whoever claims that man's free will was lost and extinguished after Adam's sin, a fabrication which the devil introduced into the Church, is cursed. This was reinforced by the Vatican Council (1870).

The atrocities of the great world wars during the first half of the 20th century have dealt the humanistic faith in man, as preached by Pelagius, a heavy blow but it recovered quickly and the old ideas of Pelagius and the Neo-Pelagians, of the men of the Groningen school and numerous liberal theologians, of Erasmus and Pighi, of libertines, Baptists, and Arminians, continue to surface with all kinds of variations and under different titles, e.g. "Moral Re-Armament" (M.R.A.).

3. Pelagius and his teaching

Pelagius was a contemporary of Augustine, also born in 354. He was a well-educated British monk, whom one could admire for his ascetic lifestyle. He worked in Rome, North Africa, and Palestine. About the year 400 he took up action in Rome against the city's immorality. He wanted nothing to do with man's incapacity to improve himself. He denied original sin. "All we received from Adam was our flesh," he claimed, "and this does not contain sin" (Manicheism). Therefore, according to him, children do not require baptism. Already at that time man taught that baptism itself washed away sin (Roman Catholicism still teaches this). However, they say that Adam's sin did introduce a bad example into the world and that people err by following that bad example. They maintain that perfection is possible if we follow Christ's example. According to Pelagius, death is a natural process and not a consequence of sin.

4. Free will?

Doesn't man have a free will? The answer depends on what one understands by "freedom" of the will. Man certainly has a will of his own. Man is no "stock or block" (Canons of Dort). Possession of a will of his own is part of man's essence. However, this will is *depraved*. His enmity against God constantly leads him to the *wrong* choice. The heart of man desires evil and therefore man constantly chooses evil. For this the term "formal freedom" is used to denote that man, as a rational-moral being, is not a machine but makes his own choices and is responsible, and that he has a kind of "material freedom of the will," the freedom to choose good or evil (Canons of Dort, III/IV, Rejection of Errors #3-5).

5. The image of God

In Genesis 1:26, 27 the words "image and likeness" denote one and the same thing. The Heidelberg Catechism restricts itself to the word "image." Here the Confession refers to Ephesians 4:24. Dogmatics also makes a reference to Colossians 3:10. The "new man" spoken of here is the man renewed by Christ. One is to recognize the "original man" in the "new man" where Christ restores what sin destroyed, and where Scripture acknowledges only one concept of man. One can compare this to a statue which has been destroyed and rebuilt. The old statue can be recognized in the new statue because the latter was made according to the drawings of the original statue.

The image of God is not reflected exclusively in specific qualities of man; then angels would also be God's image, something which is not stated anywhere in Scripture. Man was God's image, His representative, in all his conduct, by faithfully executing the office to which he was appointed. He was God's image in his righteous dominion over all creatures (Genesis 1:28; Psalm 8). God endowed man with all the gifts required for that. However, mere possession of the gifts God gave man to reflect His image did not qualify man as God's image. (The term "image-bearer" is inaccurate.)

Roman Catholic theology distinguishes between two concepts of man. First of all it recognizes "the natural man" (*puris naturalibus*). This good person already has the natural desire (*concupiscentia*), which can be a source of sin, but of itself is not sinful (note the inherent contradiction). It claims that this natural desire can be suppressed by the natural man, but only through immense exertion. That is why God also gave man the image of God as a supernatural gift and as a golden bridle to control this desire (man in the state of grace). Through sin man lost this "golden bridle." However, it argues that, just as a horse without a bridle is still a complete and perfect horse, so man after his fall into sin is still sound and good (Pelagius!). When this fallen yet sound person uses his faculties in the right way, he can do good, even though this is no more than what is naturally good. By this he does not obtain salvation, but he is not lost either. The whole doctrine of grace as a supernatural good is connected to this.

6. Could conform to the will of God

The words of our Confession: "could conform to the will of God in every respect," point to what Augustine said concerning man in the state of righteousness: He was "capable of not sinning." That had to become, "incapable of sinning." Instead, it became "incapable of not sinning."

7. Origin of sin

Outside of God's revelation, this is an insoluble question. Conflicting answers have been given. As was already done in Paradise, all blame is shifted away from man.

A. Sin originates in God like a dark background, just like a shadow and light. Therefore it is eternal and essential (Böhme, Schelling). However, see 1 John 1:5: "God is light and in Him is no darkness at all."

B. From eternity the good god existed in opposition to the evil god (Dualism).

C. Sin lies in matter (Plato). The soul as the "superior part" of man is good (Asceticism).

Dialectical theology regards the first chapters of Genesis as "saga" (not myth). It does not want to acknowledge a fall into sin in the course of history. History itself is "sinful" and the saga of the fall qualifies it as such.

In opposition to this Article 14 confesses that man's will could once conform to God's will and was in a "high position." The fall into sin took place in history, through the "deliberate disobedience" of man (Q&A 9 of the Heidelberg Catechism). A familiarity with the event of the fall into sin and the meaning of the "test command" is assumed here.

Not a single explanation will suffice for this fall into sin. Scripture calls it folly. Just as every explanation falls short, so there is not a single valid excuse for what man did. We must maintain that it was man's *deed*. Pointing to man's underlying nature amounts to blaming God for sin.

8. The "Geelkerken issue"

Dr. J.G. Geelkerken was of the opinion that among the various ideas concerning paradisal history, the Reformed opinion was not allowed to be imposed as the only plausible opinion. It could, he said, be correct, but it could also be incorrect. He wanted freedom, wishing to dispute whether the tree, the snake, etc., were observable, tangible realities. The Synod of Assen, 1926, rejected this, declaring it to be in conflict with Articles 4 and 5 of the Belgic Confession. With this the authority of Scripture had actually become an issue. Scripture clearly gives us the first chapters of Genesis as an historical description. Today there is a concerted effort afoot to undo the decisions of "Assen".[11]

9. Depravity through sin

By willingly submitting to sin, man broke the lifeline with God, terminated the covenant with God, and thereby "corrupted his whole nature." Now he is "totally unable to do any good and inclined to all evil" (Q&A 8 of the Heidelberg Catechism). This article says, "man became wicked and perverse, corrupt in all his ways." In connection with this read Canons of Dort, III/IV #1; Genesis 6:5; Romans 8:7. The disposition of the flesh is "enmity against God."

---

[11] In 1967, a number of years after the author wrote this book, the synodical Churches did indeed retract the 1926 decisions. — Editor.

10. The small *vestigia*

This article states that of all the excellent gifts God gave man in creation, he has nothing left but "some small traces." The Latin text uses *"vestigia,"* which means "traces." If "remnant" was used, one could still say: the thing itself no longer exists, but there is still *something*, just a fraction of it. The word "traces," however, nicely indicates that there is still some remembrance of those earlier gifts, but nothing at all of the actual gifts as they once were. A footprint in the snow points to the foot that was there, but it is not a part of that foot. On the basis of this expression in the Confession one cannot, therefore, build a doctrine of man losing God's image in a "narrow sense," but retaining it in a "general sense." This "doctrine" has led to some very questionable views concerning the potential of fallen man. In Genesis 9:6 God does say that whoever kills a man must himself be killed, for man was made in the image of God. However, this text does not say that fallen man was in any way still God's image. It merely says that God still regards man with a view to his mandate and purpose. Christ says concerning fallen man, "You are of your father the devil, and the desires of your father you want to do" (John 8:44). (See Canons of Dort, III/IV #4, concerning what it is that man does with these traces.)

11. Punishment

Man made himself guilty through his sin. Since God does not regard the guilty as guiltless, punishment is inevitable. Man became prey to death and the curse. In this context Article 14 speaks of "physical and spiritual death." As to what was originally meant by these terms is not so important. What is important is that we can and must understand them in a Scriptural sense. Often an additional term is suggested. One then distinguishes as follows:

A. spiritual death (which also affects the body!), which is our inability to do good (Ephesians 2:1, "dead in trespasses and sin");

B. physical (or temporal) death, dying (Hebrews 9:27);

C. eternal death, the suffering of everlasting destruction far from the presence of God (2 Thessalonians 1:9).

Scripture also speaks of the "first" and "second" death (Revelation 20:6, 14).

12. Rejection of the error concerning the "free will"

One is referred to the last part of Article 14. It is entirely constructed from quotes from Scripture. The Confession does not theorize about the error concerning the "free will," but makes it abundantly clear that this error is directly opposed to the witness of Holy Scripture so extensively presented here.

ARTICLE 15
ORIGINAL SIN

We believe that by the disobedience of Adam original sin has spread throughout the whole human race. It is a corruption of the entire nature of man and a hereditary evil which infects even infants in their mother's womb. As a root it produces in man all sorts of sin. It is, therefore, so vile and abominable in the sight of God that it is sufficient to condemn the human race. It is not abolished nor eradicated even by baptism, for sin continually streams forth like water welling up from this woeful source. Yet, in spite of all this, original sin is not imputed to the children of God to their condemnation but by His grace and mercy is forgiven them. This does not mean that the believers may sleep peacefully in their sin, but that the awareness of this corruption may make them often groan as they eagerly wait to be delivered from this body of death.

In this regard we reject the error of the Pelagians, who say that this sin is only a matter of imitation.

1. Introduction

Augustine once wrote, "In the matter of preaching, one must know most about original sin, but when it comes to understanding there is nothing more mysterious. Even the sharpest mind fails to comprehend it. The authority of God's Word alone must lead us step by step. We must submit to this authority which does not, and cannot, deceive us."

That being so, it's not at all surprising that fierce protests have been levelled at precisely this portion of our Confession.

H. Marsman, in *Tempel en Kruis* (Temple and Cross) expressed this protest as follows:

> *No deadlier wound has festered*
> *than the gnawing and lingering notion*
> *of a debt, a sin inherited,*
> *committed before we existed,*
> *causing the flesh's contamination.*

It all comes down to the question of whether we wish to submit to the sovereign God and His Word, which is the truth, or whether we prefer to honour ourselves. Here too the deciding factors are faith versus unbelief.

2. Division of the article

A. Description of original sin
   1. its cause
   2. its essence
   3. its extent

B. Consequences of original sin
   1. it is the root of all evil in man
   2. it has made us damnable before God

C. Believers and original sin
   1. it is also a fountain of sin within believers
   2. it is, however, not imputed to them to their condemnation
   3. this may not make one careless, but must be an incentive to put the old nature to death

D. Rejection of the Pelagian error that sin is only a matter of imitation

3. Terminology

Dogmatic usage of the term "original sin" implies something different from what this article understands by it. The former explains it as: original guilt + original contamination = original sin. This article, on the other hand, understands "original sin" to be the depravity that clings to us through Adam's transgression.

4. Cause

The Confession points to the "disobedience of Adam" as the cause of original sin. The Confession does not speak of the method by which Adam's disobedience affected us. (In the Compendium,[13] Q&A 11 reads as follows: "Does the disobedience of Adam affect us? Yes indeed, for he is the father of us all, and we have all sinned in him.") Basically two aspects are pointed out here:

A. Adam was our covenant head; he acted as our representative. Not only did his actions have consequences for himself, but also for all his descendants.

B. The objection of Ezekiel 18:20 ("The son shall not bear the guilt of the father") points to Romans 5:12 (compare Hebrews 7:10). Adam's sin was not imputed to us as if, but because, we ourselves were involved in it. Paul rejoices over the wisdom of God concerning "one for all" (Romans 5). In giving Adam *that* position God could, by maintaining His established order of paradise, let us share in the righteousness obtained by One.

5. Essence

This article describes original sin as the "corruption of (our) entire nature," referring to Romans 3:10. One should also take note of the subsequent verses of this chapter; see also Romans 8:7 and the Canons of Dort, III/IV #1-4. One could call sin "hereditary infirmity," this being the English translation of "vice hereditaire," but not in the sense that it has robbed us of something but for the

---

[13] *The Compendium of the Christian Religion* written in 1611 by Hermannus Faukelius, minister of the Word of God in Middelburg. The Compendium is a short form of Catechism used in some Reformed churches. Although it contains the same three parts as the Heidelberg Catechism and is based on it, the questions and answers are arranged differently. — TRANS.

rest has left us untouched (like a man without an arm). It totally corrupted our whole nature and existence. Therefore the translation "hereditary evil" as suggested by Rev. C. Vonk is better, at least clearer. The disability is active. The endeavour of the flesh "is enmity against God" (Romans 8:7). Over against this the Roman Catholic doctrine fantasizes that original sin only exists in the loss of the supernatural gifts of the image of God. Our natural existence, weakened by the loss of God's image, was left untouched (see paragraph 5 of the chapter on Article 14, and also paragraph 12 below).

6. Extent

Sin touched everyone. All are born in unrighteousness (though not created that way in Adam) and are conceived in sin. The Lord Jesus was the exception. The Roman Catholics also make Mary the exception but cannot give any Scriptural proof for doing so. The guilt of the first breach is imputed to everyone; consequently each person is born in sin.

7. Radical

Man's depravity is not just total, but also radical (Latin: *radix*; French: Racine = *root*). Man is not born as a neutral being. His heart is the source of all evil (Jeremiah 17:9; Mark 7:21-23). Original sin brought forth all kinds of sins. It is an active robbery of good.

Sins can be distinguished according to the instruments by which they principally come into action: sinful thoughts, words, or deeds. They can also be distinguished according to the commandments which they transgress; sin against the 1st, 4th, or 9th commandment. One can also make a distinction between sins of involvement versus sins of negligence. However, every distinction between great or small, between "daily" and "deadly sins," is nonsense. Both distinctions are poisonous. All sins render us guilty. One sin is unforgivable: blasphemy against the Holy Spirit (see paragraph 5 of the chapter on Article 11). Roman Catholic scholasticism speaks of seven cardinal sins.

8. Damnable

Original sin renders us damnable. "Those who are in the flesh cannot please God" (Romans 8:8).

9. In believers too

Much has been written concerning this article's pronouncement that original sin "is not abolished nor eradicated even by baptism." On this statement man has based all kinds of considerations concerning baptism, but incorrectly so. The Confession does not discuss baptism here. It will do that quite elaborately in a subsequent article. There is good reason for Rev. C. Vonk's opinion that De Brés had in mind here a decision of the Council of Mileve. This Council declared that the free will, which became powerless with the first man, can only be restored through the grace of baptism. Hence the errors of these decisions are opposed here. In this respect, too, Scripture is clear (Romans 7:18, 19). (See also Canons of Dort, V #1-4, and the text of this article.)

The sin which has remained in the believers is not imputed to their condemnation (Romans 8:1-4; 2 Corinthians 5:21; Q&A 60 of the Heidelberg Catechism).

10. "I press on" (Philippians 3:12)

God's forgiveness may not make us careless. Psalm 130:4 says, "But there is forgiveness with You, that You may be feared" (see also Romans 6:1-4; Canons of Dort, V #2).

Believers have no delight in sin (1 John 3:19). They fight against it and shall one day overcome it (Romans 16:20). Unbelievers on the other hand cover up one sin with another. Their heart remains averse.

One must not understand the expression "body of death" to suggest that sin resides in the body. This expression refers to the constitution of this life which lies in death.

11. Rejection of Pelagius

In conclusion, the Pelagian error that sin is not an "hereditary evil" but only a matter of imitation, is rejected in a few words. This is sufficient in view of the detailed Scriptural proof provided in Article 15.

12. Natural and supernatural good

With this article we will briefly pay attention to one overriding tendency of the Roman Catholic doctrine. This tendency, following in the footsteps of Thomas Aquinas, is not governed by the Scriptural contrast sin-grace, physical-spiritual, curse-acquittal, but by the scholastic co-ordination "natural and supernatural." By "natural" is understood all that constitutes the existence of every creature, hence that which makes the creature what it is. In a human being that includes all faculties and powers which make him true man. In contrast to that, "supernatural" is all that goes beyond the "natural," but which God, out of free grace, granted to people and angels. That includes beholding God, heavenly salvation and all the gifts of grace required to attain this salvation. These gifts elevate the rational creature far above the "natural" order and make him share in the divine nature.

On the basis of this distinction Rome draws a sharp dividing line between knowledge and faith, philosophy and theology. It recognizes a "natural" knowledge of God derived from natural powers and a supernatural knowledge of God derived from the powers of grace. It is sometimes said that although "natural" man is satisfied with the former, he at times desires the latter.

The supernatural is lost through sin. It can be compared to the removal of the second floor from a two-storey house. The ground-floor remained habitable, even though the windows may have been broken. According to Rome, original sin has not corrupted man. Essentially man is still good; merely weakened. Man can no longer elevate himself to the supernatural. His residence has become smaller, less comfortable. Thomas Aquinas criticized Pelagius, not in order to deny that man still had a "free will" and is inclined to do good, but to point out that Pelagius had overlooked the fact that the "natural, free will" can only strive for the supernatural if it is elevated by grace (Neo- or Semi-Pelagianism). This elevation is granted through baptism. In this way original sin (loss of the supernatural capacity) is removed. The other sacraments serve to enable man to use the supernatural grace granted in baptism. The Church of Rome, to use its own words, is the guardian of life. Where this life respects natural wisdom Rome does not condemn it but elevates it to higher grace. This leads to complete acceptance of "natural" life (carnival) and to shunning life (fasting), and to typical Roman Catholic Sunday observance. This also explains the ease with which the Roman Catholics co-operate with Humanists and Socialists.

In light of this, it must be concluded that unbaptized Roman Catholic children, who did not receive supernatural grace, cannot be saved, but are not wretched either. They consciously lack salvation, but are satisfied in their "natural" existence. One can compare this to the fact that any sensible person is not bothered by the fact that he is unable to fly, although he is thoroughly conscious of this fact.

In light of this we can understand the Church of Rome's lenient attitude toward the "good works" of unbelievers. Their deeds lack supernatural good, but that does not make them bad. A horse lacks man's ability to reason, but that does not make it a bad horse.

Against all this it suffices to say that the starting-point, the scholastic co-ordination of "natural" and "supernatural" is totally unScriptural. It is a system which totally obstructs the way to understanding the Scriptural preaching of sin and grace, of curse and acquittal.

ARTICLE 16
DIVINE ELECTION

We believe that, when the entire offspring of Adam plunged into perdition and ruin by the transgression of the first man, God manifested Himself to be as He is: merciful and just. Merciful, in rescuing and saving from this perdition those whom in His eternal and unchangeable counsel He has elected in Jesus Christ our Lord by His pure goodness, without any consideration of their works. Just, in leaving the others in the fall and perdition into which they have plunged themselves.

1. Introduction

Considering that election is said to be the doctrine which characterizes the Reformed faith the most, this article's specific placement within the Confession is rather striking. The Heidelberg

Catechism does not touch on election at all. It merely makes an incidental reference to it in Q&A 52 ("me and all His chosen ones") and Q&A 54 ("a church chosen to everlasting life"). Only the Canons of Dort elaborates on this confession, compelled to do so in response to the disputes of the Arminians. However, it approaches the subject discreetly, avoiding inquisitive prying. See in particular Canons of Dort, I #14. Meanwhile, we must not pretend to be wiser than God by considering it better to be silent about election. Indeed, the LORD clearly reveals election in Scripture for the following reasons:

A. *In order that God may be glorified.* By means of this confession we give God all the honour for our deliverance. "So then it is not of him who wills, nor of him who runs, but of God who shows mercy" (Romans 9:16; Canons of Dort, I #18).

B. *In order that we may be comforted.* Read 2 Timothy 1:3-10. Here Paul comforts and encourages his "son" Timothy. In so doing, he directs Timothy's attention firstly to the gifts granted him (vss. 6, 7), and secondly, to the holy calling by which God wished to preserve him, son of a Greek father, from heathendom (vs. 9). This calling was certainly not motivated by Timothy having made himself worthy of it by merit of his own deeds. If that were the case, his sins could make him unworthy of it again. Rather, the motivation behind this calling was God's gracious purpose by which, "before time began," He regarded Timothy in Christ. Would God change that eternal purpose? Hence Timothy must remain of good courage! Thirdly, Paul comforts Timothy, his assistant, by directing his attention to the contents of the Gospel he himself declares (vs. 10). (See Canons of Dort, I #14.)

2. Division of the article
   A. God has displayed Himself to the fallen human race as merciful and righteous
   B. 1. How He displays His mercy
   2. How He displays His righteousness

3. Starting-point and method

The Confession proceeds from mankind's depravity and what God has done for man in the course of time. It does not proceed with considerations "from eternity." The Canons of Dort, I #1-6, treat the subject in the same manner. We do well to adopt this method when we think and talk about God's election. In so doing, we must always commence with our depravity through our own fault. Whoever refuses to admit that, will, with a view to God's predestination, land himself with insurmountable difficulties. Those refusing to admit man's fallen state through his own fault always end up rejecting the confession of election. Hence all who would reject the doctrine of election must in turn reject man's depravity, for *then* the initiative to seek God would arise in man himself.

4. God's counsel

God demonstrates His mercy to fallen mankind by rescuing many from their perdition. Many . . . not all! He does not send His Gospel of salvation to all, but "to whom He will and when He wills" (Canons of Dort, I #3). Among those to whom He does send His Gospel, there are those who accept it, but also those who reject it. This is not ascribed to any worthiness or action on man's part (Canons of Dort, I, Rejection of Errors #9; and III/IV #7). This all takes place according to God's counsel. *God* decides who will hear the Gospel and who will accept it. He calls and delivers those whom He, according to His counsel, has chosen for that purpose.

Scripture refers to this counsel (deliberation) in various ways: foreknowledge, purpose, fixed counsel, decree, good pleasure. God's counsel is the sum total of His eternal decisions concerning what in the course of time shall be or shall take place. This counsel is "eternal" (Ephesians 1:4; 2 Timothy 1:9), and "unchangeable." "My counsel shall stand, and I will do all My pleasure" (Isaiah 46:10). This counsel of God, outside of which not even a hair can fall from our heads, is not merely limited to all "natural" events, but also to all man's rational actions. "The preparations of the heart belong to man, but the answer of the tongue is from the Lord" (Proverbs 16:1). God also decides our eternal well and woe. This "part" (even though with reference to God's counsel one cannot really speak of a "part") we call predestination (appointed beforehand) which we distinguish in election (choosing - Canons of Dort, I #7), and reprobation (rejection - Canons of Dort, I #15).

5. Election and rejection

Election is God's unchangeable purpose whereby, *before* the foundation of the world, out of the whole human race, He chose in Christ, out of mere grace, a definite number of persons, neither better nor more worthy than others (see Canons of Dort, I #7).

Rejection means that not all people are elected; some people have been passed by in God's eternal election, namely, those whom "God has decreed to leave in the common misery into which they have by their own fault plunged themselves" (see Canons of Dort, I #15).

6. In Christ Jesus

Election did not take place *because of* Christ. He did not bring it about for us. Those who belonged to Him are given to Him from the Father and He obtained life for them. Rather, election is *in* Christ, that is to say, in close connection with Him. God saw the elect in Him. In this way He poured out His love to them.

7. "Undeserved blessings"

Election is purely out of loving-kindness. It is not based on "foreseen faith" or any merits on our part. It occurs "without any consideration of their works." It is not based on faith, but it results in faith, not because we are, but so that we would be, holy and blameless (Ephesians 1:4). Its source is solely God's good pleasure.

8. Unjust?

One cannot call election unjust, for the Lord would not have acted unjustly if He had left everyone in the misery into which they had plunged themselves. While it cannot be said that rejection takes place because of the sins of those rejected, the fact that they are lost is their own fault. God "leaves" (active verb!) them in the perdition into which they have plunged themselves.

Our difficulty in refraining from raising objections against God's rejection of sinners and our inclination to regard it as unjust is due to the fact that we constantly want to haughtily assert ourselves as critical spectators of God's work instead of letting ourselves, as guilty sinners, be taught by Him (see Luke 13:23ff.).

9. Our guarantee

Assurance of one's election is a fruit of faith. It is certainly not something which, once acquired, is guaranteed to remain with one, even if one neglects to believe. It is ours only by faith, by living in faith (Canons of Dort, I #12). We must grow toward it. "Be even more diligent to make your calling and election sure, for if you do these things you will never stumble" (2 Peter 1:10).

10. Supralapsarianism and Infralapsarianism

This dispute is about the sequence of God's decrees, or the object of election.

"Supra" puts it this way: 1. election and rejection; 2. creation; 3. fall; and then deliverance.

On the other hand, "Infra" puts it this way: 1. creation; 2. fall; 3. election and rejection; and then deliverance.

With "Supra" the creation is merely a means of achieving an aim; with "Infra" it is something positive. "Supra" emphasizes God's sovereignty, "Infra" man's responsibility. However, the whole dispute is nonsense. With God there is no succession, nor are His decrees sequential. His counsel is a single concept. Fortunately the Reformed Confessions make no pronouncement in this respect. Yet their way of introducing election is Infralapsarian. They specify fallen man as the object of election. With "Supra" the object is man not yet fallen, nor even created.

11. Fatalism

Fatalism compares the relationship between God's counsel and what takes place over time to the making of a film on the one hand, and the showing of a film on the other hand. It excludes any responsibility on man's part. Yet that is not what Scripture teaches us. Rather, Scripture says that everything happens in accordance with God's will, *and* that God is grieved and angered about what takes place. We ourselves would have to be God in order to understand how God had already determined everything from eternity, and now directs all things according to that counsel, not compelling anyone, but leaving everyone free. According to Scripture God's decrees and our actions occur simultaneously. "Him

(Jesus) being delivered by the determined counsel and foreknowledge of God, you have . . . put to death" (Acts 2:23; see also Canons of Dort, I #13.)

We do well to differentiate between the decree of election and the execution of this decree. When Scripture speaks of "election" it does not always refer to the decree. It often speaks of God's electing work in the course of time (Deuteronomy 10:15; 2 Peter 1:10).

In the days of the Reformation, in the controversy against the Church of Rome and later against the Arminians, all attention was focussed on "without any consideration of their works." Today, in opposition to fatalism (belief in fate, destiny) and determinism (all is a closed chain of cause and effect), attention must be payed to the fact that God's purpose also does not negate our responsibility. In His counsel, God has included us as responsible creatures, and He executes His counsel in such a way that our responsibility is not removed. He does not deal with us as if we were "stocks and blocks" (Canons of Dort, III/IV #16; and see also #14).

12. Arminianism

The Arminians objected to:
A. speaking about the "*unchangeable* counsel"
B. speaking about "*those*" whom He has elected
C. the expression "without *any* consideration of their works"
D. saying that God "*leaves* the others in their fall and perdition"

In fact, they differentiate between a "preceding" and a "successive" will. They believe that the "preceding" will occurs before man's actions. Yet this is only provisional. Only the "successive" will, which succeeds man's actions, and tests them, is definitive. God's preceding will was that all should be saved. To that end He gave His Son as Saviour for all, and let His preaching go out to all men (not true!). Dependent upon the acceptance or rejection of this preaching, God decided on the gift of salvation. By this it becomes evident why the Arminians objected to exactly those points of this article listed above. The Arminians also speak of election, but they distinguish:

A. election to initial grace

B. election to effective grace (after the person had used the first grace properly)
C. election to glory (after also the second grace had been used properly)

According to the Arminians, this threefold election is "eternal." God knew beforehand who would make good use of the initial and effective grace. However, according to them, this eternal election is based on "foreseen faith."

One traces this line of thought among all kinds of groups who subscribe to "universal atonement," though at times it is expressed less theologically. Such is the case virtually everywhere outside Reformed circles.

However, Reformed circles too are threatened by a dilution of the doctrine of election. This starts when people only wish to speak of reprobation as an act of God in the history of salvation, a Divine response to man's rejection of the Gospel of grace. However, by continuing in this line of thinking, and by not taking seriously the confession of Dort concerning reprobation, all one will end up with concerning the doctrine of election is merely an Arminian denial of it.

ARTICLE 17
THE RESCUE OF FALLEN MAN

We believe that, when He saw that man had thus plunged himself into physical and spiritual death and made himself completely miserable, our gracious God in His marvellous wisdom and goodness set out to seek man when he trembling fled from Him. He comforted him with the promise that He would give him His Son, born of woman, to bruise the head of the serpent and to make man blessed.

1. Seeking love

Here the beginning of the work of deliverance is ascribed to God with thanks and praise, and confession is made of the fact that He already began the work of deliverance immediately after the fall of mankind in Paradise (Q&A 19 of the Heidelberg Catechism). Here the Confession takes a stand against the opinions of, among others, Servetus and the Anabaptists, who claim that God only gave Israel promises for this temporal life and that this nation had no knowledge of Christ or eternal salvation. Hence they claim that the Old Testament, as a "book of the Jews," is meaningless for us. However, the Gospel, out of which we live, was already revealed in Paradise. Most certainly Israel also knew that salvation was through Christ. It longed for David's great Son. The message of salvation brought to Zechariah and Mary made them mindful of the promises to the fathers of old (see also Isaiah 33:22). Paul rightly says that the righteousness of faith bears witness to the law and the prophets. The Gospel is one, beginning at Paradise. *There already, God sought us.*

In addition to that, this article praises God's wonderful wisdom and goodness (see 1 Corinthians 1:23, 24). No one could find a way leading to salvation but God; in His wonderful, divine wisdom, He opened the way for us. That God did this makes His goodness all the more praiseworthy (Luke 1:78; Ephesians 1).

2. Covenant

In Paradise God demanded from man an obedience of love. God placed before man the perspective of life unfolding completely in eternal fellowship with Him. Whether or not man wanted to walk with his God, who wanted to be a Father for him, in this way would be tested by the "test command." We call this relationship, in which God presented Himself to man, the covenant relationship.

It is striking that this article does not speak of the covenant.

Calvin, Bullinger, Olevianus, and Ursinus have written a lot about the covenant. The Confession merely refers to it in passing. There is no official ecclesiastical "doctrine of the covenant." However, the Confessions and the liturgical forms do contain building blocks. Such is the case here too. It is confessed here that God, in spite of man breaking his bond with God, did not let man go. He continued with His covenant. Hosea says (6:7a), "But like men they transgressed the covenant" (see also Romans 5:12-14; 1 Corinthians 15:21, 22). A covenant is a mutual agreement between two or more parties, whereby they bind themselves to each other by promises and demands, with the threat of retribution hanging over the one who breaks the covenant. God's promise to man was and is: Himself and eternal communion with Him ("to be God to you," Genesis 17:7). His demand is: Give me your heart. Attached to that is the threat: death. This covenant *before* the fall is at times referred to as: covenant of works, covenant of Paradise, covenant of God's favour, or covenant of creation. At the time it existed between God and the whole human race incorporated in Adam. When man broke the covenant, God did not remove the threat but placed the Mediator between Himself and mankind for the salvation of many. Then we speak of the covenant of grace. The Mediator fulfils the stipulations of the covenant. He bears the curse of the breach (passive obedience) and fulfils the demand (active obedience). In this way He obtained for all of His own eternal fellowship with God, which He offers them through faith in Him. Although the covenant is *unilateral* in its establishment (which comes across clearly in Article 34 too), and is thus God's initiative, it is indeed a *covenant*. In its continuation it is bilateral. God makes man an active "party." The covenant which originally commenced with Adam, and in him was continued with the whole human race, only continues in the line of the believers and their seed.

3. "Into physical and spiritual death"

With this expression this article does not necessarily use the exact words of Scripture, but it does use Scriptural language. Scripture calls us "dead in trespasses and sins" (Ephesians 2:1). It also says that God sent His Son so that we would live through Him (1 John 4:9). In this context dead does not mean to be "nonexistent" but it means existence in a lost state, existence in disharmony. Likewise, to be alive does not just mean "being there;" do we not also say of some places where we have been, "it's no life being there?" To have life means to be in a right relationship with God and His whole creation.

Hence fallen man is "dead." This dead state affects his whole being, body and soul. As it is stated in the Form for Baptism, "This life is . . . no more than a constant death."

Our "state of death" does not mean that we are powerless but that we exist *wrongly*, in rebellion against God and inflamed with enmity against all He has made.

While we were in this terrible state God turned back to look for us, to search for us, yes, He comforted us with the promise that He would give us His Son as Redeemer.

4. The Promise to Eve

Genesis 3:15, quoted here, conains the promise to Eve. All subsequent promises are more detailed and clearer revelations of what God already promised in Paradise when He said, "I will put enmity (i.e. break up the intended friendship) between you (i.e. the serpent, the devil) and the woman, and between your seed (i.e. the seed of the serpent, haters of God) and her seed (i.e. Christ and those who are His); He (i.e. Christ, the seed of the woman) shall bruise your head and you shall bruise His heel (the victory would not be gained in a bloody battle, but as it took place on the cross at Golgotha). Here already we have the whole Gospel (the good news) "in a nutshell."

ARTICLE 18
THE INCARNATION OF THE SON OF GOD

We confess, therefore, that God has fulfilled the promise He made to the fathers by the mouth of His holy prophets when, at the time appointed by Him, He sent into the world His own only-begotten and eternal son, who took the form of a servant and was born in the likeness of men. He truly assumed a real human nature with all its infirmities, without sin, for He was conceived in the womb of the blessed virgin Mary by the power of the Holy Spirit and not by the act of a man. He not only assumed human nature as to the body, but also a true human soul, in order that He might be a real man. For since the soul was lost as well as the body, it was necessary that He should assume both to save both.

Contrary to the heresy of the Anabaptists, who deny that Christ assumed human flesh of His mother, we therefore confess that Christ partook of the flesh and blood of the children.
He is a fruit of the loins of David;
born of the seed of David according to the flesh;
a fruit of the womb of the virgin Mary;
born of woman;
a branch of David;
a shoot from the stump of Jesse;
sprung from the tribe of Judah;
descended from the Jews according to the flesh;
of the seed of Abraham, since the Son was concerned with the descendants of Abraham. Therefore He had to be made like His brethren in every respect, yet without sin.
In this way He is in truth our Immanuel, that is,
God with us.

1. Division

A. God fulfilled His promise and sent His Son

B. Conceived by the Holy Spirit and born from the womb of Mary, He was, in the likeness of our sinful flesh, like us in every respect, sin excepted

C. Rejection of Anabaptist error

2. In the "fullness of time"

This article's close connection with the previous article is clear, and is expressed by the word "therefore." God fulfilled His promise (Article 17) and sent His Son "at the time appointed by Him." Galatians 4:4 says, "But when the fullness of time had come, God sent forth His Son, born of a woman, born under the law." The expression "in the fullness of time" means that the time which had to *precede* according to God's inscrutable decree was *full*; the specified moment had arrived.

In hindsight we admire God's wisdom in the timing. There was at the time one universal language; Greek. Travel in the one Roman Empire was easy and, moreover, a certain spiritual weariness prevailed in all nations, with people looking forward to the coming of a Saviour. However, one must not attach too much value to this. Although these circumstances may have favoured the spreading of the Gospel, they did not contribute to its acceptance.

The phrase "at the time appointed by Him" also confesses the single event of the incarnation. It rejects any idea of a progressive incarnation, which the Church calls a "continuing incarnation of Christ," as is promoted by some Roman Catholic theologians (though it is not an official doctrine of the Roman Church).

3. The mystery of godliness

This article speaks of the "mystery of godliness which is great" (1 Timothy 3:16). He who was without a mother in heaven was without a father on earth. Christ "assumed" our flesh. His birth was *His* doing. He truly assumed, and it is said with emphasis, "a real human nature with all its infirmities," sent as He was "in the likeness of sinful flesh" (Romans 8:3; Philippians 2:7.) He did not come in the full lustre of Adam's perfectly created nature but in our by-sin-affected human existence, susceptible to suffering and death. His contemporaries hence said, "Isn't this the son of Joseph, the carpenter?" Yet, though He was made like us in every respect, He was "yet without sin" (Hebrews 4:15). He did not share in original sin. Being in the bosom of His Father, He did not fall when the whole human race fell in Adam. Since He was not created in Adam, no human father could beget Him. He was conceived of the Holy Spirit. By His birth His divine nature did not change into human nature. He remained what He had been (God) and became what He was not (man). The divine Person of the Son, who has the divine nature from eternity, now also assumed the human nature. He did so totally. This article says: not only a human body, "but also a true human soul." The way in which the Confession speaks here may not use exact liturgical language, yet what is expressed is entirely Scriptural. This must also be maintained over against Apollinaris and similar heretics.

4. True seed of David

In Lord's Day 14 the Heidelberg Catechism says that the eternal Son of God was born of Mary, "thus He is also the true seed of David." The texts referred to in this article emphasize that the Son of God in human nature was born of David. In this way the promise to David was fulfilled. This promise to David was the promise of the "seed of the woman" already given in Paradise. In the course of the history of salvation God bound this promise to Abraham's generation, and through Jacob's blessing to Judah's tribe (Genesis 49), and by Nathan's prophecy to David's house (2 Samuel 7:12-16).

Christ's (self)humiliation commenced with the incarnation. This humiliation is not to be found in the incarnation per se. If that were so, Christ would still be in humiliation, for in His glory He is still in our flesh. His humiliation was that He came in "the form of a servant" (Philippians 2:7), burdened with our sins.

5. Refutation of the Anabaptists

Menno Simons pointed out that Scripture presents Adam, totally sinful, as the opposite of Christ, the Holy One. He said too that the "putrid elder tree Adam" could bear no good fruit. Therefore he totally disclaimed the fact that Christ would have assumed our flesh. According to him, He was born *in* but not *of* Mary. Subsequent ideas of the Anabaptists on this matter diverge. Sometimes it is said that Christ took with Him a new flesh from heaven, and, just as water passes through a funnel, so He passed through Mary. Sometimes it is claimed that His flesh was created in Mary by divine creation. Whatever the case may have been, He was not born *of* Mary. According to Menno Simons, if the cells of Christ's human body had grown from Mary's, He would have been contaminated with sin. To say that Christ's human nature was a new creation is to say that He broke His bond with us; this led to far reaching consequences. According to the Anabaptists redemption was not the renewal and salvation of this world but that a whole new life would come. For that reason they distanced themselves from things of this life, declined military service, rejected authority of civil governments and refused to swear civil oaths. The events in Munster[14] have demonstrated what this could lead to. It was not without good reason that our fathers so strongly opposed such fanaticism.

---

[14] See Article 36, footnote 26. — TRANS.

6. *Ex virgine natus*

Ever since Adolf von Harnack denied the "virgin birth" in the 19th century, many have dismissed it. This kernel of God's redeeming work has always been the focus of Satan's fierce hatred. Many centuries ago, he already tried to prevent the virgin birth (see Revelation 12; think also of Egypt, Saul, Athaliah). When Christ was on earth Satan tried to destroy Him. Since then, now that the Child has been snatched away to God's throne, Satan has tried to deny the virgin birth of Christ. Karl Barth wanted to hold on to the term "virgin birth," but attached no significance to it. According to him the "virgin birth" is a "sign" of man's impotence. He does not want to argue about the "sign" if we agree anyway on what it signifies. However, man may not let fact be turned into a symbolic concept. Scripture teaches us the *fact* of the virgin birth.

7. To pay for our sin

In Scripture the incarnation of the Son of God is always presented in connection with sin. Our Confessions do the same (see Lord's Day 5 and 6 of the Heidelberg Catechism; Article 19 of the Belgic Confession). Without the fall into sin it wouldn't have been necessary to bridge the "gap" between the Creator and the creature or to "reveal" that God is also free in respect to His own nature and can become man (Barth).

ARTICLE 19
THE TWO NATURES IN THE ONE PERSON OF CHRIST

We believe that by this conception the person of the Son of God is inseparably united and joined with the human nature, so that there are not two sons of God, nor two persons, but two natures united in one single person. Each nature retains its own distinct properties: His divine nature has always remained uncreated, without beginning of days or end of life, filling heaven and earth. His human nature has not lost its properties; it has beginning of days and remains created. It is finite and retains all the properties of a true body. Even though, by His resurrection, He has given immortality to His human nature, He has not changed its reality, since our salvation and resurrection also depend on the reality of His body.

However, these two natures are so closely united in one person that they were not even separated by His death. Therefore, what He, when dying, committed into the hands of His Father was a real human spirit that departed from His body. Meanwhile His divinity always remained united with His human nature, even when He was lying in the grave. And the divine nature always remained in Him just as it was in Him when He was a little child, even though it did not manifest itself as such for a little while.

For this reason we profess Him to be true God and true man: true God in order to conquer death by His power; and true man that He might die for us according to the infirmity of His flesh.

1. The issue at stake

Holy Scripture has both divine and human things to say concerning Christ; it ascribes two groups of predicates to the *one* and the same subject. We read that He is called God's Son, has the power to forgive sin, existed before Abraham, and at the same time we read about Him growing up, feeling hungry, grieving, and thirsting. Both groups of predicates concern the One and the Same: "He who descended is also the One who ascended" (Ephesians 4:10). Even to the man Jesus are attributed divine properties: "What then if you should see the Son of Man ascend where He was before?" (John 6:62). Concerning our God, Jesus Christ, Paul says to the elders of Ephesus in very human terms that Christ purchased His Church with His own blood (Acts 20:28). Furthermore, Paul declares to the Corinthians that the Jews crucified the God of glory.

None of these texts from Scripture, to which many examples could be added, may be ignored. Yet, how can the one text be reconciled with another? Here the question is not whether or not Christ is true God (Article 10) and even less is it a question of whether or not He is true man (Article 18), but it is a question of how these two, God and man, are combined in Him.

2. Acceptance of the catholic heritage

This was one of the many questions that had to be addressed in the Christological struggle of the first centuries. Already at the Council of Constantinople (A.D. 381) and at the Council of Chalcedon (A.D. 451) the Church stammered its answer and rejected the errors of Apollinaris, Eutyches, and Nestorius. This answer, as well as what Irenaeus, Athanasius, and later Augustine taught concerning it, is accepted here in its entirety. Concerning the two natures of Christ, the Council of Chalcedon pronounced that they were:

A. not mixed: each nature remained independent
B. unchanged: each nature retained its own properties
C. unseparated: each nature was constantly united in the one Person
D. undivided: the whole human nature remained united with the whole divine nature

Points A and B refuted Eutyches who taught that Christ possessed only one nature after His incarnation and that the two natures were blended, like water and wine, into a new "divine-human" nature.

Point C refuted Nestorius who separated the two natures to such an extent that the unity of the Person was in danger of being lost (like water and oil).

Point D refuted Apollinaris who imagined that the Son of God merely assumed the human body.

Note that although the Church had exposed unScriptural interpretations about this matter on four occasions, in reverence to God's Word it refrained from trying to explain "the mystery of godliness which is great" (1 Timothy 3:16).

3. Revival of errors

The days of the great Reformation saw a revival of old errors. The Anabaptists wanted nothing to do with the fact that there were two natures in Christ. The thought that Christ would have assumed our flesh was offensive to Menno Simons (see paragraph 5 of the chapter on Article 18). To use the words of Martin Micron, Simons was "a clumsy cuckoo always singing the same song" and knew no other text than John 1:14, "The Word became flesh." His explanation of this text was that the Word was the material from which Christ's flesh was made. In so doing he, like Eutyches, was merely left with the idea that Christ had a single "divine-human" nature.

Servetus, who denied the Trinity and was opposed by Calvin, claimed that Jesus was made human in a miraculous way, but he did not acknowledge Him as God. Leo Socinus wouldn't do so either. According to him, the name "God" was not a reference to Christ's essence but was rather a title of appointment by which His extraordinary calling, majesty, and authority were defined.

The Lutherans also strayed on this point. As a basis for their doctrine concerning the Lord's supper, in which they claim that Christ is bodily present in, with, and under the signs of the Lord's supper, they taught the ubiquity (omnipresence; ubiquitarians) of His human nature. In Him the properties of the one nature transferred to the other. Thereby His human nature would not have been deified, but would nevertheless have received divine properties. This can be compared to iron held in the fire: the heat of the fire is transferred to it, but it does not become fire. This transfer of properties from the one nature to the other would have been completed at His ascension. From that moment on Christ's human nature also became omnipresent (see the Heidelberg Catechism's disputation of this in Lord's Day 18, Q&A 47, 48).

This article positions itself against these errors and against those of the Anabaptists; not against the Roman Church, with whom there was no controversy on this point.

4. Division
    A. In Christ, the divine and human nature are united in one Person
    B. 1. Both natures retain their distinct properties (against Eutyches, Anabaptists, and Lutherans)
       2. The two natures are never separated (Nestorius)
    C. The reason why Christ is God and Man

5. Nature and Person
The following definitions are vague but are about as close as one could get to a definition. By "nature" we understand that which

makes a creature *what* it is. The "nature" of a horse is different from that of a man. An angel's nature is different again. By "person" we understand that which makes someone the person he is; it refers to *who* he is; his "self." There is no such thing as an impersonal human nature. The human nature is always arranged into a person. Christ's human nature had been arranged into the divine Person of the Son. Since His incarnation this Person existed in two natures. Hence in the man Jesus there were not two persons. The "self" of Jesus' human nature was the "self" of the Son of God.

6. Reason

If Christ were *not* human, He could not be our Surety and the human race could not be reconciled to God in Him (Q&A 16 of the Heidelberg Catechism). If He were not God, He would be unable to overcome death for us (Q&A 17 of the Heidelberg Catechism). Since the Person *who* suffered and paid the price in Jesus' human nature was that of the Son of God, all that He did in that nature had infinite value. The blood of Jesus Christ cleanses us from all sin (1 John 1:7b; Canons of Dort, II #4).

7. A general denial

On this issue there is no controversy with the Church of Rome, but in "Protestant" circles this confession of the two natures in one Person is, in general, practically denied. According to Karl Barth, God is totally free, not bound or limited by His own nature. He can step across the boundary between Him and us. This freedom is demonstrated in Jesus Christ. In Him God is human, and in Him God even dies. Barth's view leaves nothing of the two natures in one Person, the purpose of which is the redemption from our guilt of sin. This is essentially a revival of the Anabaptist error.

ARTICLE 20
THE JUSTICE AND MERCY OF GOD IN CHRIST

We believe that God, who is perfectly merciful and just, sent His Son to assume that nature in which disobedience had been committed, to make satisfaction in that same nature;

and to bear the punishment of sin by His most bitter passion and death. God therefore manifested His justice against His Son when He laid our iniquity on Him, and poured out His goodness and mercy on us, who were guilty and worthy of damnation. Out of a most perfect love He gave His Son to die for us and He raised Him for our justification that through Him we might obtain immortality and life eternal.

1. Context

Having dealt in Articles 17-19 with the promise, the sending, and the mystery of Christ, we now confess in Article 20 what God did through Him, and in Article 21 what He, as the One sent by God, did for us.

2. Division

   A. God has sent His Son in our nature in order to remove our punishment
   B. In so doing He demonstrated
      1. His justice over against His Son
      2. His mercy toward us

3. Perfectly merciful and just

On the one hand Scripture says that God's love also reaches out to sinful man, "For God so loved the world" (John 3:16). Yet at the same time it says, that God is wrathful toward the sinful world and that we were enemies before we were reconciled to Him through the death of His Son (Romans 5:10).

We may not try to harmonize these two facts in such a way as to create the impression that Christ persuaded the wrathful God to turn away his anger and so won His love and affection for us. This leads to "Jesus-worship" where Jesus, rather than the Triune God, is the focus of our worship (Moravian Brethren). This would also conflict with all those statements in Scripture which assure us that it was precisely God's love which surrendered Christ for sinners. "In this is love, . . . that He . . . sent His Son to be the propitiation for our sins" (1 John 4:10).

Here we encounter something which remains a mystery for us: that all God's virtues are one in Him. There is no contradiction between His virtues. Mercy and wrath, justice and love, are in many ways contrasting notions, because our wrath usually lacks mercy, and our mercy (deficient as it is) lacks wrath. However, God's justice lacks no love, and His love lacks no justice. This is the "simplicity" of God as confessed in Article 1.

God is love, but His love never lets Him "forget" His justice. The cross of Golgotha was an embodiment of both. Who had ever seen such love? And who at the same time, saw such justice and wrath? In His adorable wisdom God followed a course which perfectly demonstrated His merciful justice, which is also His just mercy. By attaining satisfaction for their transgressions through His Son, God reconciled to Himself those who were His enemies (Q&A 11 of the Heidelberg Catechism).

4. Just

God's righteousness (justice) is His loyalty, by which He fulfils His Word. Hence His justice punishes and delivers (1 Samuel 12:7). Here, as in Q&A 12 of the Heidelberg Catechism, attention is paid to God's vengeful and punishing justice. This demands — would God not also maintain His threat of the covenant? — that whoever has committed disobedience must be punished for it (Q&A 12, 14 of the Heidelberg Catechism). There is no reconciliation except through full satisfaction. The entire Old Testament, through all the offerings and purifications, impressed this upon Israel. However, the blood of goats and bulls could not obtain this reconciliation (see Hebrews 10:1-10). The human race had committed sin and had to pay for it (Q&A 12 of the Heidelberg Catechism). Hence God sent His Son in that very nature in which the disobedience was committed. He then imputed to Christ all our sins. "The LORD has laid on Him the iniquity of us all" (Isaiah 53:6). "For He made Him who knew no sin to be sin for us" (2 Corinthians 5:21). Christ was assigned the position of a sinner. One's position is one's legal status and is dependent on the Judge's decision. Until His death, Christ, though guiltless, held the position of one who is guilty. At His resurrection He had the status of one who was justified.

5. Cocceius

To be sure, God has also exercised His vengeful justice in the time of the Old Testament through the punishment of sin. One only has to think of the flood, Sodom and Gomorrah, the venomous serpents in the desert, the exile, and many more instances. However, the full discharge of His vengeful justice was postponed. He did punish, but not according to sin.

For that reason, Cocceius (1650; professor at Leyden) claimed that in the Old Testament there wasn't as yet a complete forgiveness of sin. At that time there was merely a looking past sin (*paresis*). Total forgiveness (*afesis*) only came in the New Testament; only then was the punishment removed.

The Roman Catholics fantasize along similar lines. According to them the believers in the Old Testament had to wait in the "*limbus patrum,*" the waiting room of the fathers, for the sacrifice of Christ, before they could enter heaven. Only after His death, by His "descending into hell," would Christ have come to free them from the waiting room of the fathers and have led them to heaven.

However, this contradicts Holy Scripture (see Psalm 32:1; 103:12; 130:4; Isaiah 40:1, 2).

"Cocceianism" led to a disdaining of the Old Testament, reducing it to something of historical significance only. However, the way in which the believers of the Old Testament have been saved is no different from the way in which we have been saved. Reconciliation through Christ was granted to them "on credit."

6. Merciful

How great is God's mercy. No sinner has asked Him for help or salvation. We did not love God, but God loved us and sent His Son. He did this for us who were enemies (Romans 5:6, 8).

7. "Because of" and "for"

This article says that God raised Christ *for* our justification but Romans 4:25 reads *because of* our justification. Both words are acceptable, although *for* is preferable. He is raised so that we might obtain, share, and take possession of the righteousness earned by Him.

The translation *"because of"* implies the notion that Christ was raised because by His death our debt was settled and our justification obtained. *Because* of this our Surety was released from the imprisonment of death. The resurrection is then seen as God's declaration of approval on the "It is finished" of Calvary. Both considerations are acceptable. The Heidelberg Catechism also includes both when in Lord's Day 17 it teaches us to confess Christ's resurrection as proof of payment of our debt (justification), as the power for our renewal (sanctification), and the pledge of our total deliverance (glorification).

8. Immortality

This article concludes by saying that through Christ's resurrection we might obtain immortality. Don't we already have an "immortal" soul though? Holy Scripture says that God alone has immortality (1 Timothy 6:16), and that the redeemed will receive this (1 Corinthians 15:53, 54). Outside of Christ there is nothing but death and we are physically and spiritually dead through sins and trespasses (Ephesians 2:1). Hence our Confession makes a very Scriptural statement here.

ARTICLE 21
THE SATISFACTION OF CHRIST OUR HIGH PRIEST

We believe that Jesus Christ was confirmed by an oath to be a High Priest for ever, after the order of Melchizedek. He presented Himself in our place before His Father, appeasing God's wrath by His full satisfaction, offering Himself on the tree of the cross, where He poured out His precious blood to purge away our sins, as the prophets had foretold. For it is written, Upon Him was the chastisement that made us whole and with His stripes we are healed. Like a lamb He was led to the slaughter. He was numbered with the transgressors, and condemned as a criminal by Pontius Pilate, though he had first declared Him innocent. He restored what He had not stolen. He died as the righteous for the unrighteous. He suffered in body and soul, feeling the horrible punishment caused by our sins, and His sweat became like great drops of blood falling down upon the ground. Finally, He exclaimed, My God, My God, why hast Thou forsaken Me? All this He endured for the forgiveness of our sins.

Therefore we justly say, with Paul, that we know nothing except Jesus Christ and Him crucified. We count everything as loss because of the surpassing worth of knowing Jesus our Lord. We find comfort in His wounds and have no need to seek or invent any other means of reconciliation with God than this only sacrifice, once offered, by which the believers are perfected for all times. This is also the reason why the angel of God called Him Jesus, that is, Saviour, because He would save His people from their sins.

1. Introduction

This article deals with Christ's work of reconciliation for sin (see also paragraph 1 of the chapter on Article 20); therefore only His priestly work is discussed here. His work as Prophet and King could also be discussed, but the Heidelberg Catechism does this in detail in Lord's Day 12. There we confess that as Prophet He "has fully revealed to us the secret counsel and will of God concerning our redemption," that as Priest He with "the one sacrifice of His body has redeemed us and . . . continually intercedes for us before the Father," and that as King He "governs us by His Word and Spirit, and . . . defends and preserves us in the redemption obtained for us." This is not to say that Christ had three offices. Nevertheless in His one office of Mediator three aspects can be distinguished. One can thus speak of His prophetic, priestly, and kingly work which He performed, and still performs, before, during, and after the days of His incarnation. Moreover, He does not only fulfil these offices Himself and in so doing fulfil what Adam failed to do (active obedience = obedience by doing the law), and above all bear the punishment for our sin (passive obedience = obedience in bearing the punishment), but He also makes those who belong to Him prophets, priests, and kings (Q&A 32 of the Heidelberg Catechism). The fact that this article only discusses Christ's priestly work, and restricts this to the sacrifice He offered, is because rather than deal with His office, it wished to deal with His sacrifice for removing our guilt of sin.

2. Division

A. Christ is a Priest forever after the order of Melchizedek
B. He offered Himself up to purge away our sins
C. Scriptural evidence which points out the nature of His priestly sacrifice
D. Further evidence from Scripture that we rightly call Him our Saviour

3. After the order of Melchizedek

Two priestly orders can be discerned from Scripture. Firstly, that of Aaron or Levi (Hebrews 7:11) which is hereditary. No one can serve in this priesthood of Aaron, unless he is of the tribe of Levi. The priest's task was the reconciliation for sin (Hebrews 5:1), although he could not remove sin by his sacrifices (Hebrews 10:1-4, 11). Since the priesthood of Aaron was unable to fulfil this task of reconciliation, Christ fulfilled this task and consequently abolished the priesthood of Aaron (Hebrews 10:11-14; 7:11-14). However, this did not cancel all priesthood. Apart from this temporary order of Aaron, established at Sinai and abolished by Christ, there is the everlasting priesthood in which man was placed as soon as he was created. Its purpose was not reconciliation for sin, but rather, praise, thanks, and total devotion. We find something of this original priesthood in Melchizedek, king of Salem, in the days of Abram. He was called "the priest of God Most High" (Genesis 14:18-20).

This priesthood was not bound to a specific genealogy, nor do we read that it was transferable (Hebrews 7:3). In order to characterize Christ's unique priesthood, reference is made to Melchizedek and Christ is called Priest after the order of Melchizedek (Psalm 110; Hebrews 5, 7). This is because Christ did not receive His priesthood by virtue of a specific genealogy, nor was it transferred to anyone. He is Priest forever. In order to be this in the human nature, He had to fulfil the work of reconciliation of the priesthood of Aaron. This is precisely what He did. Now He is Priest forever (Hebrews 7:24, 25). To recognize other priests besides Him or in succession to Him, as the Church of Rome does, is a serious misunderstanding of, and an insult to, the priesthood of the Lord.

4. One sacrifice for the removal of our sin

Every sacrifice must be voluntary. Christ indeed volunteered Himself (Psalm 40:7-9; Hebrews 10:5-10). He did so to "appear in the presence of God for us" (Hebrews 9:24). He made His appearance as our Surety. In so doing He stilled God's wrath. God's wrath is not an emotional response but a logical consequence of sin. His wrath is His holy aversion to, and rejection of sin; it is the terrible execution of His vengeance, His avenging justice. Christ appeased that wrath by offering to God complete satisfaction of His justice (Hebrews 9:12; 10:14). This is therefore no "acceptance theory" which holds that Christ's sacrifice did not truly satisfy but was merely accepted as such by God. Christ offered to pay the penalty of all God's just demands. Burdened with the sins of His people, in acknowledgment of God's justice, He offered complete satisfaction of this justice by submitting to God's rod. He did this throughout His life on earth, but especially at the end. Christ also referred to the latter as "His suffering" (Luke 22:15). That is when He poured out His precious blood, the blood of the Son of God (1 Peter 1:18, 19). He offered Himself as a sacrifice, entirely voluntarily. "Father, Your will be done" and "No one takes (My life) from Me, but I lay it down of Myself" (John 10:17, 18). All this He did "according to the Scriptures" (Luke 24:25-27; 1 Corinthians 15:3, 4). (See also Lord's Day 15, 16 of the Heidelberg Catechism.)

5. Punishment

The "golden psalm of suffering" of the Old Testament (Isaiah 53) uses many different words to describe the suffering of Christ: despised, smitten, bruised. One could think that all these sufferings were accidental. However, verse 5 goes on to say that He had to bear all this punishment in order to secure our peace. In Christ's suffering repayment took place. For that reason He was not robbed of life through a civil uprising, but sentenced to death by a just judgment. In its Confession the Church has rightly devoted much attention to this aspect of Christ's suffering. It has even been included in the shortest creed, The Apostle's Creed: "suffered under Pontius Pilate" (Q&A 38 of the Heidelberg Catechism). This punishment, this pouring of God's just wrath upon Him, inwardly buffeted and bruised Him. Christ's suffering is a mystery. No one can fathom it. We should not so much focus on the number of lashes or the duration of the suffering, but rather on what Isaiah calls "the labour of His soul." In His suffering "He descended into hell." He endured eternal punishment. Not bit by bit (extensive). That is the only way in which we could have done it and would therefore never have completed it. He suffered it "all at once." How could it have been possible unless it had been done "by the power of His divinity."

6. Denial

The confession concerning Christ's work of reconciliation was generally accepted for sixteen centuries. However, in the days of the great Reformation it was resolutely rejected by Socinus. Since the arguments of the Socinianists still surface repeatedly, they are listed here with refutations:

A. "Love and justice exclude each other." However, this is incorrect because love without justice is sentimentality and justice without love is cruelty. In God both are one.

B. "If redemption is obtained through justice, it is not by grace. Since it is by grace, legal terms have no place here." However, this too is incorrect because Christ took the way of justice for us, and in so doing has delivered us through grace.

C. "Transfer of moral guilt is impossible." That may be so as far as people are concerned, for each individual is guilty (Q&A 16 of the Heidelberg Catechism). However, Christ is not some arbitrary "other" to His own people. He is our Head, the second Adam (Romans 5:19).

According to the Socinianists, God is not the focus of the reconciliation. It was not, they say, a case of appeasing an "irate" God, for God is love. The focus of reconciliation is us. They claim that God was wrathful in order to free us from our delusion and convince us of His love. Therefore God demonstrated His love by declaring His solidarity with us, entering into our suffering and our death, and even when we struck Him dead, He did not strike back. One still repeatedly hears of this notion of solidarity from the side of the liberal theologians, and also from the Barthians. They know how to speak touchingly of God's love, but they cut the heart out of the Gospel!

7. I glory in the cross of Christ

Over against the Socinianist denial, but especially over against the foolishness of Rome which seeks salvation also from the saints, by good works, and otherwise (Q&A 30 of the Heidelberg Catechism), the Confession gives the assurance, using quotes from Scripture, that "we . . . have no need to seek or invent any other means of reconciliation with God than this only sacrifice, once offered, by which the believers are perfected for all times." Roman Catholic error is a revival of Judaism, against which Paul fought in his letters to the Romans and the Galatians.

8. Jesus

Jesus is the Greek form of the Hebrew name Joshua: the LORD saves, gives deliverance. It was a very ordinary name (Exodus 17:9; 1 Samuel 6:14; Haggai 1:12; Zechariah 3:1-9). Our Saviour received this name from God (Matthew 1:21; Luke 1:31). He does not merely possess this Name; He is what this name says. He saves His people from their sins (see Lord's Day 11 of the Heidelberg Catechism).

9. All sorts of comfort

Christ's work is so rich that it cannot be described in just a single word, nor can it be summarized in a single formula. In the New Testament, Christ's death is a passover offering and a covenantal offering, a sacrifice and a thank offering; a ransom and an example; a suffering and an action, a work and a service; a means to justification and sanctification, to reconciliation and hallowing, to deliverance and glorification, in other words, the source of our complete blessedness.[15] The notion of solidarity certainly contains an element of truth. However, to profess it as an adequate interpretation of the Scriptural revelation concerning

---

[15] Herman Bavinck, *Gereformeerde Dogmatiek*, III, derde onveranderde uitgave (Kampen: J.H. Kok, 1918) 423, 425.

Christ's substitutionary satisfaction is a denial of the real message of grace.

10. Limited atonement

Christ's sacrifice was sufficient for the salvation of all people, but it only benefits those who belong to Him, for whom alone He completed it (see Canons of Dort, II for an elaboration on this).

All Arminian groups claim that Christ died for all people, every single one of them, and that it is now up to each individual to accept the salvation obtained by means of this death. In their defence they love to refer to texts such as 1 Timothy 2:4 and Titus 2:11. However, this is not what these texts teach. They point to the totally different dispensation of the New Testament wherein the Gospel comes to all nations. The universalists cannot deny that not all people are saved. If Christ had died for all, He wouldn't be a perfect Saviour. However, the fact is that He did not die for all, only for His people, just as He didn't pray for the world, but for those whom the Father had given Him (John 17:9).

ARTICLE 22
OUR JUSTIFICATION THROUGH FAITH IN JESUS CHRIST

We believe that, in order that we may obtain the true knowledge of this great mystery, the Holy Spirit kindles in our hearts a true faith. This faith embraces Jesus Christ with all His merits, makes Him our own, and does not seek anything besides Him. For it must necessarily follow, either that all we need for our salvation is not in Jesus Christ or, if it is all in Him, that one who has Jesus Christ through faith, has complete salvation. It is, therefore, a terrible blasphemy to assert that Christ is not sufficient, but that something else is needed besides Him; for the conclusion would then be that Christ is only half a Saviour. Therefore we rightly say with Paul that we are justified by faith alone, or by faith apart from works of law. Meanwhile, strictly speaking, we do not mean that faith as such justifies us, for faith is only the instrument by which we embrace Christ our righteousness; He imputes to us all His merits and as many holy works as He has done for us and in our place. Therefore Jesus Christ is our righteousness, and faith is the instrument that keeps us with Him in the communion of all His benefits. When those benefits have become ours, they are more than sufficient to acquit us of our sins.

1. Context

The following articles, 22-24, are closely connected. They link up with Articles 17-21. These spoke of Christ and His substitutionary work for us (see paragraph 1 of the chapter on Article 20). Articles 22-24 continue with the fruits of this work of Christ and the manner in which we obtain these.

The Holy Spirit kindles in our hearts faith, by which we are justified (beginning of Article 22) and regenerated (beginning of Article 24). Furthermore, these articles speak of our righteousness through faith (Articles 22 and 23) and our sanctification through faith. (The same is dealt with in Lord's Day 7, 23, 24 of the Heidelberg Catechism.)

2. Division

A. Whoever believes in Christ Jesus has all he needs for salvation

B. Evidence of A
1. One or the other: either Christ is not sufficient, or He is sufficient
2. Rejection of the first possibility
3. From the second possibility the conclusion is drawn that we are justified through faith alone
4. One is not to understand that because of faith man earns justification. Christ justified us and faith is the instrument by which we accept Him

3. Core and marrow

The reformers wrote repeatedly that justification by faith alone is the core and marrow, the kernel and the heart of the Gospel. By it the Church stands or falls. Therefore Article 23 states, "therefore we always hold to this firm foundation." For the sake of the preservation of this confession the Holy Spirit, through Paul's letters to the Romans, Galatians, and Philippians, engaged in the fierce battle against Judaism. *"Sola fide"* was the main issue of the Reformation. With respect to this there yet remains the rift between the Reformed Confession and the Roman Catholic error, and between the true doctrine and all kinds of sects which have this one characteristic in common, that they do not live by faith, but by an experience or by something else. By weakening the attention span through lots of liturgy and little preaching, a deadly danger is introduced.

4. The source of faith

From the beginning the Church has confessed that faith is worked in us by the Holy Spirit. This is also clearly manifest from Scripture. "Being confident of this very thing, that He who has begun a good work in you will complete it until the day of Jesus Christ" (Philippians 1:6). "For to you it has been granted on behalf of Christ, not only to believe in Him, but also to suffer for His sake" (Philippians 1:29). "For by grace you have been saved through faith, and that not of yourselves; it is the gift of God" (Ephesians 2:8).

The question here is *how* the Holy Spirit works faith in us. The Arminians described the Spirit's method of working faith in us as a "gentle suggestion." "No more is required," they say. "When the Spirit displays for us in the Gospel the excellent treasures God gives us, man, by his own free will, automatically chooses these. His 'rational mind' sees clearly how superior these gifts of God are to those of the world."

According to the Roman Catholics a working of the Holy Spirit is necessary because natural man is not receptive to the supernatural contents of God's Word. To be able to accept God's Word we must first be raised to its level. "Therefore," they say, "elevation is necessary; one needs to be raised through the conferring of the supernatural gift" (see paragraph 12 of the chapter on Article 15). However, we confess that the working of the Holy Spirit is necessary, not because of the objective of faith, but because of our own depravity. By nature we are blind to the truth and unwilling to accept the Word of God, for it testifies against us and humbles us. No sinner is willing to accept this. The working of the Holy Spirit does not merely elevate, but regenerates, recreates. Paragraph 2 of the chapter on Article 24 says that the Holy Spirit works faith in us through the hearing of God's Word (Romans 10:17), and the Heidelberg Catechism teaches in Q&A 65 that the Holy Spirit works (not awakens) faith by the preaching of the Gospel (see also Q&A 21 of the Heidelberg Catechism; James 1:18: "Of His own will He brought us forth by the Word of truth;" Psalm 119:50: "For Your word has given me life"). Scripture thus says that faith is worked in us by both the Holy Spirit and through the Word of God. We may never separate the two: Word and Spirit. The Holy Spirit is the Spirit of the Word and the Word is the Word of the Holy Spirit. He is always present in that Word.

5. The content of faith

True faith in God does not bypass Christ. If that were possible, the Jews and Muslims could also be said to believe. A right knowledge of God does not exist outside of Christ. God comes to us in Him. Therefore faith grasps hold of Him in the promises of the Gospel. Q&A 22 of the Heidelberg Catechism states that the content of faith is "all that is promised in the Gospel." Likewise, this article confesses that faith "embraces Jesus Christ with all His merits." The Roman Catholics refute this by claiming that in this way we tear up God's Word. "The Word," they argue, "is comprised of more. It does not only contain the promise of the Gospel, but also the demands of the law. Shouldn't we also believe and obey that law?" However, this is not a matter of tearing up God's Word. Though faith accepts all that God has revealed (Q&A 21 of the Heidelberg Catechism), and although it recognizes the demands of the law as being relevant for us too, it rests on God's promises and embraces Jesus Christ. One could say it this way, faith always begins with the promises.

6. The nature and functions of faith

The Heidelberg Catechism describes faith as a "sure knowledge" and a "firm confidence." This article likewise speaks of "true knowledge" and it says that faith "embraces Jesus Christ with all His merits" and "makes Him our own." With reference to this "embracing," think of a child fleeing from the threatening danger of a fierce dog on the street. He races to his mother, flings himself into her arms, embraces her and feels safe.

In his definition of faith, Calvin only speaks of a firm and sure knowledge of God. There really is no difference here. To Calvin the "firm, sure knowledge" is not merely a dry understandable knowledge but a knowledge of love, which includes confidence. In our thoughts we may never separate the "knowledge" and "confidence" of the Heidelberg Catechism nor the "true knowledge" and the "embracing of Christ" in the Belgic Confession. This has happened too often. It was said that the essence of faith is knowledge but that confidence is also required for its well-being. That means someone can profess his faith in Church, provided he knows his catechism, even though his heart does not live for the Saviour. However, faith without confidence is no faith. Then the demons would also believe (James 2:19).

Faith is knowledge. We reject the Roman Catholic error concerning a *fides implicata*, an implicated faith, whereby the inclination to accept all that the Church believes (even if you do not know anything about it) would already be "faith." By means of this error the Roman Catholics can include in their membership count thousands of people who are still totally in the grip of the power of heathendom, such as those in Brazil, and who on the whole live in sin, such as those in Spain, and without instruction give "converted Protestants" speedy access to the sacraments. However, this *fides implicata* was a smart fabrication of the Scholastics, who were always ready to adapt doctrine to (godless) practices. How can one possibly approve and regard as true what one does not know? Faith is saying "amen" to the Word of God. Therefore the Word must be known. Faith is then also knowledge, a knowledge by which I acknowledge God's Word as truth. This does not come about without a broken heart and a trust in Christ. It is that knowledge by which we yield to the Lord and entrust ourselves to His grace in Christ.

This notion is not well received today. People do not seek insight. "What's the use of knowledge?" People do not want to hear a sermon which instructs; they prefer to hear a sermon that "does something to you," "touches the core of your existence," and makes you experience something. However, all those sermons which "do something to you" do not, in the long run, do much at all, and "faith" which seeks its existence in excitement and emotion is not what Scripture calls faith.

According to the Barthians, faith is a "momentary occurrence." It is to be overwhelmed by God, that "wholly Other." However, they say, the moment one begins to discuss it, it is no longer faith. The rapture one experiences by means of a powerful oratorio is something quite different from one's description of it afterward. That is reflection, and no longer the real thing. "Therefore," they say, "a 'confession of faith' is not possible. A believer lives between memory and expectation." Our Confession does not say that faith makes us live between the memory of a previous and the expectation of a future encounter with Christ. Rather, it states that faith embraces Jesus Christ with all His merits. This rejects all Barthian speculations concerning faith.

Apart from faith, there are also other reactions to the Word of God which seem to resemble faith. Hence people sometimes speak of historical faith, temporal faith, or miraculous faith. However, a mere intellectual acceptance of the content of Scripture (historical faith) and a superficial, yet living interest in Scripture, which does not lead to conversion in the end (temporal faith) is no *faith*. All such "faith" is no more faith than a coffee substitute is coffee. On accepting these terms, man introduced alongside it "true saving faith." Yet faith does not save. Christ saves. Therefore this term must also be rejected.

7. *Sola fide*

The first part of this article says that faith does not seek anything besides Christ. Faith is exclusive. In Him and His merits it has everything. This is proven in the second part of the article, using the same reasoning as that of the Heidelberg Catechism in Q&A 30. It poses the dilemma: *either* we *do not* have everything in Christ, *or* we do have everything in Him. To say that Christ is not a complete Saviour would be a terrible blasphemy. If we do have everything in Christ, then we rightly say with Paul that "we are justified by faith alone, or by faith apart from works of law." In the expression "by faith *alone*" the full anger of the Roman Catholics is directed against the last word: *alone*. They reproach Luther for adding this word to Scripture in his translation of Romans 3:28. Nor is it found in the Greek translation. However, Luther triumphantly defended himself against this, explaining that the insertion of the word "*alone*" promoted a correct and clear rendering in German of what Paul had written. We hold on to this word in contrast to the Roman Catholic notion that not faith alone but "faith formed through love" justifies. This faith formed through love (*fides informis* and *fides formata*) is faith *plus* its works and *this* justifies us. The Roman Catholics have their own idea of what faith is. They use the same word as Scripture but mean something entirely different by it. For them "faith" only expresses an intellectual knowledge. It is no more than an initial act that only brings you as far as the threshold. In order to have true communion with Christ this "faith" must proceed to action. The bare tree of "faith" must be decorated with "our" (!) good works. Luther rightly called this error a hellish poison. There is no such thing as "*fides informis*." This too is a scholastic fabrication. In this manner the basis for acquittal is again sought in our works. To be sure, faith never exists without works. As Luther rightly said, "We are justified by faith alone, but justifying faith is never alone." However, these works do not contribute to our justification. The Scholastics loved to philosophise that if faith is always connected with works, one cannot say that only faith justifies. To this Calvin wittily retorted that the light of the sun is never without warmth, yet no one can say that it is by the warmth that one sees the sun. Likewise, faith is never without works. Yet we are justified by faith, without any consideration of our works. Holy Scripture always ascribes justification to faith, to faith without works. James 2:24 does not contradict this either when it says, "You see then that a man is justified by works, and not by faith only." When read in the context of the whole argumentation of James it is apparent that his purpose is to oppose those who say: "since it is all grace, works aren't required." James responds, "Such faith, without works, is dead! The faith that justifies must be evident by its works." However, these works of love and faith which James refers to are not the "deeds of the law" of Romans 3:28.

8. Instrument

Not our faith but Christ alone is our righteousness before God. We are not justified because of our faith. However, Scripture does not know of a righteousness without faith either. Righteousness is always through or out of faith. Faith is the hand by which we receive Christ, the instrument that keeps us with Him in the communion of all His benefits. Then we can also call faith a condition for justification. However, it is not a condition which must precede justification as claimed by the Arminians. Yet it is an accompanying condition. The one is never present without the other. There is no justification without faith. Where God gives the one, there He also gives the other. He gives justification by way of faith (see also Q&A 60, 61 of the Heidelberg Catechism).

ARTICLE 23
OUR RIGHTEOUSNESS BEFORE GOD

We believe that our blessedness lies in the forgiveness of our sins for Jesus Christ's sake and that there our righteousness before God consists, as David and Paul teach us. They pronounce a blessing upon the man to whom God reckons righteousness apart from works. The apostle also says that we are justified by His grace as a gift, through the redemption which is in Christ Jesus. Therefore we always hold to this firm foundation. We give all the glory to God, humble ourselves before Him, and acknowledge ourselves to be what we are. We do not claim anything for ourselves or our merits, but rely and rest on the only obedience of Jesus Christ crucified; His obedience is ours when we believe in Him.
This is sufficient to cover all our iniquities and to give us confidence in drawing near to God, freeing our conscience of fear, terror, and dread, so that we do not follow the example of our first father, Adam, who trembling tried to hide and covered himself with fig leaves. For indeed, if we had to appear before God, relying — be it ever so little — on ourselves or some other creature, (woe be to us!) we

would be consumed. Therefore everyone must say with David, O LORD, enter not into judgment with Thy servant, for no man living is righteous before Thee.

1. Division
    A. Justification consists of the forgiveness of sin
    B. Scriptural evidence by quoting Romans 4:6; 3:24
    C. The twofold purpose of this confession
        1. Soli Deo Gloria (to God alone be the glory)
        2. our sure comfort

2. Before the judgment seat of the heavenly Majesty

It is not a question of how we judge ourselves, but how God judges us (1 Corinthians 4:4). "All the ways of a man are pure in his own eyes, but the Lord weighs the spirits" (Proverbs 16:2; also Proverbs 21:2). Everything, including the most secret things, is subject to God's judgment (1 Corinthians 4:5). In addition to that, God is the Holy One, before whose glory the stars pale, and by whose might the mountains shrink, whose wisdom unmasks the guiles of the wise and whose burning wrath scalds even the outermost parts of hell. Who shall be able to remain standing before His countenance? This article has been written with the understanding that we will have to appear before the judgment seat of this heavenly Majesty (2 Corinthians 5:10). Many expressions in the last section of this article point to this.

3. Righteous, but how?

In response to the question as to how we shall be acquitted before God's tribunal, the Church of Rome postulates that the following are required:
    A. a broken heart in recognition of our sin
    B. the confession of sin with our mouth
    C. the satisfaction through works

Rome says that no man is capable of doing this on his own, but is enabled to do so by the grace poured out through the sacraments. However, this is a long, hard road! Whoever travels this road, taking seriously the demands postulated by Rome, will fail to find peace. How will they know they've ever done enough? When does the broken heart equate the guilt? When are all sins confessed? When has complete satisfaction been offered? In reality the Church of Rome compromises appallingly in this respect. Thereby it promotes the very thing of which it accuses us: superficiality and careless indifference. This doctrine has tormented sincere people, creating much anxiety and fear (see e.g. *I Saw the Light* by H.J. Hegger). Luther knew this fear, and it caused him to cry out: "My sins, my sins . . ."

Over against this the Church of the Reformation in this article joyfully confesses the short route to salvation by saying that we are righteous before God through the forgiveness of our sins.

God's acquittal, by which He forgives our sins, is a synthetical judgment, not an analytical judgment! In an analytical judgment the predicate is inherent in the subject (for example, this horse is a mammal). This is how Rome presents justification. According to Rome the acquittal is acknowledgment of the presence of righteousness (good works) in the acquitted. They explain it this way: God makes us righteous and then acknowledges us as righteous and acquits us. First sanctification, then justification. According to Rome we are only justified to the extent that we are sanctified. In fact, though the acquittal is a synthetical judgment, it is a judgment where the predicate is not yet inherent in the subject, but is added to it (for example: this horse is stolen).

God justifies the ungodly by imputing Christ's righteousness. The reformers always described justification in terms of court proceedings. God is the judge and the sinner is the accused. Satan and the sinner's conscience accuse the sinner of having violated the law (Scripture) as follows:

A. he has grievously sinned against all God's commandments
B. he has never kept any of them
C. he is still inclined to all evil (Q&A 60 of the Heidelberg Catechism)

This is a true accusation. Christ then enters the court room as our advocate and says:

A. I have fulfilled all of God's commandments
B. I have borne the full punishment for the transgression
C. I cover his depravity with My holiness

God then imputes to us the work of Christ, with whom we are one body through faith, and He acquits us!

Therefore, justification is to declare just. Similarly, to magnify God does not mean one enlarges Him, but rather, one acknowledges and confesses His magnitude. This is what is meant in Scripture when the just face condemnation (Proverbs 17:15; Romans 8:33). One who is justified is not yet holy. His acquittal does not change anything in him, but alters his relationship with God. He changes from an accused to one who is acquitted. However, it does not stop there. Whoever God justifies, He also glorifies (Romans 8:30). We are not to separate His justification and glorification, but we are to differentiate between them.

This justification is a matter of justice. God is not unjust when he declares the guilty innocent and leaves the ungodly unacquitted. He does this on the basis of the work which Christ completed, through which He removed our guilt. However, the fact that this acquittal, founded upon God's justice, is also pronounced concerning me, is grace!

4. The twofold view

This confession concerning the sinner's justification recognizes no merit on the part of the sinner. To detract anything from this confession is to desecrate God's honour, for then God would no longer be the only one to receive the credit for salvation, but He would have to share His glory with a creature. In so doing the assurance of our comfort would also be undermined. This is stated in no uncertain terms at the end of this article.

5. Not once and for always!

It has often been said, and it can be read in all kinds of books on systematic theology, that God's just deed of justification is a deed He only performed once, and which once and for always acquits us of all our sins, so that we always have peace with God and He is never angry with us any more. Our sins would then hinder our realisation of that peace but not our relationship with the Lord. In that case, those justified should really continue to pray, "Dispel our awareness of sin." However, Christ taught His disciples to pray (and it was to be a daily prayer at that), "Forgive us our sins."

We need God's forgiveness and acquittal daily and continually. Justification has been completed, so that when God acquits us He no more remembers all our sins, nor our sinful nature, against which we have to struggle all our life (Q&A 56 of the Heidelberg Catechism). Considering that we increase our debt daily (Q&A 13 of the Heidelberg Catechism), we need His debt-removing acquittal constantly. We continually need to shelter under Christ's intercession.

6. Release

The presupposition underpinning the confession of justification through faith in Christ is totally lost on modern religiosity. Man calls original sin a mythological phantom, denies the divine Sonship of Christ, no longer trembles in fear of God's wrath, and consigns the whole demon world to the world of fables. This realm of thought leaves no room for the doctrine of the justification of the ungodly. For the majority of people the burning question is not how we shall be delivered from our sin, but how we shall attain the means to buy a car and how we will be able to drive it with peace of mind. Modern religious songs sing of a Jesus who makes life good for us and helps us through our problems, instead of a Saviour who became our Substitute. The joy of the Gospel of the free forgiveness of sins no longer affects the majority of people today, and theology has basically let go of this confession.

ARTICLE 24
MAN'S SANCTIFICATION AND GOOD WORKS

We believe that this true faith, worked in man by the hearing of God's Word and by the operation of the Holy Spirit, regenerates him and makes him a new man. It makes him live a new life and frees him from the slavery of sin. Therefore it is not true that this justifying faith makes man indifferent to living a good and holy life. On the contrary, without it no one would ever do anything out of love for God, but only out of self-love or fear of being condemned.

It is therefore impossible for this holy faith to be inactive in man, for we do not speak of an empty faith but of what Scripture calls faith working through love. This faith induces man to apply himself to those works which God has commanded in His Word. These works, proceeding from the good root of faith, are good and acceptable in the sight of God, since they are all sanctified by His grace.

Nevertheless, they do not count toward our justification. For through faith in Christ we are justified, even before we do any good works. Otherwise they could not be good any more than the fruit of a tree can be good unless the tree itself is good.

Therefore we do good works, but not for merit. For what could we merit? We are indebted to God, rather than He to us, for the good works we do, since it is He who is at work in us, both to will and to work for His good pleasure. Let us keep in mind what is written: So you also, when you have done all that is commanded you, say, "We are unworthy servants; we have only done what was our duty."

Meanwhile we do not deny that God rewards good works, but it is by His grace that He crowns His gifts.

Furthermore, although we do good works, we do not base our salvation on them. We cannot do a single work that is not defiled by our flesh and does not deserve punishment. Even if we could show one good work, the remembrance of one sin is enough to make God reject it. We would then always be in doubt, tossed to and fro without any certainty, and our poor consciences would be constantly tormented, if they did not rely on the merit of the death and passion of our Saviour.

1. Summary

This article's lively style, so characteristic of our whole Confession, makes an accurate division of the article rather difficult. Therefore it is more appropriate to present a short summary of its content:

    A. Like Article 22, this article also commences by discussing faith. Article 22 said that faith, for the purpose of justification, embraces Jesus Christ with all His merits. It said that faith regenerates man and makes him a new man. In connection with this it said too how this faith is "worked" in man.

B. Rome's slander, which asserts that the doctrine of justification through faith alone would make us "careless" (Q&A 64 of the Heidelberg Catechism), is rejected, and confession is made that faith is never void of good works (Canons of Dort, V #12, 13).

C. These works do not count toward our justification but, rather, they must be preceded by justification. If this were not so, the tree would not be good; how can a bad tree bear good fruit? Our good works do not earn us anything at all because God works them in us. He does not owe us any thanks for these good works, but we owe Him thanks. Furthermore, all the good that we do is no more than our rightful duty.

D. God rewards good works, not out of a sense of obligation, but out of grace (Q&A 63 of the Heidelberg Catechism). In so doing He does not crown our efforts, but crowns His own work in us, and leads that work to its completion.

E. We do not base our salvation on our good works. Firstly, our works are constantly defiled by sin (Q&A 62 of the Heidelberg Catechism), and secondly, if we did not depend on the merits of the suffering and death of our Saviour, we would remain in doubt.

2. Faith and regeneration or conversion

Concerning the source of faith, Article 22 said it is kindled in our hearts by the Holy Spirit (see paragraph 4 of the chapter on that article). Here, in greater detail, it says that faith is worked in us "by the hearing of God's Word and by the operation of the Holy Spirit." With these words the Confession turns itself against spiritualists who said at the time that the Word is merely a dead letter and that it is the Spirit who makes alive. Hence they despised the preaching and the use of the sacraments; in fact, they despised the whole official service of the Church. This error is still very much alive today. Moreover, the Confession refuted the Church of Rome which, by its view that faith is human approval (*fides implicata*!), did not do justice to the work of the Spirit. The Arminians later made it even worse. They denied the necessity of regeneration and claimed that man, by his free will, was capable of accepting God's Word in faith (Canons of Dort, III/IV, Rejection of Errors #6, 7). That is why the Canons of Dort pay so much attention to the work of the Holy Spirit in working faith.

We must beware that we never separate "Word" and "Spirit" from each other. The Heidelberg Catechism unites these two by saying in Q&A 65 that the Holy Spirit works faith in our hearts by the preaching of the Holy Gospel. Later on, theology, led by a scholastic craving to construe, separated the two. Man then began to work with the notion of an "outward preaching," as if the Word is ever independent of God's Spirit. (This term "outward preaching" originates with the Arminians; the Canons of Dort do not acknowledge any "outward preaching.") Alongside this it was thought that one could speak of the "independent" (no medium) work of the Holy Spirit, a direct working without the help of any means. It was said that such a direct working of the Holy Spirit had to precede the Word. After all, isn't a sinner dead? How can a dead person hear if he is not first made alive? One can only reason this way if one falls into the trap of believing in "outward preaching." The Arminians overlooked the fact that the Word of the Lord is always powerful and calls the dead as if they were alive.

Having first of all separated Word and Spirit from each other, man went on to say that the first "bringing to life," called regeneration, worked "directly" by the Spirit, took place without our being conscious of it. In addition to that, Abraham Kuyper spoke of an implanting of the "seed of faith" (a totally unScriptural understanding and an understanding that comes very close to the Roman Catholic understanding of grace!). This "implanting" of the seed of faith could even take place in very young babies, even *before* birth. (However, in that case these children would no longer be "born in sin"!) Hence one arrived at the following diagram:

regeneration: $\begin{cases} \textit{(intellect) faith} \\ \textit{(will) conversion} \end{cases}$

Note, that this is exactly the reverse to what this article states. There it says that faith regenerates us, but in the aforementioned theological constructions faith arises from regeneration.

Here is a variation in the use of the word "regeneration." In older theology and in our Confession "regeneration" is synonymous with "conversion." Regeneration was understood to be the act of being made alive by God's Spirit + living by God's Spirit. In more recent theology it became: regeneration = the first, the initial (direct; no medium) bringing to life by God's Spirit and the term conversion was reserved for the life by God's Spirit. We do wise to maintain the terminology of the Confession. The Confession does not know of any unconscious regeneration. The Canons of Dort do not acknowledge this either. They speak at length about the work of the Spirit, but never separate from the Word. Not in Chapter III/IV #11 either. There it is not so much as suggested that the Spirit works regeneration apart from the Word, but that regeneration does not take place by the Word alone (over against the Arminian misconception of only an "outward preaching"). When Chapter III/IV #12 says that God works regeneration "in us without us," it opposes the Arminian claim that "regeneration certainly takes place by our own will, by *our* approval." It does not at all state that it takes place outside of us and outside of our consciousness. The entire Canons of Dort teach that God makes us alive through the Gospel and regenerates us (see Chapter III/IV #6).

If one concentrates on the logical sequence then one can say that the regenerating work of God precedes faith. However, in reality both take place at the same time. The Canons of Dort say, too, that whoever is regenerated, actually believes (Chapter III/IV #12).

The thought of direct and unconscious regeneration led in turn to the delusion of a dormant regeneration. The seed of faith could be dormant within us for years. One might be a believer, but no one notices it. To illustrate this Abraham Kuyper pointed to the century old grains of wheat from the graves of the Pharaohs. However, Dr. Seakle Greijdanus astutely replied that a human being is not a coffin, but that Scripture calls him a field. Who has seen a grain of wheat dormant in a field for years? Besides, Scripture says that one knows a tree by its fruits. That would no longer hold in view of the Kuyperian construction. Then a tree could bear bad fruit while regeneration lay dormant in its roots.

The illusion of a "dormant regeneration" made it easy to speak of "presumptive regeneration" as far as little children were concerned. Furthermore, one could be of the opinion that a full administration of baptism would seal grace already present. This most logically construed system is really nothing more than human wisdom. It repeatedly contradicts Scripture and Confession and it is a fatal poison for the practice of godliness.

The Synod of 1905 also dealt with the issue of "direct regeneration."[16] However, its decision was an ambiguous compromise, so distinctively characteristic of this synod as a whole. It said that this term could be used "in the right context, to the extent that the Churches have always confessed it in opposition to the Lutheran and Roman Churches, namely that regeneration does not occur by the Word or the sacraments as such, but by the almighty and regenerating work of the Holy Spirit; this regenerating work of the Holy Spirit was not to be detached from the preaching of the Word in the sense that the two were separated from each other." The formerly approved term was thus effectively rejected. Hence everyone got what they wanted.

The question was asked that if regeneration takes place by the Word, how then can little children who die at a very young age be regenerated? Appropriate here is the humility of the Canons of Dort, I #17, which does not discuss the regeneration of children. It has not been revealed to us how God makes them partakers of Christ. What counts for us is this: Believe and you shall live. Hear the Word!

The issue of "direct regeneration" also applies to the question whether God regenerates some people in the heathen world apart from the preaching of the Word. "Utrecht (1905)" discussed this, but perhaps too cautiously. We must decide on the basis of the Word that one cannot be saved by any other name given to man than by the Name of our Lord Jesus Christ.

---

[16] Or "immediate regeneration," i.e. regeneration without the use of the means of the preaching of the Word. — TRANS.

3. New man

This article says that faith "regenerates (man) and makes him a new man. It makes him live a new life . . ." In connection with this it must be noted what the Canons of Dort, Chapter III/IV #11 say in the last part concerning the complete change worked by regeneration. This does not happen instantaneously. Q&A 115 of the Heidelberg Catechism says "more and more." It is progressive. If it were to be plotted on a graph one would not see a continuous rising curve but, rather, a line with dips and rises. Moreover, even "the holiest have only a small beginning (worked by God) of this obedience, nevertheless, with earnest purpose they do begin to live not only according to some but to all the commandments of God" (Q&A 114 of the Heidelberg Catechism).

Barthians, of course, want nothing to do with this "more and more." Karl Barth wrote, "Grace and sin do not set out on a procedural liaison in which the one gradually ousts and conquers the other." And Van Niftrik writes in his *Kleine Dogmatiek* (= *Brief Dogmatics*): "We remain the old Adam." According to them "grace from above to below is to be regarded as justification and from below to above is to be regarded as sanctification. Hence my sanctification is that I know myself as a sinner before God." In this way the most atrocious sinner could simultaneously be the most holy. Whereas the Roman Catholics merge justification with sanctification, Barthians let sanctification exist in justification. Their "rejection of sanctification that is present" is Anabaptist.

4. Against two fronts

Here too the Confession strikes a blow against both the Roman Catholic and the Anabaptist errors. Roman Catholics teach that by means of the grace of the sacraments man is enabled to completely fulfil the law. In opposition to this the Confession says that in this life we are freed from slavery to sin, but not from the taint of sin. "We cannot do a single work that is not defiled by our flesh and does not deserve punishment." Antinomians claim that we do not have to obey the law. Christ, they say, has redeemed us from the law. Moreover, they add, we cannot fulfil it either, but that does not matter any more. They attribute all sins to "the old man."[17] Over against this Article 24 confesses the renewal of man (see paragraph 3 above).

5. Remaining questions

This article gives a clear answer to questions about what good works are, whether they are perfect, how God rewards them and why they do not count toward our justification. Its coverage of these questions is similar to that of Lord's Day 24 of the Heidelberg Catechism.

ARTICLE 25
CHRIST, THE FULFILMENT OF THE LAW

We believe that the ceremonies and symbols of the law have ceased with the coming of Christ, and that all shadows have been fulfilled, so that the use of them ought to be abolished among Christians. Yet their truth and substance remain for us in Jesus Christ, in whom they have been fulfilled.
In the meantime we still use the testimonies taken from the law and the prophets, both to confirm us in the doctrine of the gospel and to order our life in all honour, according to God's will and to His glory.

1. Context

Initially it might seem strange that after having dealt with justification and sanctification the Confession now suddenly moves on to a discussion on the abolition of the ceremonial law. However, when we consider that through the previous articles the Confession fought a fierce battle against what was essentially a denial of Christ through Roman Catholic doctrine, we perceive that this article is really a continuation of this battle. Articles 17-21 were concerned

---

[17] A more literal translation of the original would read: "They debit all sins to the old donkey." The "old donkey" was an expression used by Antinomians in the seventeenth century for "the old man," by which was meant a phase that the believer had left behind. — TRANS.

with Christ and His substitutionary work; following on from that, Articles 22-24 spoke of the fruits of this work and how we obtain these fruits. In all these articles the main theme was: Christ alone! Under this same theme, Article 25 draws as it were a connecting line through the Confession; not only have all the promises to the fathers been fulfilled in Christ, but in Him the whole Old Testament worship was also fulfilled. Under the great theme of "Christ alone" Article 26 draws a second line through the Confession, namely, that His work does not need to be supplemented.

2. Division

This article can easily be divided into two sections. The first section opposes the Roman Catholics and the second section opposes Anabaptist zealots.

    A. The Old Testament worship ceremonies were fulfilled in Christ

    B. The message of the Old Testament continues to speak to us

3. Significance

This article is highly significant with respect to the relationship of the Old and New Testaments; the role of the law in our lives; the institution of the worship service, and the dispensationalist expectation of a restoration of the temple worship in Jerusalem.

4. Old Testament - New Testament

"Symbols" are representations. In this article symbols are the objects used in Israel's worship, such as the candlestick, breastplate, the ark, and many more; these were all representations. The term "ceremonies" refers to the ceremonial deeds in Israel's worship, such as circumcision, offering, and purification.

All these symbols and ceremonies served to foreshadow to Israel Christ and His work (Colossians 2:16, 17; Hebrews 8:5a). They all served to lead Israel to, and to keep Israel in the faithful expectation of, the Promised One. They instructed Israel in the righteousness of faith. Israel understood but little of this. Often the people just performed the ceremonies as external deeds, by which they thought to make themselves deserving in God's eyes. The prophets fulminated against this. They cried out that God hated such sacrifices. They taught that God was not concerned with bulls and goats, but with the hearts of His people.

Hence there is no contrast between the Old and New Testaments. Both reveal the righteousness of faith. Yet there is a difference. The Old Testament is a (child's) book with many pictures and minimal text; the New Testament is a book (for adults) with few pictures and much text. Yet together both books give one continuous story. Having reached maturity, one no longer gazes at the pictures in the first section, yet one continues to listen to its message. One does not discard the Old Testament. Christ didn't do that either. The apostles honoured it as God's Word. Essentially the New Testament is no more than an explanation and clarification of the Old Testament. Therefore Christ and His apostles often referred to the Old Testament. Without knowing the Old Testament we cannot understand the New Testament. Consider the many symbols the book of Revelation has borrowed from the Old Testament. Hence the message of the ceremonies and symbols remains relevant. For example, no priest was permitted in God's presence without a sacrifice. That does not mean that we must still sacrifice, but it does mean that only by focussing with a believing heart on the sacrifice of Christ can we come to God. We do not have to circumcise ourselves any more today, but we are to take the message of circumcision to heart and are to put our old nature to death. What Israel's law stipulated for civil and moral life has not become meaningless. The Mosaic law has received far too little attention in the Church. The theologians left it alone because it was a "law" and the lawyers bypassed it because it was in the Bible. So the one left it to the other. A renewed interest among us to understand the law is commendable.

5. Fulfilled, but where?

There is no dispute between the Church of Rome and us that the ceremonies and symbols of the Old Testament have been fulfilled. However, there is a difference of opinion concerning the question: where? In accordance with Scripture we confess that they received their fulfilment in Christ (Matthew 5:17). However, the Church of Rome says they received their fulfilment in Christ and in His body, the Church, where they are all preserved "in fulfilment." The sacrifice remained, but now as a bloodless repetition of the "fulfilling" sacrifice. The whole excessive style of worship of the Church of Rome is borrowed from Israel's worship and that pattern has been supplemented with many symbols and ceremonies.

6. Objectionable

Paul forbade adherence to the Old Testament symbols and ceremonies such as circumcision, fasting, and the feast days. To maintain these today, after God Himself had torn the curtain of the Temple, would obscure the Gospel. Therefore the reformers had many objections to Roman Catholic worship. The main points of these objections were:

A. God alone is the Church's lawgiver. We are to serve and honour Him as He has commanded in His Word. Self-invented forms of worship are commandments of man and it is futile to honour God by them (see Lord's Day 35 of the Heidelberg Catechism);

B. essentially Roman Catholic ceremonies lead to Judaism. The people believe that by carefully observing all kinds of commandments they will make themselves deserving before God;

C. Roman Catholic ceremonies foster hypocrisy. People will perform all kinds of ceremonies before God, but withhold their heart from Him. They consider faith and conversion to be too serious, but are willing to bring sacrifices. In this way they think they can still be acceptable to God despite an unconverted life.

7. In spirit and in truth

In the New Testament, baptism and holy supper are the only ceremonies prescribed for us. As far as the institution of the worship service is concerned it offers minimal direction. The worship service remains what it also was for Israel: a meeting between God and His covenant people. Not in ceremonies and "shadows" but in spirit and truth. Therefore the preaching of the Word must be central. The worship service is an alternation of Word and response. The more we add to it, the more we lose sight of this main object.

Worship includes public, family, and personal worship.

Its purpose is to strengthen us in true worship whereby we present ourselves in body as pleasing sacrifices to God by being followers of Him in love.

8. Roman Catholicising

The ecumenical movement is essentially a "liturgical" movement. Man wants the worship service to culminate in the sacramental exercising of communion with God. The sacrament becomes central. Hence it is not the pulpit which is central in modern church buildings, but the Holy Supper table is the focus of attention. This is a tendency toward Roman Catholicism and a spiritual impoverishment by the increase in ceremonies. For many the liturgical movement has been the pathway which led them to the Roman Catholic Church.

ARTICLE 26
CHRIST'S INTERCESSION

We believe that we have no access to God except through the only Mediator and Advocate Jesus Christ the righteous. For this purpose He became man, uniting together the divine and human nature, that we men might not be barred from but have access to the divine majesty. This Mediator, however, whom the Father has ordained between Himself and us, should not frighten us by His greatness, so that we look for another according to our fancy. There is no creature in heaven or on earth who loves us more than Jesus Christ. Though He was in the form of God, He emptied Himself, taking the form of man and of a servant for us, and was made like His brethren in every respect. If, therefore, we had to look for another intercessor, could we find one who loves us more than He who laid down His life for us, even while we were His enemies? If we had to look for one who has authority and power, who has more than He who is seated at the right hand of the Father and who has all authority in heaven and on earth? Moreover, who will be heard more readily than God's own well-beloved Son?

Therefore it was pure lack of trust which introduced the custom of dishonouring the saints rather than honouring them, doing what they themselves never did nor required. On the contrary, they constantly rejected such honour according to their duty, as appears from their writings. Here one ought not to bring in our unworthiness, for it is not a question of offering our prayers on the basis of our own worthiness, but only on the basis of the excellence and worthiness of Jesus Christ, whose righteousness is ours by faith.

Therefore with good reason, to take away from us this foolish fear or rather distrust, the author of Hebrews says to us that Jesus Christ was made like His brethren in every respect, so that He might become a merciful and faithful High Priest in the service of God, to make expiation for the sins of the people. For because He Himself has suffered and been tempted, He is able to help those who are tempted. Further, to encourage us more to go to Him, he says: Since then we have a great High Priest who has passed through the heavens, Jesus, the Son of God, let us hold fast our confession. For we have not a High Priest who is unable to sympathize with our weaknesses, but one who in every respect has been tempted as we are, yet without sin. Let us then with confidence draw near to the throne of grace, that we may receive mercy and find grace to help in time of need. The same letter says: Therefore brethren, since we have confidence to enter the sanctuary by the blood of Jesus . . . let us draw near with a true heart in full assurance of faith, etc. Also, Christ holds His priesthood permanently, because He continues forever. Consequently He is able for all time to save those who draw near to God through Him, since He always lives to make intercession for them. What more is needed? Christ Himself says: I am the way, and the truth, and the life; no one comes to the Father, but by Me. Why should we look for another advocate? It has pleased God to give us His Son as our Advocate. Let us then not leave Him for another, or even look for another, without ever finding one. For when God gave Him to us, He knew very well that we were sinners.

In conclusion, according to the command of Christ, we call upon the heavenly Father through Christ our only Mediator, as we are taught in the Lord's prayer. We rest assured that we shall obtain all we ask of the Father in His Name.

1. Context

Concerning this article's placement in the context of the whole Confession, see paragraph 1 of the chapter on Article 25. Reference to our Lord Jesus Christ's priestly work was already made in Article 21. There we confess His priestly sacrifice. In this article we confess Christ's priestly intercession. Our Confession focuses on the work of Christ as Priest and not so much on His work as Prophet and King because the confession of His priestly work was a crucial issue in the conflict with the Church of Rome.

2. Christ, the only Mediator

It is crystal clear that here the Confession opposes the Roman Catholic practice of invoking (praying to) the saints. Invoking those who have died (in the Bible "saints" are always living members of the Church) is no trivial matter for the Church of Rome. Nor was it a trivial matter for the reformers. In the combat against this practice Luther advised against stressing it, for in his opinion it would disappear of its own accord; as long as it was understood that Christ's intercession is sufficient for us. Luther was totally convinced of the sufficiency of Christ's intercession. Calvin no less so. Here was a radical break with Rome. Our Confession, too, completely dismisses any invoking of the saints. The positive way this article speaks is beautiful. It does not give an exhaustive list of arguments against invoking the saints, but offers a broad and persuasive argument in favour of calling on Christ alone. In so doing Article 25 restricts itself to addressing the main issue in this conflict with the Church of Rome. Unlike the French Confession, it does not address the issues of purgatory, cloistral oaths, pilgrimages, celibacy, fasting, observation of days of the saints, indulgences, etc.

Roman Catholics distinguish between a mediation of reconciliation and a mediation of intercession. Christ alone offered the first, but the second is also offered by the saints. However, one cannot separate the two. Rome does not acknowledge mediation based only on Christ's sacrifice. Moreover, Roman Catholics distinguish between worshipping (*latreia*) and venerating (*doeleia*). If someone's supernatural, unique qualities lie in the created order, then we are called upon to show veneration (*doeleia*); if they lie in the uncreated order, we are called upon to worship (*latreia*). To worship means to worship in the fullest sense of the word. To venerate involves honouring and invoking. The extent to which one venerates the various saints is relative to the varying measures of supernatural qualities and meritorious deeds of the saints. The one worthy of the highest degree of veneration is Mary, the mother of God. The Church of Rome teaches that the distinction between worshipping and venerating excludes every form of idolatry. However, reality proves otherwise!

The saints are venerated religiously and are invoked on account of their meritorious acts. Their excess works serve the communion of saints for the benefit of whoever prays to the saints.

The saints specialize in various areas. St. George is the patron saint of England, St. Patrick of Ireland. Doctors have St. Luke as their patron saint and sailors and travellers have St. Brendan and St. Christopher. The list is endless.[18]

However, Scripture does not give any example, command, or promise with regard to such invoking of the saints. To do so is, in fact, a denial of the One and only High Priest, Jesus Christ (Q&A 30 of the Heidelberg Catechism; Deuteronomy 18:11; Acts 14;14, 15; Revelation 19:20).

Do we then have no respect whatsoever for the saints who have died? That would be completely contrary to Scripture. Scripture commands us to remember them. We want to do this by thanking God for the examples of His mercy which He gave in them and by following their examples of faith and faithfulness. However, the issue at stake here is the intercession, the mediation of the saints.

---

[18] The author gave examples of some Dutch patron saints. — TRANS.

3. Division
   A. We have access to God through Christ alone
   B. We must not be afraid of this Mediator
   C. The teaching of invoking the dead arose from suspicion
   D. The argument that we do not deserve to be heard is irrelevant here
   E. Scripture preaches Christ as the High Priest through whom we may approach God
   F. The manner in which we therefore pray

With regard to the second part of the article one should remember that people in the Middle Ages perceived Christ as a harsh judge. A painting dating back to that time shows Christ and Mary sitting as it were on the edge of heaven. To each of them a ladder is extended from the earth. Many people attempt to climb these two ladders. Whoever climbs the ladder leading to Christ falls down in fright as soon as he approaches Him, but whoever climbs the ladder leading to Mary receives a friendly welcome and is led to Jesus. Moreover, the well-known painter Rubens made a painting for the Franciscan friars at Ghent, portraying Christ with flaming flashes of lightning in His hand ready to destroy the earth. Yet the entreaties of Mary and Franciscus keep Him from doing so. *That* is what the Church of Rome made of our merciful High Priest!

The remaining parts of this article require no further clarification.

How we may and ought to pray is taught in the Heidelberg Catechism in Lord's Day 45, 46, 47-52.

ARTICLE 27
THE CATHOLIC OR UNIVERSAL CHURCH

We believe and profess one catholic or universal Church, which is a holy congregation and assembly of the true Christian believers, who expect their entire salvation in Jesus Christ, are washed by His blood, and are sanctified and sealed by the Holy Spirit.

This Church has existed from the beginning of the world and will be to the end, for Christ is an eternal King who cannot be without subjects. This holy Church is preserved by God against the fury of the whole world, although for a while it may look very small and as extinct in the eyes of man. Thus during the perilous reign of Ahab, the Lord kept for Himself seven thousand persons who had not bowed their knees to Baal.

Moreover, this holy Church is not confined or limited to one particular place or to certain persons, but is spread and dispersed throughout the entire world. However, it is joined and united with heart and will, in one and the same Spirit, by the power of faith.

1. Context

In Articles 17-21 and 25-26 the Confession spoke of Christ and His substitutionary work for our deliverance. Articles 22-24 dealt with the fruits of Christ's work and how these fruits are conferred to us through faith which the Holy Spirit kindles in us through the preaching of the Gospel. Hence at this point the Confession moves on to a discussion of the Church. It is to the Church that the preaching of the Gospel has been entrusted and in whose midst the Lord wants to bestow on us Christ's gifts. The Church is the "mother of us all."

In Article 27 the words "washed by His blood" refer to what was confessed in Articles 17-21 and 25-26, and the words "sanctified and sealed by the Holy Spirit" refer to what was confessed in Articles 22-24.

2. Attention given to the Church in the Confessions

The Belgic Confession devotes no less than 6 articles (27-32) to the Church, which is almost one-sixth of its total number of articles. No less attention is devoted to it in the Apostles' Creed. Of this Creed's 115 words, 11 (10%!) speak of the Church. The Heidelberg Catechism, too, refers to the Church in various Lord's Days.

Art. 27 states what the Church is and gives a description of it.
Art. 28 states that everyone is obliged to join it.

Art. 29 differentiates between the true and the false Church.
Art. 30 states that the Church is governed by the offices.
Art. 31 states that all office-bearers are equally servants of Christ.
Art. 32 deals with Church discipline.

Lord's Day 19 of the Heidelberg Catechism confesses that "Christ ascended into heaven to manifest Himself there as Head of His Church, through whom the Father governs all things." Lord's Day 21 confesses that "the Son of God, out of the whole human race, from the beginning of the world to its end, gathers, defends, and preserves for Himself, by His Spirit and Word, in the unity of the true faith, a church chosen to everlasting life. And I believe that I am and forever shall remain a living member of it." Lord's Day 27 states that children also belong to the Church. Lord's Day 30 confesses that the Church must exclude the ungodly "by the keys of the kingdom of heaven, until they amend their lives," and Lord's Day 31 elaborates on this. Lord's Day 38 teaches what the fourth commandment requires, namely, that "especially on the day of rest, (we) diligently attend the church of God." Lord's Day 48 teaches that by means of the petition "Thy kingdom come" Christ also taught us to pray, "preserve and increase Thy church."

3. I believe . . . a Church

With the words of the Apostles' Creed I confess that I believe *in* God the Father, *in* God the Son, and *in* God the Holy Spirit. However, when it comes to confessing about the Church I do not confess I believe *in* but I *believe* . . . a Church. To "believe in" something denotes trusting in or relying on something. We trust in God but, unlike the Roman Catholics, we do not trust in the Church.

The fact that the Confession does not say "I see," but rather, "I believe the Church," is not because the Church is invisible but because the Church can only be known by faith. The same applies to Holy Scripture. Indeed, we see it, but it is only by faith that we know it to be the Word of God. Hence, it is by hearing Scripture that we know it to be the Word of God. That is also how we know the Church. What we see of the Church is but little in proportion to her totality. The Church is still a house under construction. Of such a house we see the foundations laid, walls erected, and window frames fitted. However, it is only the architect who knows the design and drawing of the house and he is able to tell us what everything actually is and shall become. So only God, the Master Builder of the Church, can let us know what we see of the Church. In this, too, no less than with respect to the doctrine of the Trinity or of God's providence, we are to live by faith and we are to let ourselves be instructed by the Word and to live according to it. As Article 27 says, we believe and profess a Church.

4. Assembly

This article says that the Church is a "holy (= "separated," called *out* of the world) congregation and assembly of the true Christian believers." The Church is an *assembly*. In the French text of the Confession we read two words for this one word "assembly:" *congregation et assemblee*. The Latin text also uses two words here: *congregatio seu coetus*. "*Congregatio*" is the bringing together or gathering to one "*grex*" or flock. "*Coetus*" is related to "*co-ire*" = to come together. The Church is the flock of the Good Shepherd, which He gathers together. When it speaks of the Church in Lord's Day 21, Q&A 54, the Heidelberg Catechism immediately points to Him, the Son of God, and confesses that He gathers for Himself (= in order for it to be His) a Church. He calls His sheep. His sheep then also hear and come to Him, and in so doing meet with each other. Therefore the Church is not just a congregatio, but also a coetus. In it both God, and through Him the believers, are active.

Close attention must be paid to this notion of the Church "being an assembly." The Church can definitely not be described as the "sum total of the elect," whereby one finds the Church wherever there are believers. Nor does the fact that here or there believers have joined themselves to a congregation make that congregation the Church. If believers have come together against the will of the Shepherd or in a manner forbidden by Him one can, at best, only speak of a small herd of disobedient sheep but not of the flock, the Church. After all, it was not the Shepherd who brought them together!

To determine whether a certain assembly of Christians may be recognized as the Church, one must assess whether they meet there in response to the call of the good Shepherd, in obedience to His command. It is a question of whether the laws which constitute and govern the meeting originate with God or with man.

Scripture uses many images to illustrate the glory of this assembly. She is the Bride of the Lamb, God's wife, the body of Christ, the House of God. We must not isolate one of these images from the others and then use it to promote our own ideas about the Church; rather, we must remember that they all speak of the *assembly*.

Concerning this Church (assembly), this article confesses that it "has existed from the beginning of the world." Already in Paradise the Son of God started gathering His Church from the lost human race (Genesis 3:15). He has continued to do so, against the fury of hell. Already in Genesis 4 we read of believers *coming* together, drawn together by the Son of God. When we read there that man, in the days of Enosh, began to call on the name of the Lord, this does not mean that this was the first time man prayed but, rather, this was the first time man assembled for prayer; they were going to do it *together*. There was also every reason to do so in the face of rapid and terrible apostasy in the line of Cain. Already at that time the believers stood as a "small flock" over against the pride and the concentration of power of unbelieving brutes. Against this they found shelter with each other and sought their strength in God. Later the Church existed in the tents of the patriarchs and within the boundaries of Israel; until Christ gathered it out of *all* nations at Pentecost and it will continue "to the end." Toward the end its freedom will be forcefully restricted and there will be little room for its official service, but despite the oppression and dispersion that will take place during "Satan's release," (Revelation 20), the Church will continue to exist. Christ is an eternal King who cannot be without subjects.

Precisely because the Church is an *assembly*, every reference to an invisible Church is as foolish as speaking of dry water or cold fire, a contradiction in terms.

To argue whether Article 27 or Q&A 54 of the Heidelberg Catechism speaks of a visible or invisible Church would be contrary to the aim of the Confession. The Confession and the Heidelberg Catechism, which both confess the Church to be an assembly, do not recognize such a distinction. No, the Church is not overseeable. Who is able to trace perfectly its boundaries through the course of history, or even today? However, this incalculable Church does have a fixed address, and *that* is precisely where it is and nowhere else. It is there where Article 29 teaches us to find it.

Neither are all things pertaining to the Church visible. Its faith and the indwelling of the Holy Spirit, its unconquerability and still many more aspects are *invisible*. Yet, this is no ground for speaking of an "invisible Church."

The fact that Article 27 states that the Church is an assembly *of* true Christian believers (Latin: *omnium vere fidelium Christianorum*) does not mean that all believers are always found inside her. This is a statement of the norm and it makes a strong appeal to everyone. There are sheep outside the fold who belong to the flock, and according to Article 28 "are obliged to join it."

5. Attributes of the Church

A. *Holy*. The Church has been chosen by God, bought by Christ's blood, and has been separated from the world by the Holy Spirit with the Gospel, to serve and glorify God (1 Peter 2:9, 10). In this way it is guided toward its future state of perfection, but has not as yet attained it.

B. *Catholic or universal*. The Church is not confined to a specific time, a specific nation, or a specific view. At all times and among all nations the Church is always the same. It is gathered from the beginning out of the whole human race and continues to confess the same faith.

C. *Christian*. The Church belongs to Christ and shares in His anointing (Lord's Day 12 of the Heidelberg Catechism). It stands or falls according to whether or not it confesses that Jesus is the Christ, the Son of God (Matthew 16:16, 18; 1 John 5:1).

D. *Apostolic*. The Nicene Creed correctly calls the Church apostolic, for it is built on the foundation of the apostles (Matthew 16:18; Revelation 21:14). The Church is bound to the words of the apostles (Matthew 10:40; John 20:23). The faithful Church perseveres in what the apostles have taught (Acts 2:32; 2 Timothy

3:14), and rejects anything which contradicts or goes beyond it (Galatians 1:8).

E. *One*. Despite the many differences that can be found within the Church, it is one in the unity of faith (Q&A 54 of the Heidelberg Catechism). "It is joined and united with heart and will in one and the same Spirit, by the power of faith." Any unity not based on this unity is deceit.

6. Universal and local Church

By "universal" Church we mean the Church of all times and all places. The Church is everywhere, in every place where Christ gathers it. By being a member of a local Church, one is a member of the universal Church.

Concerning this universal Church we confess that it "will be to the end." However, this does not exclude the possibility that we may appear very small for a prolonged period of time and seem extinct in the eyes of man. Then the Church will be removed in many places, as it was, for example, in Asia Minor and along the northern coast of Africa. In Revelation, Christ also threatens some Churches that He will remove the candlestick if they do not repent. Hence the promise that the Church shall always be there is no pillow on which to sleep peacefully in sin, but a comfort for those who at times discover much oppression during the good fight.

7. One . . . Church

The word "one" (French: *une seule eglise*; Latin: *unicam ecclesiam*) means that there is only one Church. Article 29 though, in its last sentence, says with reference to the true and false Church, "These two Churches are easily recognized and distinguished from each other." Isn't that a contradiction? No, because not only does the word "Church" have many meanings, but it is also used in different ways. It means: 1. a building; 2. a meeting or service; 3. a congregation. The Confession uses the last definition, but it does so in two ways. In Article 27 the word Church is used in terms of what we believe concerning the Church, but in Article 29 it is used in accordance with common usage. For example, we speak of the Church of England even though we cannot recognize it as the

Church. For convenience sake one turns to the common usage of the term.

No objections need to be raised against this twofold usage of the word Church, as long as we distinguish between the two and use each correctly. However, the sad reality is that people do not test the common usage of the word against the Confession, but increasingly conform their confession to sinful practice. Experience confronts people with the hard reality that there are many Churches, and an increasing variety. Instead of testing this situation against the norm of Scripture and Confession, and issuing a summons to act in accordance to this norm, the weakening confessional insight, whereby the norm was no longer correctly understood, resulted in man more and more basing his confession concerning the Church on observable reality.

After all, one saw many Churches. To be sure, they differed from one another in many respects, yet they also had much in common. In that which they had in common one thought he saw in every Church something of *the Church*. Hence man began to say *the* Church is dispersed among all Churches. Every Church is a manifestation of *the* Church, the latter being regarded as a timeless ideal. This timeless ideal (invisible Church) was more apparent in one Church than another, and hence one started to speak of "more" or "less" pure Churches. In short, this is what is called the "doctrine of pluriformity,"[19] the doctrine of multiple forms of the Church. The one invisible *Church* would more or less manifest itself in every Church. Some people (e.g. Abraham Kuyper) commended this doctrine of pluriformity while others (e.g. Herman Bavinck) deplored it.

Neither Scripture nor Confession recognize any such speculation cast on the mould of Plato's philosophies. In 1892 Kuyper still admitted that this confession of the pluriformity of the Church was taught by neither Scripture nor Confession. According to him it only came to light in later developments of Church history. However, since Dr. Buizer's petition there have been many attempts within Reformed circles to read this view into the Confession. Moreover, man utilised many ingenious distinctions which

---

[19] Also known as denominationalism. — TRANS.

resembled the truth, but which gave rise to countless misunderstandings. We mention here the visible and invisible Church; Church as organism and Church as institution; militant Church (on earth) and triumphant Church (in heaven), in between which the Roman Catholics still know of a "suffering" Church (in purgatory).

We believe and confess *one . . . Church*, for the Shepherd has one flock. The Son of God gathers the Church and He and His work are inseparable.

8. Orientation

The confession concerning the Church is presently the focus of the battle of the spirits. Just as the Christian Church's concern of the first centuries was the dogma of the Trinity and the two natures of Christ, and in the time of the Reformation particularly the dogma of sin and grace, so in the twentieth century the issue has been the dogma of the Church.

In Reformed circles this became very clear when in 1917, Dr. C.M. Buizer, a teacher at Middelburg, submitted an appeal against Articles 27-29 of the Belgic Confession. He gave an historical, confessional explanation of these articles which on the whole could be accepted as true. However, he went on to argue that this view did not agree with the insights generally recognized at the time (or at least were said to be generally recognized) in the Reformed Churches and concluded that Articles 27-29 ought to be amended. Dr. A.A. van Schelven delivered a report on this to Classis Middelburg in which he argued that the explanation of the incriminated articles as presented by Dr. Buizer was incorrect because he tried to read into the Confession the general conceptions concerning the Church at the time. In Van Schelven's opinion Articles 27-29 were not in need of revision. Classis decided likewise. However, the matter was appealed at the Regional Synod of Middelburg. To this synod a totally different report on the issue was submitted by Rev. G. Doekes. He accepted as correct the explanation of Articles 27-29 presented by Dr. Buizer, but rejected his conclusions. This matter was still an agenda item at the General Synod of Leeuwarden (1920), to which Professor Dr. H. Bouwman submitted a report. The Synod agreed with his conclusions and declared that the petition of Dr. Buizer was not really directed against Articles 27-29 as such, but against his own inaccurate explanation, and therefore did not really contain an objection to these articles. Consequently it was put aside. Synod found this easy to do because it had set up a committee with the mandate to advise on whether the Confession, with regard to Holy Scripture and the Church and the Church's relation to the government, required amendment or needed to be supplemented.

However, nothing came of it. No declaration was ever made about the matters raised. However, just "putting a lid on the matter" in this way did not make the issue disappear. Since then the struggle about the confession concerning the Church has continued unabated. Evidence of this struggle is: 1. the extensive series of letters on this subject by Dr. H.H. Kuyper in *De Heraut* (No. 2087-2096); 2. the speech of Dr. K. Dijk to an academic assembly of the Free University in 1920 titled "No salvation outside the Church;" 3. numerous publications by Dr. V. Hepp, who endeavoured to defend the new doctrine of pluriformity; 4. in opposition to this, since approximately 1930, the many articles of (later) K. Schilder in *De Reformatie* and several small publications of his such as *Ons aller Moeder* (= *Mother of Us All*).

In 1936 the General Synod of Amsterdam decided to set up a committee. Its task was to make a declaration concerning the "differences of opinion" about the covenant of grace and self-examination, "common grace," the two natures of Christ, the "immortality" of the soul, and the pluriformity of the Church. The Synod of 1942 issued several declarations on all except the last one of these matters. These declarations led to the Liberation of 1944. Several years later, the synod of the synodical Reformed Churches decided against making a declaration concerning the pluriformity of the Church, as this was no longer considered "opportune." Thereby the issue was once again suppressed by putting the "synodical lid" on the matter. Meanwhile, however, the new doctrine of pluriformity had in practice triumphed on all fronts within the bond of the synodical Reformed Churches.

In broader circles, the confession of what the church is has also become a topical issue. At the turn of the century the Church was still generally seen as a free body of religious people without a single divine right. Interest in the Church was minimal. Instead, interest was focussed on religious and personal experiences of the individual. The religious ideal was individualistic and democratic. That is why the papal institution of the Roman Catholic Church was mocked as a relic of original Christianity. The slogan, "Jesus preached the kingdom of God, and what came was the Church" (Loisy), typified the situation. Likewise, Pietism and the Reveille paid scant attention to the Church. Today the wind has changed direction. The flourishing realm of sects may indeed belittle the Church, but "official" theology retains its interest in the Church and does not merely regard it as a human institution but as a creation from above, the body of Christ. At times, strong Roman Catholic tendencies are active here. The "ecumenical" movement had a great influence in this sudden change, making the issue of the Church a central theme.

The ecumenical movement, desiring to organize the Church throughout the world (ecumenical), gained strength in the 19th century. There were some voices in favour of it prior to that, but they did not receive a widespread hearing. In the nineteenth century these books were heard and can be attributed to the following three motives:

A. *the mission motive*. Man wished to prevent the divisions within the Church of the West from being transferred to the East and wanted to increase the effectiveness of the witness through unified organization;

B. *the secularization motive*. This came about especially in the twentieth century. After the two world wars there arose a general apostasy and a conformity to worldliness. Man hoped to oppose this, and especially the rise of world communism, with greater effect by joining forces.

C. *the global motive*. The world opened up; distances shrank due to faster modes of transport. "We think in terms of world proportions."

Many worldwide organizations arose in the nineteenth century. Some were confessional, such as the Lutherans, Baptists, Methodists, and Anglicans; others were categorical, such as the World Sunday-School Assembly, the World Alliance of Young Men's Christian Associations, and the World Federation of Christian

Students. All this was conducive to creating an ideal climate for the ecumenical movement.

Initially, action was stimulated by the mission motive. In 1910, John Mott convened the first world mission conference in Edinburgh. Subsequent well-known conferences were the one in Jerusalem (1928) and the one in Tambaran (1938). In 1962 the International Mission Council was incorporated with the World Council of Churches.

This World Council resulted from two widespread ecumenical movements.

Faith and Order (1910, Edinburgh). The first movement, which was driven by William Brent, correctly discerned that the cause of Church differences lay in the confession of faith and the method of Church government. The aim therefore was to examine these in an endeavour to come to an agreement. After holding several smaller conferences the large conference of Lausanne was held in 1927 where Brent said, "Here we seek truth and unity; preferably truth with unity; but if necessary, truth without unity." However, no agreement could be reached. Nor could they come to any agreement at the large conference led by William Temple at Edinburgh in 1937.

Also in 1937, a world conference of the second ecumenical movement *Life and Work* was held. This conference was led by Nathan Soderblom, who said, "Doctrine divides, service unites." After its large conference in Stockholm (1925) this movement held a conference in Oxford in 1937.

In that year, during which both large movements assembled in England, they sought unity. In order no longer to operate independent of the Churches, the ecumenical movement decided to try and establish a World Council of Churches.

A committee responsible for preparing this was established (fourteen members; seven from each movement). This committee met in Utrecht in 1938 and drafted a foundation and a constitution and prepared an invitation to the Churches. An office was set up in Geneva which sent out these invitations to the Churches and introduced itself as the "World Council of Churches in formation." However, progress was stagnated by the commencement of the second world war. Meanwhile, much work was carried out by the

"World Council of Churches in formation." It mediated to keep correspondence going between Churches in countries cut off from each other because of the war. Much work was done in prisoner-of-war camps and for escapees; "orphaned mission posts" were supported. All this achieved much good will. Meanwhile, a spirit of unity developed in the concentration camps and among the resistance.

Such was the climate in 1948 when the first meeting was held in the New Church of Amsterdam, a meeting keen to establish the World Council of Churches and to formulate a mandate for it.

Over against this "World Council," which despite its laudable foundation does not bind itself to any Confession, the International Council of Christian Churches (I.C.C.C.) was established, a kind of Biblical World Council, with its own statement of belief which, among other things, keeps silent about the sacraments and does not exclude the Baptist view.

Alas, all these ecumenical organizations work in a way which conforms to the world. The standard of faith has been discarded and therefore it can only obtain false unity.

Originally the Church of Rome stood clearly opposed to these ecumenical endeavours. As far as Pius XI and Pius XII were concerned, the only way to unity was via a return to the Church of Rome. However, John XXIII amended this stance, and Pope Paul VI appeared to continue in the same vein. The Second Vatican Council invited Protestants to attend as guests and referred to them as the separated (not even deviating) brothers.

However, this development does not imply that there is even the slightest change in doctrine, structure, or pretensions on the part of the Roman Catholic "mother-Church."

The Reformed Ecumenical Council[20] must also be mentioned here. In it various Churches throughout the world which consider themselves Reformed work together. This Reformed Ecumenical Council also admits into its circle Churches which are members of the World Council of Churches. The Reformed Churches (liberated)

---

[20] Formerly known as the Reformed Ecumenical Synod. Please note that the author wrote this in the 1950s. Certain specific matters of of that time are ommited here. — TRANS.

delivered an elaborate pronouncement concerning this at the General Synod of Amersfoort (1948).

This ecumenical endeavour, which again mistakenly appeals to John 17:20, 21, is gaining increasing support and by means of its influential organization is a fearful and dangerous power in this world.

ARTICLE 28
EVERYONE'S DUTY TO JOIN THE CHURCH

We believe, since this holy assembly and congregation is the assembly of the redeemed and there is no salvation outside of it, that no one ought to withdraw from it, content to be by himself, no matter what his state or quality may be. But all and everyone are obliged to join it and unite with it, maintaining the unity of the Church. They must submit themselves to its instruction and discipline, bend their necks under the yoke of Jesus Christ, and serve the edification of the brothers and sisters, according to the talents which God has given them as members of the same body.

To observe this more effectively, it is the duty of all believers, according to the Word of God, to separate from those who do not belong to the Church and to join this assembly wherever God has established it. They should do so even though the rulers and edicts of princes were against it, and death or physical punishment might follow.

All therefore who draw away from the Church or fail to join it act contrary to the ordinance of God.

1. The main point

This has been stated accurately in the title. Though this article contains more, none of which is insignificant, the concern here is the confession that everyone is obliged to join the true Church. Compare Q&A 55 of the Heidelberg Catechism. In detail it describes how one must "join it and unite with it". That is, by maintaining the unity of the Church, given in Christ and through faith, by submitting to the instruction and discipline of the Church. This is called bowing the neck under Christ's yoke. By this yoke is meant the institution of the offices. One must subject oneself to the admonition and discipline of the office-bearers for Christ's sake, in as far as they are faithful servants of Christ. Should office-bearers impose burdens that are not of Christ, we are to refrain from obeying them.

In addition to this one must, in brotherly communion, employ his gifts and talents for the benefit and well-being of other members, keeping a watch over each other in order to build up one another in love.

This is the duty of *all*, more specifically, of all believers, of everyone who seeks his salvation in Christ.

2. To which Church?

To the Church confessed in Article 27. Here it is not a matter of belonging to the so called "invisible Church." According to this article's line of reasoning, everyone is obliged to join "this holy assembly," which is a clear reference to Article 27. Some have wanted to make a distinction here between "assembly" and "gathering" claiming that the words "outside of her is no salvation" refer only to "gathering." They understood this article to be an admonition not to resist the pull of Christ by which He gathers the Church. However, the article in fact says that assembly is the same as gathering. Here then we are also called to unite with the universal Church confessed in Article 27, which can be found locally.

3. Why?

The reasons the article gives for its exhortation are spread throughout the article. We can arrange them sequentially as follows:

Everyone is obliged to join himself to the true Church
- A. because the Lord commands this: "according to the Word of God" (Hebrews 10:25)
- B. because we ourselves cannot do without the communion of the Church. It is to the Church that the Lord entrusted the means of salvation, which we can then only expect in its midst (Ephesians 4:11-16)

C. because we are responsible for our fellow believers and each of us must therefore see to it that the other is built up in faith

Merely to be listed as a member of the Church will not suffice. Even within the Church one can be "content to be by himself!"

This article says that there is no salvation outside of the Church, and it is of paramount importance to understand this correctly. It does not say that no one shall be saved outside the Church, nor does it say that there is no saved person outside the Church; rather, salvation is not outside of her. Salvation is what God gives to His Church. That is why we must seek it *there* and not anywhere outside of the Church. Neither does this article say anywhere that whoever withdraws himself from the Church cannot be saved, but rather, that this is "contrary to the ordinance of God."

4. The disloyal and non-committed

This article directs itself in particular to those who withdraw themselves from it (see the Latin translation) and to those who consider themselves self-sufficient. These days people put it this way: faith is what counts and not whether you are a member of the Church. Here De Brés also directed himself against the fanatics of his time who, for all kinds of futile reasons, turned their backs on the Church and went their own way.

The second part of the article speaks against those who refrain from joining the Church in fear of trouble and persecution: the Nicodemites (see paragraph 1 of the chapter on Article 1).

ARTICLE 29
THE MARKS OF THE TRUE AND THE FALSE CHURCH

We believe that we ought to discern diligently and very carefully from the Word of God what is the true Church, for all sects which are in the world today claim for themselves the name of Church. We are not speaking here of the hypocrites, who are mixed in the Church along with the

good and yet are not part of the Church, although they are outwardly in it. We are speaking of the body and the communion of the true Church which must be distinguished from all sects that call themselves the Church.

The true Church is to be recognized by the following marks: It practises the pure preaching of the gospel. It maintains the pure administration of the sacraments as Christ instituted them. It exercises Church discipline for correcting and punishing sins. In short, it governs itself according to the pure Word of God, rejecting all things contrary to it and regarding Jesus Christ as the only Head. Hereby the true Church can certainly be known and no one has the right to separate from it.

Those who are of the Church may be recognized by the marks of Christians. They believe in Jesus Christ the only Saviour, flee from sin and pursue righteousness, love the true God and their neighbour without turning to the right or left, and crucify their flesh and its works. Although great weakness remains in them, they fight against it by the Spirit all the days of their life. They appeal constantly to the blood, suffering, death, and obedience of Jesus Christ, in whom they have forgiveness of their sins through faith in Him.

The false church assigns more authority to itself and its ordinances than to the Word of God. It does not want to submit itself to the yoke of Christ. It does not administer the sacraments as Christ commanded in His Word, but adds to them and subtracts from them as it pleases. It bases itself more on men than on Jesus Christ. It persecutes those who live holy lives according to the Word of God and who rebuke the false church for its sins, greed, and idolatries. These two Churches are easily recognized and distinguished from each other.

1. Summary and division of the article

There are two "Churches" which must be distinguished from each other in order that people are not drawn away from the true Church, but stay with it. Here the word "Church" is used in accordance with common practice, just as in the time of the Reformation one spoke of the Jewish Church and the Islamic Church. Then the word "Church" has the general meaning of religious organization and not the more discerning meaning of Christ's real Church.

This differentiation between true and false Church is Scriptural. Scripture indeed warns us not to regard every prophet as a prophet of the Lord, nor to accept every teaching as God's Word, but to "test all things" (Matthew 7:15; 24:5, 24, 25; John 10:1ff.; Acts 20:29, 30; 2 Peter 2:1). There are shepherds in sheep's clothing who are inwardly ravenous wolves, and the people who crowd around them might look like the Church but are, in fact, the opposite.

This article can thus be divided into the following sections:
A. 1. why it is necessary to diligently discern which is the true Church
   2. further explanation of what is being dealt with here
B. 1. the marks of the true Church
   2. the marks of the true believers and true Church members
C. the marks of the false Church
D. conclusion based on the above

2. Why and how the true Church must be sought

All sects in the world call themselves by the name Church. There is no clear definition for the word "sect." Different sects seem to have their own unique characteristics. The word is derived from the Latin word "*sequi*" which means "to follow," and it was used by the Romans in order to identify a particular line of thought, school, or party. With them it had no negative connotation; today it usually does. During the time of the Reformation it was used to identify groups which propagated a false teaching. Hence it was used for Anabaptist groups and also for the Church of Rome which we do not have to consider as an exception to the first part of this article, even though it is mentioned separately further on. Since all these groups claim that they are the real and true Church, one cannot rely on the name by which an assembly presents itself in order to indeed find it. Nor can one go by its appearance. Countless unlawful groups display in their manner and actions much that makes one think of the Church. They too preach, sing, collect money, and in many cases administer the sacraments. How, then, is one to discern whether a particular assembly is the true Church?

The Word of God alone, which reveals what the Church is, can enable us to make a definite decision. For that reason this article confesses "that we ought to discern . . . from the Word of God what is the true Church." It says too that one must do this "diligently" (zealously) and "very carefully" (with precision)! Implied in this is a condemnation of all indifference with respect to the Church.

3. It concerns the assembly, the organization

Even the lawful and true Church is never perfect. Among all grain is chaff, and in every Church hypocrites mingle with the believers. The word "hypocrite" originally referred to an actor, someone who acts differently than the person he really is. Hence by this term we mean "fake believers," those who outwardly, and for appearance sake, conform to the teaching of the Gospel, but do not do the will of the Father, even though they say to Jesus, "Lord, Lord." As in the field when the wheat is just sprouting the real wheat cannot yet be distinguished from the sprouting weeds, so we likewise cannot distinguish the hypocrites from the believers. God knows them. When He gathers the wheat into the barns, He will burn the chaff. The hypocrites *can* know themselves too, even though they do not because of their carelessness and superficiality.

The hypocrites are to be found in the Church but they are not of the Church, they do not belong to it (like gallstones in the human body). Since we cannot know them, we cannot separate them from the Church by discipline. The Anabaptists believed they could do so. Therefore this article says in its warning against the false Church, from which one must withdraw oneself, that it is not speaking of hypocrites but of the body and the communion of the Church and the sects (groups) that call themselves Church. Hence the concern here is not the members of a group, but the way they are grouped, gather together, and are organized. One must not ask, do the people measure up (for one would arrive at the same conclusion for each group) but rather, does the assembly, the body, the way it functions, measure up?

4. The marks of the true Church

The marks of the true Church are not its characteristics (see paragraph 7 of the chapter on Article 27 in which the unique existence of the Church always emerges defective) but the norms for its functioning which God has made known in Scripture. The believers, in accordance with the clear teaching of Scripture, are to unite with respect to the preaching of the Gospel and the administration of the sacraments, and to watch over one another, nurturing one another in love and admonishing wrongdoers. Together they ought to ensure that the offices, as instituted by Christ, are able to function. Therefore the question for each union of believers is whether the communion is faithful in this respect and functions in the manner commanded by the Lord. If this, by God's grace, is indeed the case, then in this assembly, too, many weaknesses will remain and the characteristics of the Church will still reveal many defects. Nevertheless, it is still an assembly, brought together and kept together in accordance with the Word of God.

It is from Scripture alone that we derive the criteria (standards) by which to know the Church. According to the Church of Rome one does not get very far by doing that. The Church of Rome places the Church above Scripture, claiming that only the Church can explain Scripture. In that case Scriptural evidence would offer no certainty here.

The Church of Rome therefore specifies totally different marks. Belarminus listed fifteen: ability to do miracles; the multitude of believers; the evil befalling its opponents; age and apostolic succession, and others. Yet Scripture explicitly says that we cannot identify the true prophets and therefore also the true Church on the basis of *these* marks!

The Confession lists three marks:
A. *it practises the pure preaching of the Gospel as the rule.* The question is not whether, in a particular gathering someone preaches from the Bible, but whether there is "the pure preaching of the Gospel." That is, preaching which passes on the Gospel faithfully: not subtracting anything, not adding anything, not contradicting anything! And then the question is not whether there are still preachers in a particular congregation who preach in such

a way, but whether it is the rule, law, that the preaching shall be done like this and in no other way (note the Latin word: *"uti"*);

B. *it maintains the pure administration of the sacraments.* Pure administration is such "as Christ instituted" it, namely, only the two sacraments of baptism and the Lord's supper and not the seven sacraments of the Roman Catholics. This rules out any neglect of the administration of the sacraments as is the case with the Salvation Army (!) or using the sacraments out of custom or superstition as is often the case in the Church of England in which anyone presented for baptism is baptized. This means too that the cup of the Lord's supper may not be withheld, as is the practice in the Church of Rome, nor are the sacraments to be regarded as a seal on what exists or is presumed to exist within us. Here too it is the "rule" which is of concern, namely, that the sacraments are administered only in the manner as prescribed by Christ, and to those people as directed by Him;

C. *it exercises Church discipline for correcting and punishing sins.* The false Church exercises "discipline" too, not to punish sins, but to rid itself of those who witness with the Word of God against her false teaching and idolatry. That is how the Pope placed Luther under the Papal ban and the Dutch Reformed (State) Church deposed Rev. de Cock and others.

These three marks form a unity and are related. A deterioration in the one inevitably leads to a deterioration in the other. They can all be traced back to the command which the Confession summarizes as follows: that the Church "governs itself according to the pure Word of God, rejecting (not just "tolerating" despite reservations) all things contrary to it and regarding (acknowledging and accepting) Jesus Christ as the only Head."

Note that nothing is said here concerning the origin or history of any Church. The history of a Church may be beautiful and good, but that does not negate the fact that over time the Church itself may have become degenerate. This was the case with the Church of Rome. It is not a question of which assembly *once* "regarded Jesus Christ as its Head," but which assembly does so *now*.

Every believer can know the true Church by these marks and no one to whom this Church can be known has the right to separate himself from it.

5. The marks of Christians

These are presented so clearly in this article that repetition and explanation is unnecessary. Yet why are these mentioned separately here in this article about the Church? There are two reasons for this. First, no one can be content with the statement that he is a member of the true Church. The Church is always a mixture of believers and hypocrites. The Church of Rome denies this, claiming that all who subject themselves to the Pope are true members. However, in opposition to both the Roman Catholics and the Anabaptists, we confess that the Church is mixed.

Second, in opposition to the Anabaptists, it is confessed here that the true members of the Church have many weaknesses and shortcomings. The Anabaptists desired a perfect Church of pure members. Therefore they repeatedly separated themselves whenever they noticed that not all their fellow members were pure.

Over against the Roman Catholic view we must pose the command of self-examination. Not all members are living members. There are unfruitful branches and everyone must see to it that he believes, in accordance with what is described here.

Over against the Anabaptists it must be said that even in the holiest there remains much weakness, but that they fight against it, as is also pointed out by this article.

6. The false Church

The adjective "false" can be understood in both a passive and an active sense. (Passive: a fake coin, artificial hair; then it means: counterfeit, imitation, unfaithful. Active: false teaching, false witness, false evidence; then it means a teaching or directive which leads onto the wrong track and so to downfall). Here it should especially be understood in the passive sense, though that need not exclude the active meaning. For the false Church is first of all unfaithful, illegitimate, but it also leads many to ruin.

In summing up the marks of the false Church the contrasting image of the true Church is portrayed.

Here it is not stated that in the false Church there remains nothing of the Gospel or the sacraments but rather, that it is all subjected to the superiority of the Church's teaching and the rulers of the Church. There one finds not Christ on the throne, but man. This can be more, or less, obvious. There are degrees of unfaithfulness and falsehood. The deciding factor is whether or not the congregation will bow before the Word. The fact that errors, sins, and shortcomings are apparent in a Church does not make the Church false. A Church demonstrates that it is false when it hardens itself in these sins and rejects warnings based on the Word of God and when it kills the prophets. In the dark Middle Ages the papal Church was the lawful Church, but when it rejected God's call to reformation and killed the prophets it became a false Church.

It is clear that in pointing out the false Church the Confession did so with a view to the Church of Rome. This does not mean that this is the only false Church in existence today. History continued. Since then there appeared more groups which called themselves Church, but which increasingly reveal the marks of the false Church by not wishing to bow before the Word of the Lord. Therefore, albeit possibly to a lesser extent than the Church of Rome, they must nevertheless be called false.

7. The conclusion of this article and the "third way"

This article concludes that the two "Churches" with which it dealt "are easily recognized and distinguished from each other." Of course this must be understood in the context of what was said at the beginning of the article. In view of the multitude of Churches the route for unbelievers is not an easy one. Yet, whoever lets himself be taught by the Word of the Lord, never needs to doubt. The *Lord* clearly points His sheep in the direction of the sheepfold. No one *has* to lose the way.

Modern Christianity has lost hold of this confession. In the so called ecumenical movement, to mention the World Council of Churches for example, no one wants to know of a "black & white scheme," which the Confession is accused of adhering to. Over against the two ways pointed out by the Confession, they point out a "third way" which is derived from all kinds of theories of pluriformity. They claim that the true Church is made up of the sum total of all Churches. Here of course the truth is sacrificed to unity.

8. The call to believers

Taking into account the various circumstances in which a believer can find himself, this call, according to what our Confession now continues to describe, is as follows:

A. should he come to a foreign place and not find the Church there, he ought to seek contact with fellow believers there and, together with them, through the installation of the offices, institute the Church

B. should he discover that the Church to which he belongs shows or begins to show the marks of the false Church, he ought to call the Church to repentance (Hosea 2:2). Should it refuse to listen, he then ought to separate himself from it and join himself to the true Church, and if one cannot be found, to institute it with other fellow believers. In effect, then, he is not separating himself from the Church, but from those who are outside the Church

C. should he be allowed to note, with joy, that "his" Church is faithful as "true Church" he, for his part, must ensure that it stays faithful

ARTICLES 30 AND 31
THE GOVERNMENT OF THE CHURCH

We believe that this true Church must be governed according to the Spiritual order which our Lord has taught us in His Word. There should be ministers or pastors to preach the Word of God and to administer the sacraments; there should also be elders and deacons who, together with the pastors, form the council of the Church. By these means they preserve the true religion; they see to it that the true doctrine takes its course, that evil men are disciplined in a spiritual way and are restrained, and also that the poor and all the afflicted are helped and comforted according to their need. By these means everything will be done well and in good order when faithful men are chosen in agreement with the rule that the apostle Paul gave to Timothy.

THE OFFICERS OF THE CHURCH

We believe that ministers of God's Word, elders, and deacons ought to be chosen to their offices by lawful election of the Church, with prayer and in good order, as stipulated by the Word of God. Therefore everyone shall take care not to intrude by improper means. He shall wait for the time that he is called by God so that he may have sure testimony and thus be certain that his call comes from the Lord. Ministers of the Word, in whatever place they are, have equal power and authority, for they are all servants of Jesus Christ, the only universal Bishop and the only Head of the Church. In order that this holy ordinance of God may not be violated or rejected, we declare that everyone must hold the ministers of the Word and the elders of the Church in special esteem because of their work, and as much as possible be at peace with them without grumbling or arguing.

1. Summary of the contents of these articles

Since these two articles essentially deal with the same subject, they will be discussed simultaneously.

Art. 30
A. Which office-bearers there must be
B. The task of these office-bearers
C. Which prerequisites they must meet

Art. 31
A. One may only take on these offices by lawful election
B. How these office-bearers must be honoured
  1. by fellow office-bearers
  2. by the congregation

2. "Spiritual police"

Here the word "police" refers to governing or ruling. By its very nature the Church, being an assembly, a body, cannot be without a government, a head, which keeps the body together and rules. How this governing must take place is not for us to decide. The government of the Church ought to be "spiritual," that is to say, it must take place according to God's Word. Since the previous century it has often been said, from the side of the Dutch Reformed (State) Church, that the New Testament does not teach us anything concerning the government of the Church; that the way the Church is organized is a matter of common sense, in which its historical development plays an influential role. They pointed out that in the congregational life of the early Christians there were no fixed rules: things were all rather vague and in a state of flux. That is true. However, in addition to giving us some glimpses of the early days, the New Testament also presents what ultimately resulted from the Holy Spirit's leadership through the apostles. One can read of that in the pastoral epistles. They do not just deal incidentally with the institution of congregational life, but purposely. They teach very clearly what is confessed here in the Confession. If in reading these epistles we also keep in mind what earlier epistles outlined, though less clearly, then we find contained in them all kinds of evidence for these articles.

Scripture clearly preaches Christ as the only Head of the Church. We already see in the Gospels that He called twelve apostles, whom He also prepared and empowered to perform their future task. Hence immediately after Pentecost they acted as leaders of the congregations. Their offices, in turn, led to the three offices referred to in our Confession being introduced under their leadership. The Church may not exist without these offices. If these offices are not all maintained, something is lacking and must be rectified (Titus 1:5). Yet in all this Christ remains the only "Bishop," the only Head of the Church. He rules it by His Word and Spirit, but utilises the services of the office-bearers. Hence office-bearers have been given power to serve rather than to dominate. They exercise the power of Christ through instruction with the Word. They do not rule through coercion but by expounding the Word. Their task is not to subject the believers to themselves, but to subject them to Christ and His Word.

3. Three offices

In the early Church there existed, besides the apostles, the extraordinary offices of *prophet* and *evangelist*. When the New Testament was not yet complete, Christ often spoke to His congregations through prophets. Evangelists were assistants to the apostles. However, they served in the early days only for the establishment of the Church. In time to come the following three regular offices only are commanded:

A. *shepherds and teachers* (one office), who are to serve in the public preaching of the Word, in catechism instruction, home visits, and visits to the sick, and who have been commissioned to administer the sacraments. In so doing they are "elders . . . who labour in the word and doctrine" (1 Timothy 5:17);

B. *elders* (*presbuteros* = eldest, alluding to age or worthiness; *episcopos* = overseer, alluding to the work). Together with the servants of the Word they are to give leadership, to rule and to take care that "all things are done decently and in good order." They must watch over the doctrine and conduct of the ministers, the administration of the sacraments, and the exercise of Church discipline (Acts 20:28);

C. *deacons*. Their work is to exercise mercy and to ensure that everyone has what he needs for the service of the Lord. When Article 30 speaks of "the poor" one is to understand the needy, and by "the afflicted" one is to think of those persecuted on account of their faith (Acts 6:1-6).

4. Prerequisites for office-bearers

For the exercising of the office certain requirements apply. These are elaborately described for us in 1 Timothy 3 and Titus 1.

5. "By lawful election of the Church"

Article 30 already states in its conclusion that the persons must be chosen and Article 31 elaborates on this. Over against the Roman Catholics, Article 31 states that it must be done through a "lawful election of the *Church*." The Roman Catholics, by having the "higher curia" make appointments, totally exclude the involvement of the Church. Over against the Anabaptists, Article 31 states that "good order" must apply. Anabaptist practice was such that whoever considered himself called presented himself as office-bearer. The election takes place under the leadership of the office-bearers, with the involvement of the congregation, and accompanied "with prayer" so that God may give wisdom and insight for a correct choice. Every office is a duty that is bestowed upon a person. No one may take that honour upon himself (Hebrews 5:4). Whoever is lawfully elected by the congregation in this way is called by God and appointed by the Holy Spirit (Acts 20:28).

With regards to the question whether women of the congregation should be voting, the Synod of Arnhem (1930) declared that the New Testament appears to speak more negatively than positively on the matter.

6. "Do you feel in your hearts"

In the Form for Ordination, those to be ordained are asked, "do you feel in your hearts that God Himself, through His congregation, has called you to these offices?" This does not imply any "inner experience." In the past, "to feel" had a broader meaning. Likewise, here, it has nothing to do with feelings but has everything to do with understanding. Hence the question means: are you inwardly, or firmly and most certainly, convinced . . . etc. Can you give an assurance that your election is no pursuit of simony in whatever form, but that it is lawful, so that consequently you are called to serve by God Himself? Through lawful election there is the certainty of divine calling.

Hence an office-bearer is not a representative of, or set apart from, the congregation, nor is he a servant of the consistory. He is a servant of *God*! He is responsible to Him and is to seek his instructions from Him (Holy Scripture).

7. No hierarchy

By hierarchy we understand a ranking among the offices whereby the one office-bearer has authority over the other (Church of Rome). Our Confession explicitly rejects this hierarchy. All servants of the Word, irrespective of the size of the congregation they serve, have the same power and authority. In the Church there is but one Bishop, set over all office-bearers: Christ Jesus. This also applies in relation to the three distinct offices. One is not higher than the other, but different. Each office has its own task, but all are equally servants of Christ.

8. "In special esteem"

Scripture exhorts us to honour the office-bearers. No one is to esteem a member of the government higher than a member of the consistory. The consistory too is a governing body. The Lord commands us to "hold the ministers of the Word and the elders of the Church in special esteem." The deacons should also have been mentioned here. In the Church of Rome these were reduced to being helpers at the mass. It was the Reformation which finally gave this office its proper place. The office-bearers are to be honoured "because of their work." What a wonderful meaning this work has for the believers and the children of the Church. Failure to honour the office-bearers leads to, and is a consequence of, a disregard for the Word. However, there are limits to obeying the office-bearers of the Church. If they are unfaithful and impose what God has not commanded, then they must be rejected (2 John 1:10). Therefore Article 31 says too that we are to "be at peace with them as much as possible."

9. What about the synod?

Due to the appalling Romanizing of Protestant life, there is generally more respect for a synod these days than for a consistory. Therefore it is striking that the Confession only speaks of the consistory (see Article 30: "by these means . . ."). Classes and synods are of great significance for the well-being of the Church, but not essential for its existence. Also during times of war when no classes or synods could be held, the life of the Church continued on its blessed path.

The Confession does not acknowledge any authority above the consistory. In the first edition of the Confession, Article 31 contained a sentence which dismissed it explicitly. In Article 31, Guido de Brés wrote after the sentence concerning the equality of the servants, "And therefore no Church has any authority or dominion over the other, to rule over it." The Synod of Antwerp (1564) removed these words because they were not relevant here where office-bearers (not Churches) are discussed. Unfortunately these words were not inserted elsewhere.

However, in the Church Order of the Synod À la Vigne (May 1, 1564) they were included as Article 1. They also express one of the basic principles of Reformed Church government. We then also find them in Article 74 of our Church Order.[21]

Christ has organized the government of His Church locally. Note how in His letters in Revelation 1-3 He addresses each congregation separately and not communally; they do not have a communal address. The consistory is the only governing power in the Church. Nevertheless, the various local Churches are to form a federation. However, major (= broader) assemblies, in which delegates from several local Churches meet, are not higher forms of government. Although the Churches have voluntarily decided not to do certain things (for example, excommunication) without the judgment of these major assemblies, so that they can avail themselves of each other's help in difficult matters, that does not make these major assemblies governing bodies. They do not have an official authority, but merely a delegated authority; a "second-hand-authority." After all, who is greater, the sender or the one sent?

Once every three months two delegates (minister and elder) of each Church in a group of local Churches meet as a Classis. Once a year, delegates of classes meet as a regional synod. Once every three years, delegates of regional synods meet as a general synod. The decisions of these major assemblies are to be considered as settled and binding (against independentism) unless (and not until) they are proven to be in conflict with the Word of God or the adopted Church Order (against hierarchy and synodocracy; see Article 31 of the Church Order). This touches on the fundamentals of Church government and concerns the honour of Christ. Hierarchy has always been the way to progressive decay of the Church (the Church of Rome; Dutch Reformed (State) Church in 1816; and the synodical Reformed Churches in 1944, and especially also in 1957 when they adopted a revised Church Order).

---

[21] As found in the *Book of Praise* published by the Standing Committee for the Publication of the *Book of Praise* of the Canadian Reformed Churches. — TRANS.

ARTICLE 32
THE ORDER AND DISCIPLINE OF THE CHURCH

We believe that, although it is useful and good for those who govern the Church to establish a certain order to maintain the body of the Church, they must at all times watch that they do not deviate from what Christ, our only Master, has commanded. Therefore we reject all human inventions and laws introduced into the worship of God which bind and compel the consciences in any way. We accept only what is proper to preserve and promote harmony and unity and to keep all in obedience to God. To that end, discipline and excommunication ought to be exercised in agreement with the Word of God.

1. Establishment of order

The Church has been delegated a threefold power:

A. establishing doctrine (1 Timothy 3:15. See paragraph 2 of Chapter I)

B. establishing regulations to promote order (1 Corinthians 14:40)

C. jurisdiction and discipline (Matthew 18:18; 1 Corinthians 5:13; Titus 3:10)

It is almost needless to say that in exercising this threefold power the Church is absolutely bound to Scripture. This article concerns itself with the powers as listed above in B and C.

When Luther burned the papal bull and the *Corpus Canonis Juris* in 1522 he, according to some, permanently did away with all Church laws; and correctly so, they considered, for the congregation ought to be led by the Spirit directly. Such thinking was prevalent in the nineteenth century. Every regulation was regarded as an attack on freedom and a sign of deprivation, serving only to cover up a want for the Spirit and gifts of the Spirit. Later this thought did change somewhat. People ascribed to the Reformation something which was specifically Anabaptist. The Anabaptists cast aside all regulations. Admittedly, regulations were the cause of much misery in the Church of Rome. There the Church people sighed under the heavy yoke of human inventions and laws. For that very reason this article gives such a strong warning against wrong regulations. However, one does not find here the radicalism of the fanatics.

Scripture commands us, "Let all things be done decently and in good order" (1 Corinthians 14:40). To this end agreed upon regulations need to be in place. After all, how can a society exist without them? They are essential in order "to maintain the body of the Church."

The Reformed Churches have recorded their rules for conduct in the Church Order. It contains agreements regulating both local Church life and relations between the Churches. In addition to these, each congregation has its own particular rules, for example, concerning the times for Church services, how attestations can be requested, etc. All these rules and regulations are "useful and good."

Yet with this a twofold danger exists:

A. that by means of a large number of pious rules one burdens the congregation with an oppressive yoke of man-made, false religious service (Judaism)

B. that by a multitude of organizational rules the freedom of action in the offices is restricted and a false domination is introduced

This article warns against these two wrongs, though more elaborately against the first than against the second. It is then indeed the second danger to which the liberated Church of the Reformation has often fallen victim in later centuries (1816 and the new Church Order of the synodical Reformed Churches!). Man considered he was promoting unity by centralizing the power of the higher assemblies in the broader assemblies; but it merely served to scatter the sheep.

2. Excommunication or ban

This article teaches that for the sake of ensuring that the body of the Church is kept in good order and for the promotion of harmony and unity, excommunication or ban are most definitely required. John Calvin also called discipline the nerve of the Church; its existence in this life depends on it.

Excommunication = to exclude from the communion. A ban prohibits membership in the church and means the same as excommunication.

Discipline of the Church is spiritual. It does not have the power of the sword as the government has, nor does it discipline through restraint of freedom or corporal punishment, but spiritually. Article 30 already said, "that evil men are disciplined in a spiritual way," which means to say "in accordance with the command of the Spirit in His Word." It is to be exercised through admonition, and if this is not heeded, through excommunication from the communion of the Church.

The aim of this discipline is preservation. Its purpose is:
A. to save the sinner. Even the ban is still an ultimate remedy, a "last-ditch effort" to save. The Heidelberg Catechism therefore discusses discipline in its section on deliverance (1 Corinthians 5:5)
B. to defend the congregation against the domination of evil
C. to sanctify the Name of the Lord

3. Task of the congregation

All discipline begins and ends with the congregation. The believers serve the communion of saints in no minor way when they take heed to each other for the sake of each other's salvation; they so badly need each other, also for admonition and punishment (Matthew 18:15; Hebrews 3:13; 10:24, 25; James 5:19, 20). The congregation's cooperation is therefore enlisted in every step taken in Church discipline. Without the congregation's faithfulness in this respect a good administration of discipline is impossible. A relaxation of Church discipline — the beginning of the Church's downfall — is always the fault of the *congregation*! "If your brother sins against you go and tell him his fault between you and him alone. If he hears you, you have gained your brother. But if he will not hear you, take with you one or two more, that "by the mouth of two or three witnesses every word may be established." (These witnesses are to serve as witnesses of the Scriptural admonition, not of the sin committed.) If he does not listen to this either, "inform the congregation" (consistory: see Article 68 of the Church Order).

This all pertains to the so called secret sins, which are only known to a few and are not such that they have to be made known to everyone. In the case of public sins one can go directly to the consistory.

4. Process of Church discipline

If the above mentioned brotherly admonition does not lead to repentance and an improvement in conduct and the sinner is made known to the consistory, the latter must first establish if the informant has acted in accordance with Matthew 18 and, if so, if the accusation is correct. In that case it too will go and admonish the sinner. Here Article 68 of the Church Order applies, which states, "Anyone who obstinately rejects the admonition by the consistory or who has committed a public sin shall be suspended from the Lord's supper" (silent censure). If this leads to repentance then reconciliation shall take place in a manner which the consistory determines to be of benefit to the congregation (i.e. in a manner which serves the building up of faith); this can be through public confession of sin before the whole congregation, before the consistory or before two or three office-bearers (see Article 69 of the Church Order). Should continued admonition by the consistory not lead to repentance, the consistory must then proceed with the following:

First public announcement. The sin is made known and the congregation is urged to pray for the sinner whose name has been withheld, thereby supporting the work of the office-bearers. In the absence of repentance, this is followed by:

Second public announcement. In addition to the sin, the name of the sinner is made known and the congregation is urged not only to pray for him but also to admonish him as a brother. This second announcement does not take place until advice of Classis has been obtained so that, as much as possible, everything occurs in a just manner. If this is to no avail, it is followed by:

Third public announcement, in which — again, subject to the advice of Classis — it is announced on which date the excommunication shall take place if there is no repentance before such time.

This *excommunication* takes place by the public reading of the form for that purpose. Read it! Here it is officially declared that "... because he obstinately persists in his sin, he is ... excluded from the fellowship of Christ and from His kingdom. He may no longer use the sacraments. He has no part any more in the spiritual blessings and benefits which Christ bestows upon His Church." In this way those who are excommunicated are, by being "forbidden the use of the sacraments ... excluded ... from the Christian congregation and by God Himself from the kingdom of Christ" (Lord's Day 31, Q&A 85 of the Heidelberg Catechism).

If the Church sins and in the capacity of a false Church excommunicates those "who live holy lives according to the Word of God" (Article 29), then this has no effect whatever (Proverbs 26:2).

5. Readmission

Should an excommunicated person by God's mercy come to repentance later, he may, after promising to amend his life and having demonstrated this, again be received into the midst of the congregation. Then a brother, who was dead, has come to life again (Form for Readmission). Read this form too.

6. Two keys

In Lord's Day 31 the Heidelberg Catechism says that for exercising her power in opening the kingdom of heaven to believers and closing it to unbelievers the Church has received two keys: not only the Christian ban discussed above but also "the preaching of the holy Gospel" (Q&A 83 of the Heidelberg Catechism). This is the high calling of the preaching: it may not just be a genial speech on religious matters, but it must proclaim eternal well and woe and God's judgment according to this testimony of the Gospel, both in this life and in the life to come.

The preaching *opens* the kingdom of heaven. It directs attention to the kingdom of heaven and reveals it. The preaching also points out the way to that kingdom: Jesus Christ. In the Name of the Lord it proclaims to each who follows that way that his sins are forgiven him. In this way it opens the kingdom and ushers one in to the joy of the Father.

The preaching also *closes* the kingdom of heaven. It does not only speak of salvation but also of wretchedness and says that whoever disobeys the Son will remain subject to God's wrath.

This "general" exercising of the keys is not enough. Therefore this article also says that "discipline and excommunication ought to be exercised."

ARTICLE 33
THE SACRAMENTS

We believe that our gracious God, mindful of our insensitivity and infirmity, has ordained sacraments to seal His promises to us and to be pledges of His good will and grace toward us. He did so to nourish and sustain our faith. He has added these to the Word of the gospel to represent better to our external senses both what He declares to us in His Word and what He does inwardly in our hearts. Thus He confirms to us the salvation which He imparts to us.

Sacraments are visible signs and seals of something internal and invisible, by means of which God works in us through the power of the Holy Spirit. Therefore the signs are not void and meaningless so that they deceive us. For Jesus Christ is their truth; apart from Him they would be nothing. Moreover, we are satisfied with the number of sacraments which Christ our Master has instituted for us, namely, two: the sacrament of baptism and the holy supper of Jesus Christ.

1. One of the points of contention in the struggle of the Church

Our Confessions discuss the sacraments in great detail. The Belgic Confession devotes three articles to this subject, including two very long ones, and the Heidelberg Catechism no less than six Lord's Days. The Confessions were, among other things, also documents of defence. Just remember that the confession concerning the sacraments was one of the crucial issues in the spiritual battle in the days when the Confession was written. Today it is no different. This is not surprising really, for in the doctrine of the sacraments everything else is interwoven. What we confess concerning Christ, concerning His sacrifice and His ascension, concerning the Holy Spirit and the redemption of the sinner, is all of decisive importance here. That is why, throughout the centuries, the Evil One has directed his fierce blows against this stronghold of the Confession regarding the sacraments, in the hope that this might deprive the congregation of one of the strongest pillars on which her only comfort rests. For this very reason it is necessary for every believer to have a clear and well-founded understanding of the sacraments.

People have objected to this article on the grounds that Holy Scripture does not speak of sacraments in general; it speaks only of baptism and the Lord's supper. To speak of sacraments in general was regarded as scholastic speculation. This is incorrect, however, for when the New Testament speaks of baptism and the Lord's supper the two have so much in common that a wise teacher would precede a study of the two with an introduction, just as this article does. Our Confessions are also text books.

2. Sacrament

The word sacrament is not to be found in Scripture. However, that need not be an objection to usage of the word. It has received a lawful place. In Latin it suggests an action by which man is dedicated, bound, to something or someone. For example, one is bound to his word when swearing a military oath, or when giving evidence in a law-court. Christians used this word to refer to baptism and the Lord's supper, for by these they were "dedicated to the Lord." The advantage of the word sacrament is that this one word lets us refer to that for which Scripture uses two. It speaks of sign and seal (Romans 4:11).

3. Why are they necessary?

This article states that "our gracious God . . . has ordained sacraments . . . and . . . added these to the Word of the Gospel." He did not do so because that Word of the Gospel was inadequate, incomplete, or weak. That Word was not in need of any additions.

It is us who make these additions necessary because of our "insensitivity and infirmity." Insensitivity is characteristic of all mankind. We respond obtusely to what the Word of God says to us. Our depravity has dulled our minds and made us uneducable and impervious. Add to this the infirmity which remains in every believer. In spite of the fact that the Holy Spirit works faith in us, the old unbelief remains in us too, constantly opposing God's Word and causing our faith to doubt. In addition to that, reality may seem to contradict God's Word and then those realities can make such an impression on us that we again doubt the Word. We remain weak, "as newborn babes" (1 Peter 2:2). Consider now that our "gracious God" takes all this into consideration! He even gave *two* signs to the doubting Gideon. God did so repeatedly, to Abraham, Ahaz, and many others. He also gave permanent signs: the rainbow; circumcision and Passover; baptism and the Lord's supper. The latter two He "ordained." He gave them to us as "institutions" which we ourselves are to maintain. Whoever is negligent in this, acts contrary to the ordinances of God!

4. Sign and seal

This article calls them "visible signs and seals" and the Heidelberg Catechism adds to that the adjective "holy" because they are instituted by God. Q&A 66 of the Heidelberg Catechism gives a more succinct and complete definition of the sacraments than this article does; the latter is more like an eulogy of God's goodness than a concise definition.

The sacraments are *signs*. They serve to "portray" what is invisible, to represent this symbolically and so offer a graphic instruction so that it "might the more fully (be) declared . . . to us."

In addition to that they are also *seals*. They guarantee something to us, just like a seal on a document guarantees its trustworthiness (signature, trade-mark).

Appreciation for the sacraments is attacked from two sides. According to the Roman Catholics we underestimate the sacraments. Roman Catholics regard the sacraments as "vehicles of grace." Not only do they signify and seal grace to us, but deliver it to us. According to them grace is contained in the sacrament and cannot be obtained without the sacrament. On the other hand, Anabaptists and Socinianists, and Zwingli too, claim that we over emphasize the sacraments. Zwingli only recognizes the sacraments as representative signs and does not want to know of any other purpose for the sacraments. Many Anabaptists and other fanatics view the sacraments as mere actions on our part and accuse us of attributing to earthly things such as bread, water, and wine that which only the Holy Spirit can give. They say this in spite of what this article says, that God gives us confirmation through the sacraments. Note too the words in Q&A 66 of the Heidelberg Catechism, "by *God* so that . . ."

5. Purpose

The Confession says that the Lord uses the sacraments "to seal His promises to us," so that we would embrace them and without any hesitation rely on them. He gives them to us as "pledges" of His good will and grace toward us. In the sacraments He gives us His promises as tangibles in our hands, just as one receives a pledge (engagement ring, cheque) in order to guarantee the trustworthiness and sincerity of a promise made. This is how God nourishes our faith. Faith is strong as long as it holds on to God's promises and puts its trust in Him.

Therefore the purpose of the sacraments is the strengthening of faith. They promote this because they make the promises of the Gospel visible to us, seal these promises, and place them in our hands as it were.

Should anyone disregard this and deem the pledges God places in his hands to be meaningless, then the receipt of those pledges will one day testify against him! The sacraments *can* serve to our damnation (Article 35). However, just like the Gospel, they are given to us as a pledge of God's *grace* toward us.

6. Word and sacrament

The previous paragraph made it clear that the contents of the sacraments are the promises of the Gospel. This is what they seal. They are appended "to the Word of the Gospel." They do not add anything to it. They are like the pictures in an illustrated book, "a visible preaching." What the Lord teaches us through the Gospel

He illustrates through the sacraments, namely, that our complete salvation rests in Christ. The Lord comes to us with the Word through the "doorway" of hearing and with the sacraments through the "doorway" of sight, taste, and touch, bringing to us the one promise of the Gospel. Their instruction is revisional.

Since they are appended to the Word, they cannot be understood without the Word. Instruction by the Word must precede, otherwise no one is able to use the sacraments, just as nothing can be understood of a photo of the moon unless one has first learnt much about this heavenly body.

Contrary to what the Church of Rome does, one cannot esteem the sacraments higher than the Word. The Word is essential for salvation. This cannot be said of the sacraments. Nevertheless, they are necessary on account of God's good and wise command.

Sacramentalism, which is on the increase in Protestant worship services, where on centre stage one finds the pulpit replaced by the Lord's supper table, is a very disturbing Romanizing of life.

7. Sacrament and faith

According to the Roman Catholics, faith is given through the sacraments. This "*ex opere operato*," is only through the completed work; thus it is automatic.

This article only speaks of "nourishing" and "sustaining" faith (keeping faith in existence), and it does not take place automatically.

Neither the administration (issuing) nor the receipt of the sacraments is sufficient for the nourishment of faith. The "use" of the sacraments entails more (Q&A 66 of the Heidelberg Catechism). In order for our faith to be nourished it is necessary that we accept the promise of the Gospel pointed out by, and sealed in, the sacraments; to work with the sacraments. Hence the sacraments *require* faith. They point out to us our sin (baptism) and weakness (the Lord's supper), God's promise of forgiveness, and renewal through Christ. They convince us of these so that we might be mindful of our infirmity and totally entrust ourselves to Christ. They call us to faith in a different way, but no less so than the Gospel. Only by heeding this call do we receive the strengthening of faith.

The absence of faith does not make the sacrament an empty shell, a pretence. It does mean though that the "truth" of the sacrament, Jesus Christ, is not received. Just as a portrait is real, clear, and genuine regardless of whether the person portrayed is present or not, so likewise the sacraments are true, even when, as a result of unbelief which rejects Christ, He who is their truth is not received (Article 35).

Over against this it has been asserted that if faith is lacking, the sacraments lack content. Hence the baptism of an unbeliever was then called an incomplete baptism, a feigned baptism, merely a spillage of water. It was argued that if one were to give someone something which would "the more fully declare," (Q&A 66 of the Heidelberg Catechism), he must first already have received and understood something that was declared to him previously, (whereas in actual fact "more fully" is a reference to the manner of giving). The "complete" sacrament was regarded as a seal on faith already present (presumptive regeneration). It was claimed that this could also be deduced from this article where it states that the sacraments represent better to our external senses "both what He declares in His Word and what He does inwardly in our hearts."

If that were so, the sacraments would speak of God's Word (outside of us) and of the work He has done inside us. However, one must note that it does not say "what He has done inwardly," but "does." He teaches us this through the Word, and lets it be represented to us through the sacraments, so that the full Word of God, concerning both His work for us and His work in us, is made visible to our eyes.

The sacraments do not seal anything in the recipient; they seal the promise. Therefore they have nothing to say concerning the recipient, but they testify of God; they are pledges of His good will and grace toward us.

8. The number of sacraments

The two sacraments of the Old Covenant, circumcision and Passover, have been replaced by no more than the two sacraments of the New Covenant, baptism and the Lord's supper. With the shedding of blood fulfilled in Christ, the sacraments of blood were no longer necessary. Whereas the Old Testament sacrifices emphasized that a sacrifice was necessary for reconciliation, the New Testament sacrifices assure us that reconciliation has been obtained. The Roman Catholics have instituted seven sacraments: baptism (to confer grace); confirmation (to strengthen in grace); reconciliation (formerly called confession — to restore to grace); the mass or communion (to maintain grace); the anointing of the sick (formerly called extreme unction or last rites — to confer grace for death); marriage; and ordination to the priesthood. As far as marriage and priesthood are concerned, one can only receive the one or the other, not both. Apart from baptism and communion, the other five Roman Catholic "sacraments" lack institution by the divine Word. They are not instituted by God but invented by man in order to maintain the distinction between the clergy and laity and to make the latter dependent on the former.

ARTICLE 34
THE SACRAMENT OF BAPTISM

We believe and confess that Jesus Christ, who is the end of the law, has by His shed blood put an end to every other shedding of blood that one could or would make as an expiation or satisfaction for sins. He has abolished circumcision, which involved blood, and has instituted in its place the sacrament of baptism. By baptism we are received into the Church of God and set apart from all other peoples and false religions, to be entirely committed to Him whose mark and emblem we bear. This serves as a testimony to us that He will be our God and gracious Father for ever. For that reason He has commanded all those who are His to be baptized with plain water, into the Name of the Father and of the Son and of the Holy Spirit. By this He signifies to us that as water washes away the dirt of the body when poured on us, and as water is seen on the body of the baptized when sprinkled on him, so the blood of Christ, by the Holy Spirit, does the same thing internally to the soul. It washes and cleanses our soul from sin and regenerates us from children of wrath into children of God. This is not brought about by the water as such but by the sprinkling of the precious blood of the Son of God, which is our Red Sea, through which we must pass to escape the tyranny of Pharaoh, that is, the devil, and enter into the spiritual land of Canaan.

Thus the ministers on their part give us the sacrament and what is visible, but our Lord gives us what is signified by the sacrament, namely, the invisible gifts and grace. He washes, purges, and cleanses our souls of all filth and unrighteousness, renews our hearts and fills them with all comfort, gives us true assurance of His fatherly goodness, clothes us with the new nature, and takes away the old nature with all its works.

We believe, therefore, that anyone who aspires to eternal life ought to be baptized only once. Baptism should never be repeated, for we cannot be born twice. Moreover, baptism benefits us not only when the water is on us and when we receive it, but throughout our whole life. For that reason we reject the error of the Anabaptists, who are not content with a single baptism received only once, and who also condemn the baptism of the little children of believers. We believe that these children ought to be baptized and sealed with the sign of the covenant, as infants were circumcised in Israel on the basis of the same promises which are now made to our children. Indeed, Christ shed His blood to wash the children of believers just as much as He shed it for adults. Therefore they ought to receive the sign and sacrament of what Christ has done for them, as the Lord commanded in the law that a lamb was to be offered shortly after children were born. This was a sacrament of the passion and death of Jesus Christ. Because baptism has the same meaning for our children as circumcision had for the people of Israel, Paul calls baptism the circumcision of Christ.

1. Place in the Belgic Confession and the Heidelberg Catechism

Both the Belgic Confession and the Heidelberg Catechism discuss baptism in great detail. The Heidelberg Catechism deliberately positions itself against the Roman Catholics. The Belgic Confession does this too but also, and especially, against the Anabaptist errors.

The Heidelberg Catechism devotes two Lord's Days to holy baptism (26 and 27), discussing in:

- Q&A 69: the sign and the promise it signifies and seals
- Q&A 70: the content of the promise
- Q&A 71: Scriptural references to the promise
- Q&A 72: what the relation between the sign and the promise does not consist of
- Q&A 73: what the relation between the sign and the promise does consist of
- Q&A 74: the entitlement of children of believers to holy baptism

In Article 34, one of its lengthiest articles, the Belgic Confession discusses this subject in great detail. We divide it as follows:

A. 1. who instituted baptism in place of circumcision
    2. the purpose of baptism
       a. in relation to man
       b. in relation to God

B. What we *are*, and are *not*, bound to by becoming partakers of that which is promised in baptism
    1. method by which baptism is administered
    2. what can be seen and believed in baptism
    3. a. rejection of the Roman Catholic error
       b. rejection of the Anabaptist error

C. No rebaptism
    1. we cannot be born twice
    2. because baptism benefits us throughout our whole life

D. 1. rejection of the Anabaptist error of rebaptism
   2. rejection of the Anabaptists' condemnation of infant baptism
   3. evidence for infant baptism
      a. the promises are for them too
      b. so is the content of the promise: Christ
      c. therefore the seal of the promise is for them too

2. Institution of holy baptism

Christ instituted holy baptism (Q&A 69 of the Heidelberg Catechism; Article 34 of the Belgic Confession) shortly *before* His ascension (Matthew 28). Prior to that, Israel practised not only all kinds of ritual cleansings but also the baptism of proselytes. John the Baptist already baptized *before* its institution by Christ. His baptism is actually similar to Christian baptism. Scripture calls both of these baptisms a baptism of repentance for the forgiveness of sins. However, John the Baptist only baptized in Israel and then only those who came to him. Only after Pentecost could baptism be administered among all nations and was man permitted to go out and baptize. The baptism of John looked *forward* ("He who is coming after me"), while Christian baptism looks back on the fulfilled work of the Lord.

This article says that Christ instituted baptism in the place of circumcision. Circumcision was first given to Abraham as "a seal of the righteousness of the faith" (Romans 4:11), and after that to Israel as a nation with the sealing of the covenant in the desert. Christ did not simply abolish circumcision and discard it; He fulfilled it, and gave that which it signified. For this He gave a new, bloodless sign: baptism. It contains the same promise as circumcision, only it is administered in a different way.

It is incomprehensible that, whereas Christ commanded so explicitly to baptize "all nations," the Salvation Army, for example, maintains that baptism was merely for the early days of Christianity.

3. Sign

The sign of holy baptism is water, by which we are baptized into the Name of the Father and of the Son and of the Holy Spirit.

In Q&A 69, the Heidelberg Catechism calls this the "outward washing" and the Belgic Confession speaks of "the water as such." This is not to say that holy baptism is only something external, but that on the outside it is a washing. Just clean water is to be used; no blend of water and salt as used by the Roman Catholics, and preferably not water from the River Jordan as is often used for royal children and other "important baptisms." Neither the Confession nor the Catechism touch on the issue of baptism by sprinkling of water versus immersion. In early times it was customary to baptize by immersion. For example, John the Baptist baptized by immersion. It is questionable whether the three thousand on the day of Pentecost, and the jailer who was baptized in his house during the night, were baptized by immersion. Later on, in colder climates and due to infant baptism, sprinkling came into practice. One cannot call this wrong. The value of baptism does not lie in the quantity of water used. Holy Scripture speaks of the "blood of sprinkling" (Hebrews 12:24), and says, "I will sprinkle clean water on you" (Ezekiel 36:25). Granted, with immersion the symbolism is richer. When immersed, the person receiving baptism disappears in the water: he is gone. It symbolises his burial with Christ into death, a dying to sin. He then arises from the water as a new, cleansed person, which symbolises how he is raised with Christ in newness of life (Romans 6:3, 4). One really shouldn't make an issue of the question of immersion as the Baptists, Pentecostals, and others do.

4. Baptismal formula

It is very much a question whether the Lord prescribed the use of a particular formula for baptism when He gave the command to baptize in Matthew 28. The New Testament also uses other expressions, such as baptizing in (on) the Name of the Lord Jesus (Acts 2:38; 8:16; Romans 6:3; Galatians 3:27). Already very early in the Christian church it became common practice to administer baptism into the Name of the Father and the Son and the Holy Spirit. "Into the Name of" does not mean by order of, or on the authority of. When in holy baptism we are "baptized into the Name of . . ." then we are closely bound to that Name. Note Galatians

3:27, "For as many of you as were baptized into Christ have put on Christ." Baptism speaks of a most intimate, overriding union with God in an eternal covenant of grace.

5. The graphic, revisionary instruction through the sign

The sign of holy baptism makes visible for us and repeats for us what the Gospel has already taught. It says to us that, *as* water removes dirt from our body, the blood *and the Spirit* of Christ remove the impurity of our soul, our sin. The "blood of Christ" is the sign of all His suffering which climaxed in the shedding of blood on Calvary. In that suffering He bore the punishment for our sins and so paid our debt. Therefore we can say that His blood, His suffering, cleanses us from sin, namely, from the *guilt* of sin (*justification*). The Spirit of Christ renews us, frees us from the slavery of sin, makes us die to sin and teaches us to live lives pleasing to God. He increasingly removes the *pollution* of sin (*sanctification*) (see also Q&A 70 of the Heidelberg Catechism).

6. Seal

By holy baptism we are "admonished" (instructed) and "assured."[22] This article says that it serves as a testimony to us. Baptism is not only a sign. This sign is a seal, a seal of the same promise portrayed by the sign. Holy baptism assures us that the promise is true and trustworthy and that it applies to us, concerns us; that we have "an eternal covenant of grace with God."

Holy baptism itself does not cleanse us of our sins. The Roman Catholic notion that baptism provides supernatural grace must be refuted. The connection between the sign and what it represents is not automatic. The Roman Catholics teach that baptism is essential for salvation. According to them an unbaptized person is unable to receive grace (therefore they administer emergency baptisms). This leads to the error of the possibility of losing grace and the falling away of the saints. For more details concerning the Roman Catholic

---

[22] Here the author makes a reference to the Dutch text of the Heidelberg Catechism in A. 69, current at the time, which used the terms *vermaand en verzekerd*. The English version uses the terms "signify and seal," which is a little weaker, because in old Dutch *vermanen* means: to remind of, to call back to. The original German text has *errinert* (reminds). — TRANS.

errors see the text of this article and Q&A 72 of the Heidelberg Catechism.

Baptism does not seal a cleansing from sin either; it does not seal a cleansing which is already present and at work as if each baptized person therefore has to be regarded as regenerated.

Holy baptism is joined to the Gospel; it seals the *promise*. The Form for Baptism also says that it is an ordinance of God to seal to us and our seed His covenant.

The connection between the sign and what it signifies is federal or covenantal. God promised in His covenant to bind His grace to the use of the sacraments (Q&A 69 of the Heidelberg Catechism "and with it gave"). This usage entails more than giving or receiving. The promised benefit of cleansing is only received in the way of faith, to which the Lord also encourages us through holy baptism.

Over against this some say that baptism does not assure us of an entitlement to forgiveness through grace, but that we *have* forgiveness already. They base this on what is stated in the Heidelberg Catechism, Q&A 69: that I *am* washed, and in Q&A 73: that we *are* spiritually cleansed from our sins. However, one may not forget that in these answers it is the believing confessor who speaks; he who trusts the LORD. It can be compared to the receipt of a cheque. The cheque itself does not say you have $100, but that you are entitled to $100. That cheque is a pledge, a proof of that entitlement, proof of the promise. The recipient who trusts the reliability of the cheque will say, "I *have* $100." Yet that cheque itself is not $100, nor the guarantee that its owner *has* it, but the evidence and the guarantee of the promise made and his entitlement to the $100. In order to receive the amount stated in the cheque, one needs to go to the bank and cash it. Likewise, to receive what is promised in holy baptism one must go to the Lord Jesus Christ.

7. No rebaptism

The Anabaptists only acknowledged a baptism to be genuine if it was administered 1. to a holy person; 2. in a holy Church; 3. by a holy servant.

This led to endless rebaptizing. Whenever it was discovered that one of these criteria had not been met, baptism was re-administered.

The Anabaptists did not regard baptism as God's work, by which He sealed His covenant with us, but merely as a deed of the believer, by which he testified to what God had done to "his soul."

Over against this Article 34 says that we ought to be baptized only once, for we are only born once. Baptism is the sacrament of being grafted into the Church. Yes, children of believers are born into the Church as members of the Church, but this is officially declared and sealed in baptism. We are not baptized with "a view to" membership of the Church but "as members of His Church" (Form for Baptism). (Profession of faith is not for the purpose "of being accepted as a member.")

8. Lifelong benefit

According to the nature of the sacraments one can also distinguish between the following in holy baptism: 1. its administration; 2. its receipt; 3. its practice. Administration and receipt only take place once. However, holy baptism is given and received for a life-time (certificate of faithfulness) and we are to honour it for our entire life, to be at work with it, that is to say, to take to heart what it teaches. It teaches us 1. our misery, in telling us that we are filthy and in need of cleansing; 2. our deliverance, in teaching and assuring us that the blood and the Spirit of Christ purify us so that we entrust ourselves to Him and His work; 3. our obligation to be thankful, in telling and assuring us that God laid His hand on us, is our Father, adopted us as His children, and that we bear His "mark and emblem."

9. Who ought to be baptized

This article says, "For that reason He has commanded all those who are His to be baptized," namely, all those sanctified in Christ Jesus, who belong to God's covenant and to His congregation; all converted unbelievers and all children of believers. It is not permissible to baptize all who are presented for baptism in the hope that they will come to understand it later, and so to some extent bind them to the Church (Roman Catholic practice on the mission fields and the practice of the Church of England).

10. The entitlement to infant baptism

The Heidelberg Catechism confesses this in Q&A 74, stating that children also "belong to God's covenant and congregation" (Genesis 17:7; Acts 2:39).

This article also presents three arguments in favour of infant baptism:

- A. the children in Israel had the same promises as our children and by means of circumcision received the sign of the covenant; for that reason our children must also receive the sign of the covenant
- B. Christ also laid His hands on the children and blessed them, and acknowledged them as heirs of His kingdom. He is also their Saviour
- C. baptism replaced circumcision (Colossians 2:11, 12)

Infant baptism was very early a custom already, as is apparent from the writings of Tertullian.

11. Objections to infant baptism

A. "In the New Testament there is no command for infant baptism." This was also not necessary. That children should also receive the seal of the covenant was already commanded in the days of Abraham. If one is to be consistent with such "rigid" evidence, women should not be permitted to participate in the Lord's supper either, for neither is that commanded anywhere.

B. "In the New Testament there is no example of infant baptism." This is not surprising, for at that time the Church was gathered through conversion from heathendom. Meanwhile, we read repeatedly, He and all his family were baptized (Cornelius, Acts 10:48; the jailer, Acts 16:33). No, this does not prove beyond a doubt that there were also children in that family, but the point is that, according to the rule established in the Covenant of the Old Testament, the family also belonged to the congregation through the father.

C. "Children do not understand baptism." However, they didn't understand circumcision either and yet the Lord commanded them to be circumcised.

D. "We do not know if children indeed believe." However, we do not baptize on the basis of their faith but on the basis of God's command and promise.

In our time many doubt and even oppose the entitlement to infant baptism, especially since the time of Karl Barth. He differed from the Anabaptists in that he did not regard infant baptism as invalid, and he rejected rebaptism. Yet he pointed out that in the whole of the New Testament one reads of letting oneself be baptized and not of being presented for baptism. This is the old objection mentioned under 2. He believes that there is only one fine thread one can hold onto in support of infant baptism, namely, that the New Testament speaks of "all his family." Although Barth acknowledged that according to the New Testament children belong to the kingdom of God, he argues that the kingdom of God is not the same as the Church. That is true, but not in the sense that the number of citizens in God's kingdom is different to that of the members of the Church. Whoever wants to know more about this should read a beautiful little book by Rev. G. Visee, *Ons aller Moeder* (*Mother of Us All*, published by Oosterbaan & Le Cointre N.V., Goes, 1961), pp 126-129.

12. On the Anabaptist track

The difference between the Reformed Confession and the opinions of all kinds of Anabaptists of earlier and later times can be seen in the following three points:
- A. according to Anabaptists the sacraments are not signs and seals, but only signs
- B. according to Anabaptists the sacraments are not signs of the salvation God promises and also gives to those who believe His promises, but signs of what God "has done to the soul"
- C. according to Anabaptists it is not *God* who speaks in the sacraments, but the believer

According to Anabaptists faith and confession must precede baptism. The person baptized must first have *received* the benefits and this can only be by way of faith. Yet according to the Reformed

Confession the sealing through holy baptism can also precede faith. In this respect too baptism is not "void or meaningless" (Article 33) for not faith but God's promise is the content of baptism and faith receives and accepts this promise.

However, in the struggle against Anabaptists of earlier and later times those of the Reformed faith have let themselves be lured into adopting an Anabaptist method of questioning, by which they sometimes ended up on Anabaptist tracks.

It was then said that although a child can't yet profess faith, it is possible that faith is already in him in the form of "potential faith" (Scripture does not know of such a "potential faith"!) and we may "presume that this faith is there." However, on what grounds must this be presumed? That is how eventually, even in ecclesiastical decisions, it was said of children of believers that one must presume them to be regenerated . . . until they should show the opposite through their way of life or doctrine (Synods of 1905 and 1939-1943) or one was to consider them "as being partakers in the regenerating grace of the Holy Spirit" (Replacement Formula, 1946). This formula was set aside in 1959. However, all objections to this formula were dismissed and its doctrinal content was maintained.

Not only do these theories neglect many Scripture references, but they also contradict texts and undermine the certainty of the sacraments. Every baptism is "complete," real, and *well-meant*. Differences between those baptized certainly become apparent as they grow up. However, this is not because the Lord didn't promise anything to some of them (1 Corinthians 10:4) but rather because they are unwilling to believe what He has promised (1 Corinthians 10:5; Hebrews 4:6).

13. The sealed covenant

The opinions that baptism seals "regeneration already present and at work" and that each baptized person is to be "presumed regenerated," or at least is to be presumed "as being partaker in the regenerating grace of God" are related to an incorrect understanding of the covenant of the Lord. Refer, too, to what has already been said about this covenant in the chapter on Article 17.

The Form for Baptism points from the covenant, which is sealed by baptism, to God's covenant with Abraham, which we read about in Genesis 17. There it is apparent that this covenant proceeds completely and exclusively from God. He establishes it. The covenant does not come into existence through an agreement of God with man; God imposes it. In this way the covenant is one-sided (unilateral) in its origin.

It is clear that this covenant does not only apply to Abraham personally, but that all his descendants are partakers in it too. It is an eternal covenant, which means that it applies right through to the last generation.

In this covenant the Lord promises: "I will be a God to you and to your descendants." The Form for Baptism describes clearly what this entails. God the Father wants to care for His covenant children, God the Son wants to ransom them by His blood, and God the Holy Spirit wants to renew them and lead them to eternal life with God.

With this comes what is clearly expressed in Genesis 17, namely, that the members of the covenant must keep this covenant. God wants them to recognize Him, and to cling to Him as their covenant God. Through faith, by which they entrust themselves to Him who works salvation, they ought to love and serve Him. This "second part" of the covenant is also described in detail in the Form for Baptism.

In this way the operation of the covenant is two-sided. Both the Lord, and Abraham and his seed, maintain the covenant (bilateral).

Acts 2:39 draws this covenant through to the time of the New Testament. The letter to the Romans teaches us that Abraham is the father of all *believers* and that all believers, as his spiritual seed, share in the covenant established with him. It applies to all believers that God is their God and the God of their children.

Later on there arose the misunderstanding that God's covenant really only applies completely to the elected and regenerated children. The others, it was said, do not belong to God and do not share in His covenant. They only have an external place. God merely has an "external covenant" with them, or: "they only belong to the earthly appearance of the covenant." Therefore, it was claimed, they do not have a right to the sealing of the covenant in baptism either. They are baptized, and they must be baptized, because we cannot distinguish them from the real members of the covenant, but then their baptism is "a baptism in the incomplete sense," a "feigned baptism," a "spillage of water."

So man went on to distinguish between those who really belonged to the covenant and those who belonged externally to the covenant, between those who had received the complete baptism and those who had received an incomplete baptism. For the former, the Gospel was an unconditional promise of God's salvation, but for the latter it was no more than an external offer which is extended to all who hear the Gospel, but extended more powerfully to those baptized.

As far as the members of the covenant were concerned, it was said that they were regenerated, or would at least become certain of it. It was for that reason that they were baptized: on the grounds of this presumed regeneration. Hence those children who merely belonged externally to the covenant were also baptized, but if it appeared as they grew up that they did not believe, then it was apparent that they had not received a complete baptism.

Thus a distinction was made between a twofold Gospel (an unconditional promise for the elect *and* an external offer of salvation; that is to say, a powerful Word *and* an external preaching), a twofold sacrament and two kinds of covenant members.

All these divisions and distinctions served to constitute an impressive and exclusive system of reasoning but meanwhile the living Word of God was robbed of its power. Where did one hear the promise to Abraham and his seed mentioned? These unbiblical notions were laid down in the synodical doctrinal declarations of 1942 and, even though these were superseded in 1946 by a "Replacement Formula" which in 1959 was not rejected or abolished but "put aside," they have never been condemned or revoked. With each act of "replacement" and "setting aside" all previous decisions were concluded to be, and maintained and praised as being, "in accordance with the Word of God" and "to have been a blessing."

This impressive, exclusive system of reasoning neglected matters clearly taught in God's Word because they were matters which did not fit the system. It is a system which brings one into conflict with the Word of God on more than one issue, and by it God's people are robbed of the certainties they receive in grace.

God's promises are for all who are baptized and no one needs to question whether his baptism was a complete baptism. That question can never be answered in this life. However, everyone is to see to it that he keeps the covenant and, clinging to God's promises, conforms to His demands. For . . . children of the kingdom will be thrown out and branches of the true vine cut off when they are disobedient and unfruitful. However, if we through weakness fall into sin and are heartily sorry for this, then we "must not despair of God's mercy nor continue in sin, for baptism is a seal and trustworthy testimony that we have an eternal covenant with God" (see Form for Baptism; John 15:6; 1 Corinthians 10:1-5; Hebrews 4:6, 12:16).

ARTICLE 35
THE SACRAMENT OF THE LORD'S SUPPER

We believe and confess that our Saviour Jesus Christ has instituted the sacrament of the holy supper to nourish and sustain those whom He has already regenerated and incorporated into His family, which is His Church.
Those who are born anew have a twofold life. One is physical and temporal, which they received in their first birth and it is common to all men. The other is spiritual and heavenly, which is given them in their second birth and is effected by the word of the gospel in the communion of the body of Christ. This life is not common to all but only to the elect of God.
For the support of the physical and earthly life God has ordained earthly and material bread. This bread is common to all just as life is common to all. For the support of the spiritual and heavenly life, which believers have, He has sent them a living bread which came down from heaven, namely, Jesus Christ, who nourishes and sustains the spiritual life of the believers when He is eaten by them,

that is, spiritually appropriated and received by faith. To represent to us the spiritual and heavenly bread, Christ has instituted earthly and visible bread as a sacrament of His body and wine as a sacrament of His blood. He testifies to us that as certainly as we take and hold the sacrament in our hands and eat and drink it with our mouths, by which our physical life is then sustained, so certainly do we receive by faith, as the hand and mouth of our soul, the true body and true blood of Christ, our only Saviour, in our souls for our spiritual life.

It is beyond any doubt that Jesus Christ did not commend His sacraments to us in vain. Therefore He works in us all that He represents to us by these holy signs. We do not understand the manner in which this is done, just as we do not comprehend the hidden activity of the Spirit of God. Yet we do not go wrong when we say that what we eat and drink is the true, natural body and the true blood of Christ. However, the manner in which we eat it is not by mouth but in the spirit by faith. In that way Jesus Christ always remains seated at the right hand of God His Father in heaven; yet He does not cease to communicate Himself to us by faith. This banquet is a spiritual table at which Christ makes us partakers of Himself with all His benefits and gives us the grace to enjoy both Himself and the merit of His suffering and death. He nourishes, strengthens, and comforts our poor, desolate souls by the eating of His flesh, and refreshes and renews them by the drinking of His blood.

Although the sacrament is joined together with that which is signified, the latter is not always received by all. The wicked certainly takes the sacrament to his condemnation, but he does not receive the truth of the sacrament. Thus Judas and Simon the sorcerer both received the sacrament, but they did not receive Christ, who is signified by it. He is communicated exclusively to the believers.

Finally, we receive this holy sacrament in the congregation of the people of God with humility and reverence as we together commemorate the death of Christ our Saviour with *thanksgiving and we confess our faith and Christian religion. Therefore no one should come to this table without careful self-examination, lest by eating this bread and drinking from this cup, he eat and drink judgment upon himself. In short, we are moved by the use of this holy sacrament to a fervent love of God and our neighbours. Therefore we reject as desecrations all additions and damnable inventions which men have mixed with the sacraments. We declare that we should be content with the ordinance taught by Christ and His apostles and should speak about it as they have spoken.*

1. Place in the Belgic Confession and the Heidelberg Catechism

This second sacrament too is discussed in great detail by these two Confessions. This is not surprising, since the struggle about the sacraments at the time of the Great Reformation was a struggle about the Lord's supper. Wasn't Guido de Brés condemned to be hanged because he had dared to administer the Lord's supper? The Heidelberg Catechism devotes three Lord's Days to this sacrament and the article devoted to it in the Belgic Confession is even longer than its article on baptism.

The Heidelberg Catechism discusses in:

- Q&A 75: the sign and the promise it signifies and seals
- Q&A 76: the content of the promise
- Q&A 77: Scriptural references to the promise
- Q&A 78: what the relation between the sign and the promised benefits does not consist of
- Q&A 79: what the relation between the sign and the promised benefits does consist of
- Q&A 80: the distinction between the Lord's supper and the papal mass
- Q&A 81: who the Lord's supper has been instituted for and who are to attend as guests
- Q&A 82: that the congregation must keep the Lord's supper holy and how it must do so

Note that in the Heidelberg Catechism the discussions on baptism and the Lord's supper both follow the same pattern (see paragraph 1 of the chapter on Article 34).

This article is divided as follows:
A. the Lord's supper has been instituted to feed us. Our spiritual life is nourished when we eat of Jesus Christ
B. for by eating the bread and drinking the wine in faith we indeed receive Jesus Christ. The Holy Spirit works this in a way incomprehensible for us
C. this makes it a spiritual meal for the believers
   1. in which Christ shares Himself with them
   2. (the unbelievers receive no portion of Him)
   3. which the believers attend with thanks and reverence
D. rejection of errors

2. Institution

The oldest account of the institution can be found in 1 Corinthians 11:23-28. It is also recorded for us in all three synoptic Gospels: Matthew 26:26-28; Mark 14:22-24; Luke 22:19, 20.

From all these accounts it is clear that the institution of the Lord's supper contains a *command* for all ("drink from it, all of you" (Matthew 26:27) and for all times and places ("proclaim the Lord's death till He comes" (1 Corinthians 11:26). The Church obeyed this command immediately (Acts 20:7), and Paul "delivered" the institution of the Lord's supper with the preaching of the Gospel. If the Church is negligent in the administration of the Lord's supper it acts "contrary to God's ordinance" and every believer who neglects the Lord's supper does likewise.

In the accounts of the institution we notice small differences in the wording, but in principle there is complete agreement.

These accounts clearly demonstrate:
A. that the Lord Jesus gave His disciples broken bread, and wine poured into a cup
B. that concerning this bread He declared, "This is My body" and concerning the wine poured out, "This is the blood of My (or of the) covenant" or, "This is the new covenant in My blood"

C. that Christ said that His body would be broken and His blood poured for the sake of those who are His (for many) for the forgiveness of sins
D. that the Lord's supper has not only been instituted so that Christ would speak through it to those who are His, but that they would also confess Him as the One sacrificed for them: they "proclaim the Lord's death" (1 Corinthians 11:26)

The different formulations used in the various accounts indicate that a specific formulation for the celebration has not been prescribed. Moreover, we are not to consider the words of institution as a magic formula. After all, the words are not directed to the bread and wine but to the receivers, in order to teach them the meaning of the death of Christ and to seal the salvation which this death would bring.

3. The signs of the Lord's supper

These signs are bread and wine, which signify the body and blood of the Lord. The bread is broken and the wine poured out, signifying that the body of the Lord was broken and that His blood was shed.

These signs of bread and wine are:

distributed and apportioned, signifying that the sacrifice of Christ was for us, made for the payment of our debt of sin;

accepted and received with the hand and the mouth as a sign of our heartfelt acceptance in faith of the promised Christ who was sent and crucified;

eaten and drunk, signifying that through faith we are so closely united with Christ, that the payment of the debt by His suffering and the renewal by His Spirit have become ours, just like bread and wine become united with us through eating and drinking. In as much as bread and wine nourish and refresh our physical lives, so He nourishes us. Above all, the *eating and drinking* with our mouth signifies our heartfelt trust in Christ alone.

Thus the signs of the Lord's supper speak of what Christ did for (on behalf of) us: His sacrifice completed on the cross. They also speak of what He does in us by His Spirit, feeding and refreshing us, strengthening and renewing us to eternal life.

They speak of the forgiveness of sins (Matthew 26:27, 28), eternal life (John 6:54), and of the communion of saints (1 Corinthians 10:17). For just as we all eat of the same bread, so we all share in the same Christ; just as one bread and wine enter us through the celebration of the Lord's supper, so is there, through Christ, one life in all the believers and they are members of each other.

4. Aim and purpose of the Lord's supper

The holy supper has been instituted for the believers. This article calls them "born anew" and describes them as those whom He has "incorporated into His family, which is His Church." It is for all believers, also and especially for the weak in faith, "who desire more and more to strengthen their faith and amend their life" (Q&A 81 of the Heidelberg Catechism). Baptism, by which we are engrafted into the Church, ought therefore to precede the Lord's supper. Baptism is the sacrament of engrafting; the Lord's supper is the sacrament of remaining incorporated in the congregation of God.

The Lord's supper serves to "nourish and sustain" us. Therefore we are baptized once, but celebrate the Lord's supper repeatedly.

5. Spiritual nourishment

This article gives a broad explanation of a "twofold life" in the regenerated, the believers, namely, the physical life and the spiritual life (see also Canons of Dort, III/IV #17). We may not understand this to mean that this physical and spiritual life exist next to, and independent of, each other. Hence it is not as if the spiritual life, brought about by regeneration, leaves our physical life unaltered. After all, regeneration also sanctifies our physical life and teaches us to present it as a spiritual sacrifice to the Lord (Romans 12:1). This article does not deal with regeneration but with the Lord's supper. And in order now to make it clear that the Lord's supper has been given for spiritual nourishment and that it serves to strengthen our faith, this article gives an elaborate comparison of this "twofold life." Read it carefully. It is so clear that nothing more needs to be said about it.

Note that the "living bread which came down from heaven," and which God sent to sustain our spiritual lives, is not the bread of the Lord's supper, but Jesus Christ (John 6:51). Therefore the bread we must eat is Jesus Christ, who is the bread of life. We must eat His flesh and drink His blood (John 6:35; see also Q&A 76 of the Heidelberg Catechism). This eating and drinking of the flesh and blood of Christ is not done with the physical mouth, but it takes place when Christ is "spiritually appropriated and received by faith." Compare John 6:35 with John 6:51 and see also John 6:56. The Heidelberg Catechism describes the eating of Christ's crucified body and the drinking of His shed blood in a most Scriptural way when it states that it is "to accept with a believing heart all the suffering and the death of Christ" and "to be united more and more to His sacred body through the Holy Spirit."

The bread of the Lord's supper is given to us in order to represent (sign) and testify (seal) to us the "spiritual and heavenly bread," which is Christ, so that "as surely as I receive from the hand of the minister and taste with my mouth the bread and the cup of the Lord (as sure signs of Christ's body and blood) so surely does He Himself nourish and refresh my soul to everlasting life with His crucified body and shed blood" (Q&A 75 of the Heidelberg Catechism).

The manner by which Christ works in us that which He sets before our eyes through the signs of the Lord's supper surpasses our understanding, just as all the work of the Holy Spirit is a mystery and remains hidden from us.

If the Lord's supper is accepted in faith we do not merely eat bread and drink wine but "the true body and true blood of Christ." Then the value and meaning of Christ's sacrifice is given to and accepted by us so that we have the forgiveness of sins and are more and more united with Christ Himself. In this way we do not eat Him with our physical mouth but by faith in the spirit. Faith is "the hand and mouth of the soul."

This act of communion by faith, this "eating" of Christ's flesh and this "drinking" of His blood we may and must do every day.

However, at the Lord's supper we receive the visible signs and seals of this. By those signs and seals Christ's own natural body and His own blood are pledged, and in that pledge also given to us, just like a cheque for $10 pledges to give us ten dollars. If one fails to cash that cheque, one does not receive the ten dollars, and this is then entirely one's own fault. Likewise, whoever does not work with the pledge in faith, and does not desire and accept what was pledged, will not receive what was pledged and given. Hence, giving and receiving are to be distinguished from each other!

6. Meal at a table

The Lord's supper was instituted during the celebration of the Passover meal. This Old Testament sacrament was a sacrifice and a meal. Christ now revealed that He was going to fulfil the sacrifice which each Passover yearned for, and from then on ordained a meal only. This is also how the Lord's supper was celebrated in the ancient Christian Church: as a simple meal. However, it has degenerated into a sacrifice, and this degeneration has become the "be all and end all" in the Church of Rome. Therefore the Church of Rome does not celebrate the sacrament of the death of the Lord at a table but at an altar. Thereby the papal mass has become something entirely different from the Lord's supper. The Roman Catholic mass is not a remembrance of the sacrifice of Calvary, but a repetition of that sacrifice. According to Rome the mass is a bloodless repetition of the sacrifice of Christ since on its altars the body and blood of Christ, considered to be physically present by means of transubstantiation, are separated from each other. They claim that without this repetition "the living and the dead do not have forgiveness of sins" (Q&A 80 of the Heidelberg Catechism). In the mass they also worship Christ in the form of the bread. For that reason the Beggars[23] of the Sixteenth Century called the Roman Catholics "worshippers of the bread-

---

[23] The word Beggars (Dutch: *Geuzen*) derives from the French *gueux* or *gueses*. "It was the name first given contemptuously to Dutch Protestant nobles when they presented a petition to the Spanish Regent of The Netherlands, Margaret of Parma. The name was subsequently adopted by partisans, mostly seafarers, in the Eighty Years' War, the Dutch war of independence and for religious freedom against Spain." (A.H. Oosterhoff in J. van Bruggen, Annotations to the Heidelberg Catechism [Neerlandia, AB: Inheritance Publications, 1991], p. 192). — TRANS.

god." Therefore Q&A 80 of the Heidelberg Catechism, is stating it none too strongly when it teaches that the mass is basically a denial of Christ's one sacrifice. The mass does not confess redemption by the one sacrifice of Christ (Hebrews 10:11-14). Instead, man intends to work his own salvation via the services of the priest in repeating that sacrifice. Worshipping what essentially is nothing more than mere matter is "an accursed idolatry." The Roman Catholic mass is, despite all its pomp, so very poor. In contrast the Lord's supper, in its simplicity, is so very rich. In the Lord's supper we are confronted with the (visible) preaching of our accomplished redemption. Therefore a simple celebration of the Lord's supper in a barn is richer than a pontifical high mass in a cathedral.

(Apparently the term "mass" is the result of a misunderstanding. In former days, according to an incorrect custom, baptized members vacated the church when the Lord's supper was about to be celebrated. The minister then said, "*Ite, concio missa est*," or "*missa est*," meaning, "Depart, the meeting is closed." However, when Latin was no longer understood, this was misinterpreted as: "it is mass.")

7. Christ's presence in the Lord's supper

The signs of the Lord's supper are "earthly and visible" bread and wine. We call them "holy bread" and "holy wine" (Form for the Celebration of the Lord's Supper) because they are set apart for a specific purpose, but they nevertheless remain "earthly and visible" bread and wine. No change in substance occurs, contrary to what the Roman Catholics claim (transubstantiation). According to them, although the properties (flavour, odour, etc.) of the bread remain unchanged, their *essence* changes into the essence of Christ's body. This is nonsense. If the "essence" changes, then the properties must also change. (The water that was changed into wine at the wedding feast in Cana also tasted like wine.)

When Christ says "This *is* My body," it is clear that this "is" must be understood in the same way as when one points to a dot on a map of The Netherlands and says, "This is Amsterdam." Scripture sometimes calls the bread His body and the wine His blood. This is sacramental language, in which the sign is spoken of as if it were the depicted matter itself (see Q&A 79 of the Heidelberg Catechism).

The Lutherans taught co-existence of substance (consubstantiation). According to them, the body of Christ was simultaneously present with (under and in) the signs (ubiquitarians).

Hence, with reference to Christ's presence in the Lord's supper there are the following differences:

Roman Catholics: Bodily and materially present (transubstantiation); He is eaten with the mouth.

Lutherans: Also bodily present (consubstantiation) and eaten with the mouth.

Zwingli: Not present; the Lord's supper is nothing more than a meal of remembrance.

Reformed: Truly present, but in a spiritual sense. Christ's body is in heaven. In the Lord's supper He is eaten with the mouth of faith (Q&A 78 of the Heidelberg Catechism).

(The Lutherans based their doctrine of the Lord's supper on their strange teaching that Christ became omnipresent at His ascension — See Lord's Day 18 of the Heidelberg Catechism.)

8. The sacrament and the believers

Article 33 said that the sacraments are never "void and meaningless so that they deceive us." In agreement with this, Article 35 now teaches that the bread and wine of the Lord's supper are always "joined together with that which is signified." In other words, the bread and wine are always joined with what they signify, namely, the body and blood of the Lord, the whole payment of the debt through His sacrifice and the renewal by His Spirit. The Lord gives each participant of the Lord's supper the full sacrament and never just an empty sign. The person who in unbelief only eats bread and wine, not accepting the Christ pledged in them, will only receive just bread and wine. He remains estranged from Christ. The bread and wine then make his judgment heavier. He did not value what he was given and made the hypocritical gesture of accepting Christ, while his heart was closed to Him.

Here this article gives Judas and Simon the sorcerer as two examples; a regrettable choice. Many Bible commentators claim that Judas didn't participate in the actual Lord's supper any more. Furthermore, where do we read that the Lord's supper was served to Simon? Nevertheless, they do serve as clear examples.

9. The celebration of the Lord's supper

This article describes it as a celebration:

A. which is to take place "in the congregation of the people of God." The Lord's supper is a communal meal of the believers. Hence, no separate administrations at homes (communion for the sick). Nor a "mass" without communion, where the priest is the only one to partake in the Lord's supper.

B. which is to take place "with humility and reverence." The Roman Catholics accuse us that our celebrations lack the pompous splendour of their celebrations. However, the Church confesses that it comes in humility and reverence to the holy meeting with God, which is what the Lord's supper is.

C. which is to take place "as we together commemorate the death of Christ our Saviour with thanksgiving." This thanksgiving is beautifully described in the second section of our Form for the Celebration of the Lord's Supper.

D. which is to take place in order to "confess our faith and Christian religion." At this celebration we proclaim the death of the Lord (1 Corinthians 11:26) as the only ground of salvation.

This article does not discuss how frequently we ought to celebrate the Lord's supper. Scripture is not prescriptive here. However, it is worth noting that the way in which God regulated the Old Testament worship service is an exhortation to sobriety. Each week there was only one Sabbath and each year there was only one great day of atonement. A free-will offering was only allowed to last for a day at the most. The Lord's supper is commonly celebrated once per season. Article 60 of the Church Order stipulates: "The Lord's supper shall be celebrated at least once every three months."

10. Self-examination

Although unbelievers receive the sacrament to their condemnation, believers do not automatically receive it to their comfort. They can eat judgment upon themselves. This judgment is not necessarily *the* judgment. The opportunity to repent remains. However, they eat judgment upon themselves and call God's wrath upon themselves if they eat and drink in an unworthy manner, without exercising faith. Celebrating the Lord's supper in an unworthy manner will dull the conscience and cause us to become more ensnared in sin. Then we become accustomed to treating dishonourably that which is honourable.

This has led some to say, "It is better not to attend the Lord's supper, for then it cannot be profaned either." However, in that way it is also profaned, not through misuse, but through lack of use. Paul exhorts us to both examine ourselves as well as to eat of the bread.

This self-examination is not just a question of: shall I or shall I not attend? The command is to attend! However, it is a matter of ensuring that we do not attend in a manner unworthy of, or unsuited to, the Lord's supper. This self-examination does not serve to make us worthy of the Lord's supper. We are always unworthy of it, but we are made worthy by the Lord. Self-examination serves to let us partake in the Lord's supper *to our comfort* (and not to our condemnation). It consists of the following three parts:
- A. the consideration of our sins and accursedness, so that we humble ourselves before God; also to put sin aside and to live uprightly with God and our neighbour
- B. embracing in faith the promise of forgiveness
- C. renewing our resolve to serve the Lord according to His Word and to love our neighbour as ourselves. See also the beginning of the Form for the Celebration of the Lord's supper.

Apart from this self-discipline, Church discipline is also necessary (Lord's Day 31, Q&A 82 of the Heidelberg Catechism, and Article 32 of the Belgic Confession).

11. The fruit of the Lord's supper

This article points out to us that by the use of the Lord's supper "we are moved . . . to a fervent love of God and our neighbours." The fruits of the Lord's supper, like all fruit, ripen slowly. It is

12. Rejection of errors

In this article the Confession gives a very sober coverage of errors. Of all the "additions and damnable inventions which men have mixed with the sacraments" it does not list a single one. It does not explicitly mention transubstantiation, withholding the cup, adoration of the host, a procession with the host, etc. All deviations are rejected by the simple warning to "content oneself with the ordinance taught by Christ and His apostles." Yet in all that it confesses, this article is one big protest against Roman Catholic corruption of the Lord's supper. This is evident from the repeated references in this article to the Lord's supper as a meal at a table.

ARTICLE 36
THE CIVIL GOVERNMENT

We believe that, because of the depravity of mankind, our gracious God has ordained kings, princes, and civil officers. He wants the world to be governed by laws and policies, in order that the licentiousness of men be restrained and that everything be conducted among them in good order. For that purpose He has placed the sword in the hand of the government to punish wrongdoers and to protect those who do what is good. Their task of restraining and sustaining is not limited to the public order but includes the protection of the Church and its ministry in order that (all idolatry and false worship may be removed and prevented, the kingdom of antichrist may be destroyed) the kingdom of Christ may come, the Word of the gospel may be preached everywhere, and God may be honoured and served by everyone, as He requires in His Word.
Moreover, everyone — no matter of what quality, condition, or rank — ought to be subject to the civil officers, pay

taxes, hold them in honour and respect, and obey them in all things which do not disagree with the Word of God. We ought to pray for them, that God may direct them in all their ways and that we may lead a quiet and peaceable life, godly and respectful in every way.

For that reason we condemn the Anabaptists and other rebellious people, and in general all those who reject the authorities and civil officers, subvert justice, introduce a communion of goods, and confound the decency that God has established among men.

1. Division of the article

A. God has instituted the governing authorities in order that the licentiousness of man may be restrained
B. For that purpose He gave them the power of the sword
C. The obligation of governing authorities with respect to public worship
D. The obligations of subjects toward governing authorities
E. Rejection of errors

2. Overstepping the boundaries?

It is claimed by numerous Reformed people (among others Dr. K. Dijk, Rev. S.G. de Graaf, Dr. I.A. Diepenhorst) that with Article 36 the Church "has overstepped the boundaries of its prophetic authority." According to them an article on the government does not belong in the Confession.

Admittedly, the Church is not to intervene with the technical details of government policy. It is not for the Church, in spite of what the Synod of the Dutch Reformed (State) Church repeatedly did in its "messages," to prescribe what the government ought to do with regards to all kinds of policy matters. The World Council of Churches also interfered far too frequently with such matters; matters which are not at all the Church's concern. However, this does not take away the fact that the Church in her Confession, which is to echo the Word of God, ought also to confess what this Word teaches with respect to the government and particularly the Church's relationship to it. This is what the Belgic Confession does in this article. It does not give an elaborate teaching about authority, or about the state, but confesses here, over against the threats of Anabaptist error and revolution, how Christians are to act in relation to the authorities. Scripture is clear on this issue (Romans 13). In addition to this, something had to be said about the role of the government. Yet on the whole the article is more an appeal to the protection of the authorities than a statement telling the authorities what their obligations are. De Brés' original text reads as follows, *"Nous croyons finalement . . ."* (= finally, we believe . . .). Later the word *"finalement"* (= finally) was deleted, apparently because Article 37 also begins with: *"Finalement nous croyons . . ."* However, it appears that De Brés intended a double conclusion. His intention was to make a double appeal, first with respect to the earthly government (Article 36) and secondly with respect to the heavenly government (Article 37). Such an appeal to those whom God has given to be the "shields of the earth" (Psalm 47), makes the inclusion of this article in the Confession most appropriate.

3. Only because of sin?

This article begins with the confession, that "our gracious God has ordained (instituted) "kings, princes, and civil officers." This is clearly taught by Scripture (Romans 13:1; 1 Peter 2:13ff.; Titus 3:1). By means of this statement our Confession refutes the revolutionary Anabaptists who would have nothing to do with it. In fact, the whole article is an attack on the grave danger that threatens the Church from these quarters. It is a struggle to keep the believers out of the grip of revolution. At the same time this article wants to make clear to the Roman Catholic government, which "tarred the Reformed and the Anabaptists with the same brush" and therefore persecuted them as revolutionaries, that the Reformed are most faithful subjects to authority. The Reformed recognize that the office of government represents God (not the sovereignty of the people).

Furthermore, this article says that God instituted the authorities "because of the depravity of mankind . . . in order that the licentiousness of men be restrained." This does not mean to say that without the fall into sin there would have been no government. It is impossible to say exactly how the world would have looked without the fall into sin. However, there are grounds for saying that even without the fall into sin there would have been governments. After all, governments also exist in the world of the good angels. For the sake of good unity, as far as we can judge, leaders would also have been necessary without the fall into sin, but the authority of the governments would then not have had a forceful character. The government would not have required the sword to assert itself. However, our Confession does not say anything about this and limits itself to what the situation is today. The government as we know it is there "because of the depravity of mankind" and "in order that the licentiousness of men be restrained." That the punishment of wrongdoers is not its only task is apparent from what follows in the article. The government is also there for the sake of our protection. Christ has all power, also over all authorities placed under Him. All kings ought to serve Him, the King of kings, and promote the kingdom of Christ. This is the best service they could ever offer their country and people! Pay attention to 1 Timothy 2:1-5.

Take note of the fact that the Confession here too, just as in Article 33 for example, speaks of "our gracious God." We may indeed be thankful that God instituted the authorities. What would become of the world otherwise?

4. Power of the sword

The government does not exercise its authority in the way that office-bearers of the Church do it, through teaching, but rather, by force. Due to sin this cannot be otherwise. For that purpose God gave it the sword. He lent it the power to exercise force and, if necessary, to apply capital punishment. The infliction of punishment also belongs to this "power of the sword."

5. Obligation of the government toward public worship

The third part of this article has given rise to much contention. The seventeen words one finds in brackets have been the centre of many debates. At the General Synod of Middelburg (1896) eight members submitted an objection to these words. A decision on this objection was finally made at the Synod of Utrecht (1905).

This Synod deleted these words. The Christian Reformed Church (in The Netherlands) and the Dutch Reformed (State) Church did not do so. The matter was raised again at the Reformed Ecumenical Synod[24] in Amsterdam (1949), because the overseas Churches had not withdrawn these words either.[25]

At the Reformed Ecumenical Synod in Edinburgh (1953), a decision was made concerning the relationship between Church and government. The Dutch Reformed (State) Church too was constantly occupied with this matter.

In its extremely lengthy report the General Synod of Utrecht (1905) argued as follows: One ought to read the Confession according to the intention of the authors. (This is wrong! We must read it in the light of Holy Scripture.) The intent of the authors, it was claimed, was that the government had to burn the heretics. (This also is wrong! Though Reformed people have also made mistakes, their overriding consideration was that the government ought to be tolerant. Later, when Petrus Dathenus of Ghent called upon the government to take strict measures against the Roman Catholics he was opposed by Reformed people). However, being of the opinion that the Reformed people in the 16th century were "burners of heretics" the Synod of 1905 judged that these seventeen words implied that it was the calling of the government to destroy heretics. Synod correctly judged such an idea to be in conflict with Holy Scripture. Therefore it deleted the seventeen words.

This is regrettable. The real question is not what one or another Reformed person might once have pleaded for, but whether the words written here make good sense in the light of Scripture. This they do, if only one would read them carefully.

"The protection of the Church and its ministry" does not mean that the government must organize the Church and perform this ministry, but that it ought to protect it, safeguarding it from hindrances and providing it with room. This is also meant by the words "that the kingdom of Christ may come (and) the Word of the Gospel may be preached everywhere." Furthermore, it does not say here that the government must destroy worshippers of idols,

---

[24] Today known as the Reformed Ecumenical Council. — TRANS.

[25] The 1958 Synod of the Christian Reformed Church in North America also approved the removal of these words. — Editor.

but that "all idolatry and false worship may be removed and prevented," meaning that in its domain, the domain of public life, the practices of idolatry and false religion ought to be prevented and forbidden. Here the government is not to bind people's consciences. That is not its duty. Rather, it may not permit public practice of idolatry and false worship, the reason being that it is not to open the door to the "kingdom of Antichrist;" instead, it is to destroy this kingdom in its domain.

Understood in this way, the deleted words do have a valid and Scriptural meaning. Those in the office of government (of whom this article is speaking) must, like all people, let themselves be directed by both tables of the law of the Lord in carrying out their tasks.

6. Church and civil government

Roman Catholics subject the civil government entirely to the Church. Lutherans give the civil government authority over the Church.

However, neither the government nor the Church have authority over the other. God instituted both. Each has its own task. The Church has the task of governing the Church, the practice of worship, and the preaching of the Gospel. The government has its task in public life, to establish and maintain law and order according to the Law of the Lord.

The government is to protect the Church in carrying out its task in public life.

The Church is to respect the government and to encourage such respect. To that end it must also proclaim in its Confession and preaching what the Lord teaches us concerning the task and calling of the government.

7. Obligation of subjects

This is so clearly stated by this article, that no further explanation is required. The obligation described here does not only apply to Christian and just governments, but also to harsh and unjust governments. Read 1 Peter 2:13-25; and consider that Romans 13 was written when Nero reigned! There is only one restriction here: "We ought to obey God rather than men" (Acts

5:29). Only when the government commands us to sin, we must disobey. Yet even then there remains the obligation to show respect!

8. Rejection of errors

Here we must keep in mind that the Confession dates back to the time of the episode at Munster[26] and the revolt in Amsterdam. How easily the innocent could have been caught up in this resistance to a government which had killed their loved ones in a gruesome manner. Such events have happened repeatedly. This last section, in fact our whole article, is still relevant in every respect.

ARTICLE 37
THE LAST JUDGMENT

Finally, we believe, according to the Word of God, that when the time, ordained by the Lord but unknown to all creatures, has come and the number of the elect is complete, our Lord Jesus Christ will come from heaven, bodily and visibly, as He ascended, with great glory and majesty. He will declare Himself Judge of the living and the dead and set this old world afire in order to purge it. Then all people, men, women, and children, who ever lived, from the beginning of the world to the end, will appear in person before this great Judge. They will be summoned with the archangel's call and with the sound of the trumpet of God. Those who will have died before that time will arise out of the earth, as their spirits are once again united with their own bodies in which they lived. Those who will then be still alive will not die as the others but will be changed in the twinkling of an eye from perishable to imperishable. Then the books will be opened and the dead will be judged according to what they have done in this world, whether good or evil. Indeed, all people will render account for

---

[26] A peasant revolt in the small German town of Munster. Under the leadership of Jan Mathijs and John of Leiden, many refugees settled in Munster in 1534 and took control of the city. In 1535 the city was captured and the Anabaptist leaders were tortured and killed. — TRANS.

every careless word they utter, which the world regards as mere jest and amusement. The secrets and hypocrisies of men will then be publicly uncovered in the sight of all. And so for good reason the thought of this judgment is horrible and dreadful to the wicked and evildoers but it is a great joy and comfort to the righteous and elect. For then their full redemption will be completed and they will receive the fruits of their labour and of the trouble they have suffered. Their innocence will be known to all and they will see the terrible vengeance that God will bring upon the wicked who persecuted, oppressed, and tormented them in this world. The wicked will be convicted by the testimony of their own consciences and will become immortal, but only to be tormented in the eternal fire prepared for the devil and his angels. On the other hand, the faithful and elect will be crowned with glory and honour. The Son of God will acknowledge their names before God His Father and His elect angels. God will wipe away every tear from their eyes, and their cause — at present condemned as heretical and evil by many judges and civil authorities — will be recognized as the cause of the Son of God. As a gracious reward, the Lord will cause them to possess such a glory as the heart of man could never conceive. Therefore we look forward to that great day with a great longing to enjoy to the full the promises of God in Jesus Christ our Lord. Amen. Come, Lord Jesus!

1. Character and division of this article

This article offers "doctrine concerning the last things." Many matters relating to that receive no mention here. No reference is made to the interim state between death and resurrection, the thousand year reign, the Antichrist, signs of the times. Nor is this article just a bit of dogma but an urgent appeal from the heart. Here the tormented Church of martyrs makes a passionate appeal to her heavenly Judge and confesses her hope in the face of persecution. This appeal simultaneously serves to warn these persecutors of their destruction. To subdivide such a cry rising from the depths of despair is almost unnatural. However, in order to assist our memory, we will follow the set pattern and do so anyway. The last day of history, on which this article sets its hope, is a day of judgment. In discussing the last judgment, a judgment which has significance for eternity, this article speaks of:

A. the majestic arrival of the Judge
B. the summoning of all people, the living as well as the dead
C. the books that will be opened
D. the rehabilitation of the saints, who await this great day with eager longing

2. The majestic arrival of the Judge

The Judge will be our Lord Jesus Christ (Matthew 25:13; Acts 1:11; 2 Timothy 4:1). This is a comfort to those who are His. Here the Church calls Him "our Lord" and the Heidelberg Catechism describes Him as "the very same person who before has submitted Himself to the judgment of God for my sake, and has removed all the curse from me" (Q&A 52 of the Heidelberg Catechism). However, for those who rejected Him this will be dreadful, for they will receive as Judge "Him who they pierced" (Revelation 1:7). He will come at the time ordained by the Lord. This time is "unknown to all creatures." He will appear suddenly and unexpectedly, as a thief in the night (Matthew 24:36, 37; 1 Thessalonians 5:2). No one knows of that day and hour, not the angels who are in heaven, nor the Son, but only the Father. Scripture does mention many signs which point to Christ's return: increased lawlessness (Matthew 24:12); the revelation of the man of sin, the Antichrist (2 Thessalonians 2:1-12); wars and rumours of wars (Mark 13:7, 8); earthquakes in various places (Luke 21:25-27); severe persecution of the Church (Matthew 24:9-12); preaching of the Gospel to all nations (Matthew 24:14). These signs serve as a constant warning to all mankind: Behold, He comes!

Christ will return bodily and visibly (Acts 1:11; Revelation 1:7). Then He will complete His work as Redeemer and Judge. As such He will come with great glory and majesty, surrounded by all the holy angels. Then He will seat Himself "on the throne of His glory" (Matthew 25:31). His power will be so great that He will "set this old world afire in order to purge it" (2 Peter 3:7-10).

3. Premillennialism[27]

Premillennialism is derived from the Latin words *pre* (before), *mille* (thousand), and *annus* (year), and it denotes the error concerning the thousand year reign of Christ (see Revelation 20:2, 4, 6). Premillennialism has been around for a very long time and has been widely propagated in America and on its mission fields. It originates from the schools of the Jewish rabbis. They considered the Messianic era to be the time of Israel's political reign over the nations, a time of great prosperity, to be followed by the Last Judgment. These views gave rise to expectations of an earthly kingdom in which the Christian Church would come to glory. Premillennialists can be found among the Pentecostals, the Jehovah's Witnesses, the Mormons, and all kinds of Adventists. Each has its own interpretation of the millennium but all have the same basis.

Premillennialists believe that Christ will return twice. During the era of His first return He will defeat the anti-Christian powers, bind Satan, raise the believers who have died, gather around Himself the congregation and especially the converted Jews who returned to Palestine, govern the world with that congregation and usher in for His people a time of spiritual and material prosperity. Some expect Christ's seat of government to be in Jerusalem, others (Mormons) expect Him to reside in Utah, and there are others again who point to heaven as His residence. At the end of this era, which will last a thousand years, Christ will return to heaven and Satan will be released. He will engage the Church in the last and most terrible battle. When the darkest hour arrives, Christ will come a second time. Then the dead shall be raised and eternal judgment will take place. Different explanations on how it will all take place (for example, the duration of this kingdom, its commencement, the position of the Jews in it) abound but there is agreement on the main points.

In order to justify this error an appeal is made to the Old Testament prophecies concerning the coming Messianic kingdom

---

[27] The author used the term "*Chiliasm*," a word derived from the Greek word "*chilios*" meaning thousand. Since *premillennialism* is the term more commonly used in English, that is how this error is referred to in this translation. — TRANS.

of glory. The main evidence is drawn from Revelation 20. It is claimed that the above is clearly discernible from that chapter.

However, Revelation 20 does not say that Satan will be totally powerless on earth for one thousand years, but that he will not be able to deceive the *nations*. He has not been able to do that ever since Christ ascended to the throne of the Father. Christ's ascension marked a sharp turning point in world history. Prior to it, God's nation Israel had no influence at all in the vast world. Satan dominated the world unhindered. However, since Christ's ascension to the throne, the Roman eagle had to yield to the cross. World dominion was placed and kept in the hands of the nations influenced by the Gospel. The Gospel proceeded triumphantly from nation to nation. That is the reign of Christ, His thousand year empire. Thousand (ten times ten times ten) is then to be understood symbolically, as are all numbers in the book of Revelation. It denotes a lengthy period which will not be terminated prematurely but which will be completed and in which all that must be accomplished will be accomplished.

Revelation 20 does not say that the believers will reign with Christ on earth after a "first resurrection" as promulgated by the millennialists. John does not say in verse 4 that he saw all those who were beheaded for Christ's sake rise from the dead but that he saw them (the souls!) alive (in heaven), participating in the dominion exercised by Christ.

Premillennialism is a dangerous error. Firstly, it gives an incorrect impression of the relationship between the Old and New Testaments. It does not recognize the New as a fulfilment of the Old, but sees such a fulfilment as taking place only in the "thousand year reign." According to this view we are presently living in an interim period in which one cannot speak of a people of God on earth. Premillennialism is an impediment to a correct understanding of Scripture.

Furthermore, premillennialism is deadly for the Christian life. It claims that Christ's dominion is still to come. But the truth is that He is already King now and must be served everywhere. The millennialists however, despise all Christian activity. In all their activities they are content to passively wait for the Rapture. They desire a minimum of preaching and discussion.

It is worth noting that the positive direction world history took at the time of Christ's ascension has decreased since the last two world wars. The hegemony of the nations upon which the Gospel had placed its stamp, and in which the Church is degenerating and unbelief is gaining victory, is nearing its end, indeed has ended. The release of Satan is clearly apparent from the increasing power of the heathen nations. Clearly the last battle is rapidly approaching. Be sober and watchful! And, fear not: the last battle leads to the complete victory!

4. The summons to all people, both the living and the dead

All people, without exception, will be called to appear before the Judge by a voice which will be heard by all, compelling them to come forward (see 1 Thessalonians 4:16). Those who have already died will arise from the earth. The Confession says that they will again receive "their own bodies in which they lived." This does not mean that this body will be made up of the same particles as before. Even on earth these particles are continuously renewed. Yet despite all these renewals, our bodies stay the same. Hence we will later receive the same body in which we presently live. However, it will be a body of a totally different quality. With reference to the believers Paul, in 1 Corinthians 15, speaks of the distinctions between their physical and glorified bodies in terms of perishability versus imperishability; dishonour versus glory; weakness versus power; mortality versus immortality; physical versus spiritual. "Spiritual" does not mean that it will not be physical but that it will be totally subservient to the spirit, perfectly adapted to the life of glory. It no longer needs food; propagation is discontinued because renewal and growth give way to being perfected for eternity (Matthew 22:30; 1 Corinthians 6:13). With respect to the resurrection of the unbelievers Scripture says that they shall awaken "to shame and everlasting contempt" (Daniel 12:2) and "to the resurrection of condemnation" (John 5:29). The curse will then continue to affect their bodies totally. Through the resurrection they will not rise to life eternal nor attain the glorious immortality, but, as this article says, "will become immortal, but only to be tormented in the eternal fire."

Those still alive at the appearance of the eternal Judge will not first die but "be changed in the twinkling of an eye" (1 Corinthians 15:51, 52).

5. The interim state

The old Anabaptist error concerning the sleep of the soul (*pyshopannychy*) was presented anew in a slightly modified version in the publications of Rev. B. Telder. According to Telder man returns to dust when he dies. That is the end of the matter. Man is dead when he enters the grave and no longer exists. He merely remains in God's thoughts. God does not forget His own and will awaken them some time in the future.

However, Scripture says concerning those who have returned to dust and dwell among the dead that God "is not the God of the dead, but of the living, for all live to Him" (Luke 20:38). And these last words do not speak of what God is doing, but what the "dead" do! Not only are the dead carried to the grave, but they immediately leave the body and go to Christ in order to proceed with eternal life, but now outside the dead body, in fellowship with Him until the day that they, completely glorified, will be resurrected from the grave (Q&A 42, 57a of the Heidelberg Catechism; see also J.R. Wiskerke, *Leven tussen sterven en opstanding* [= *Life Between Death and Resurrection*], published by Oosterbaan en Le Cointre N.V., Goes, 1963).

These publications emphasized that the dichotomy of body and soul originated from the schools of the Greek philosophers and penetrated Christian doctrine, but that the Bible does not speak in this way. Rather, it is said that the Bible sees man as one unit. However, the Bible also makes a distinction between the two. The Bible also speaks of body and soul (Matthew 10:28) and would have us understand that the "soul" also lives after death (see Luke 23:43; John 11:25; 2 Corinthians 5:8; Philippians 1:23; Revelation 20:4).

This error concerning soul sleep, which says that there is no conscious life for us between death and resurrection, is not an isolated idea. Such is never the case with an error. The issue at stake here is what one understands by eternal life. It is a matter of how great and glorious one confesses Christ's power as the Prince of Life to be, how we see the renewal by the Spirit and the relationship between "nature" and "grace."

6. The books that will be opened

All deeds and words, even all man's thoughts, will be tabled like in a lawsuit (Matthew 12:36; 2 Corinthians 5:10; Revelation 20:12). The point will be whether our deeds were evidence of our faith, the faith which unites with Christ who is our righteousness.

Immediately after death each person receives a "provisional" judgment; believers may go to Christ and the ungodly go into temporary custody; after that the final public judgment will take place.

7. The rehabilitation of the saints

This article confesses the return of Christ to be "a great joy and comfort." The Heidelberg Catechism does likewise in Q&A 52. On earth the Church is oppressed and her cause is reviled and despised. However, no matter how many judges and rulers condemn her cause as heretical and evil, when Christ comes it will be apparent that her cause was the cause of the Son of God. He will then cast all His and the Church's enemies into everlasting condemnation, but all His chosen ones He will take to Himself into heavenly joy and glory. "And so for good reason the thought of this judgment is horrible and dreadful to the wicked and evildoers but it is a great joy and comfort to the righteous and elect. For then their full redemption will be completed and they will receive the fruits of their labour and of the trouble they have suffered." Therefore the Bride prays with the Spirit, Come Lord Jesus! (Revelation 22:17). Those who in this life choose God's cause as their own are familiar with this longing. Wherever the Maranatha prayer has fallen silent, faith has given up. The stronger faith is, the more earnestly the prayer will resound, "Come, Lord Jesus, yes, come quickly!"

INDEX

A. = Article
# = Paragraph

Aaron's priesthood .... A. 21 #3
Agnosticism .... A. 1 #9
Anabaptists .... Chapter II #6;
.... A. 34 #7, 11-12; A. 36 #2-3
Angels .... A. 12 #9
Apocryphal books .... A. 4 #4;
.... A. 6 #1-3
Apollinaris .... A. 19 #2
Apostles' Creed .... Chapter I #5
Arianism .... A. 10 #2
Arminianism .... A. 16 #12
Atheism .... A. 1 #9
Ban .... A. 32 #2
Baptism .... A. 34 #2-9
- of infants .... A. 34 #10-11
Barthianism .... Chapter I #6
Baston de la Foy .... Chapter II #2
Bible .... A. 4 #4
Bible criticism .... A. 3 #7
Canonical books .... A. 4 #3; A. 5 #2
Ceremonies .... A. 25 #4
Chiliasm SEE: Premillennialism
Christ:
   - divinity .... A. 10 #3-4
   - intercession .... A. 26 #2-3
   - natures .... A. 5; A. 19 #1-3
   - obedience .... A. 21 #1
   - person .... A. 19 #5-7
   - return .... A. 37 #2
   - sacrifice .... A. 21 #4
   - suffering .... A. 21 #5
Christians .... A. 29 #5
Church:
   - and civil government ... A. 36 #6
   - assembly ...... A. 27 #4; A. 29 #3
   - attributes .... A. 26 #5
   - bond of churches .... A. 30/31 #9
   - consistory .... A. 30/31 #9
   - discipline .... A. 32 #3-4
   - false .... A. 29 #6
   - government .... A. 30/31 #2
   - marks .... A. 29 #4
   - true .... A. 29 #2
Cocceianism .... A. 20 #5
Confession .... Chapter I #1
Confessions .... Chapter I #5
   - appreciation .... Chapter I #6
   - authority .... Chapter I #3
   - character .... Chapter II #6
   - of the Church .... Chapter II #4
Consubstantiation .... A. 35 #7
Conversion .... A. 24 #2
Covenant .... A. 17 #2; A. 34 #13
Creation .... A. 12 #3-5
- days .... A. 12 #7
Darwin .... A. 12 #6
Deacons .... A. 30/31 #3
Death (between death and
   resurrection) .... A. 37 #5
De Brés, Guido .... Chapter II #1
Deism .... A. 1 #9; A. 13 #2
Denominationalism
   SEE: Pluriformity
Devils .... A. 12 #10
Doctrinal authority (Roman Catholic
   Church) .... A. 7 #4
Ecumenical movement ..... A. 25 #8;
.... A. 27 #8
Elders .... A. 30/31 #3
Election, doctrine of ... A. 16 #1, 5-9
Eutyches .... A. 19 #2, 4
Excommunication .... A. 32 #2
Evolution .... A. 12 #6
Faith .... A. 22 #4-6
   - and sacraments .... A. 33 #7
   - origin .... A. 24 #2
Fatalism .... A. 13 #2; A. 16 #11
Free will .... A. 14 #4
   - errors .... A. 14 #2, 12

INDEX

Geelkerken .... A. 14 #8
God:
- attributes .... A. 1 #4-8
- proofs .... A. 1 #3
God's counsel .... A. 16 #4
God's image .... A. 14 #5
Good works (fruits of faith) A. 24 #1
Government (civil) .... A. 36
- and church .... A. 36 #6
- and worship services ...... A. 36 #5
- power of the sword .... A. 36 #4
Grace, means of .... A. 33
Heaven .... A. 12 #8
Hierarchy .... A. 30/31 #7
Higher criticism .... A. 3 #7
Holy Spirit, the .... A. 9 #1-3; A. 11
- sin against .... A. 11 #5
Immortality .... A. 20 #8
Incarnation of Christ .... A. 18
Inspiration .... A. 3 #5
Interim state (between death and resurrection) .... A. 37 #5
Judgment (last) ... A. 37 #1-2, 4, 6-7
Justification .... A. 22 #3
- *sola fide* .... A. 22 #7; A. 23 #3-6
Limited atonement .... A. 21 #10
Lord's supper .... A. 35 #2-9
- celebration of .... A. 35 #9
Lower criticism .... A. 3 #7
Lumen internum .... A. 7 #2
Mani .... A. 12 #11
Manicheans .... A. 12 #11
Mass .... A. 35 #6
Mediator .... A. 26 #2
Melchizedek's priesthood .... A. 21 #3
Miracles .... A. 13 #5
Natural law .... A. 13 #5
Nature (of Christ) .... A. 19 #5
Nestorius .... A. 19 #2, 4
Office-bearers (election) A. 30/31 #5
Offices:
- in the Church .... A. 30/31 #3
- of Christ .... A. 21 #1
Original sin .... A. 15 #1-7
Pantheism .... A. 1 #9; A. 13 #2

Pelagianism .... A. 14 #3
Pentecostalism .... A. 11 #6
Person (of Christ) .... A. 19 #5-7
Pluriformity .... A. 27 #7
- history .... A. 27 #8
Polytheism .... A. 1 #9
Pope (infallibility) .... Chapter I #6; .... A. 7 #4
Predestination .... A. 16 #1, 5-9
Premillennialism .... A. 37 #3
Priesthood .... A. 21 #3
Priesthood of Aaron .... A. 21 #3
Priesthood of Melchizedek A. 21 #3
Promise to Eve, the .... A. 17 #4
Providence of God .... A. 13 #2
Racine .... Chapter II #3
Regeneration .... A. 24 #2
Remonstrantism SEE: Arminianism
Resurrection of the dead .... A. 37 #5
Revelation (means) .... A. 2 #6
Sacraments .... A. 33 #1-5
Sacraments:
- and faith .... A. 33 #7
- and Word .... A. 33 #6
- Roman Catholic Church .... A. 33 #8
Sadducees .... A. 12 #11
Saints (honouring of) .... A. 26 #2
Sanctification .... A. 24 #3
Satan (release of) .... A. 12 #10; .... A. 37 #3
Scripture:
- attributes .... A. 7 #7
- authority .... A. 5
- sufficiency .... A. 7
Self-examination .... A. 35 #10
Septuagint .... A. 4 #4
Sin:
- against the Holy Spirit . A. 11 #5
- cause .... A. 14 #7; A. 15
- consequences .... A. 14 #4; .... A. 15 #3-9
- terminology .... A. 15 #3
Son of God .... A. 10 #4
Soul (after death) .... A. 37 #5

Supernatural .... A. 14 #5
Text criticism .... A. 3 #7
Traditions (Roman Catholic
   Church) .... A. 7 #3
Transubstantiation .... A. 35 #7
Trinity .... A. 8 #3-5
  - evidence .... A. 9 #2-4
Word and sacraments .... A. 33 #6
World Council of Churches A. 27 #8
Worship service .... A. 25 #7

The Belgic Confession and its Biblical Basis
by Lepusculus Vallensis

The Belgic Confession is a Reformed Confession, dating from the 16th Century, written by Guido de Brès, a preacher in the Reformed Churches of The Netherlands. The great synod of Dort in 1618-19 adopted this Confession as one of the doctrinal standards of the Reformed Churches, to which all office-bearers of the Churches were (and still are) to subscribe. This book provides and explains the Scriptural proof texts for the Belgic Confession by using the marginal notes of the Dutch *Staten Bijbel*.

Subject: Creeds   Age: 15-99
ISBN 0-921100-41-8   Can.$17.95 U.S.$15.90

Annotations to the Heidelberg Catechism
by J. Van Bruggen

John A. Hawthorne in *Reformed Theological Journal*: ... The individual Christian would find it a constructive way to employ part of the Sabbath day by working through the lesson that is set for each Lord's Day. No one can study this volume without increasing his knowledge of truth and being made to worship and adore the God of all grace. This book will help every minister in the instruction of his people, both young and not so young, every parent in the task of catechizing and is commended to every Christian for personal study.

Subject: Catechism   Age: 13-99
ISBN 0-921100-33-7   Can.$15.95 U.S.$13.90

The Church
Its Unity in Confession and History
by G. Van Rongen

This book deals first of all with what the Belgic Confession says about the Church, since they contain the Scriptural fundamentals. Then it deals with what Church history teaches us about unity of faith as something basic to Church unity. Finally, it deals with the unity of the Church as it was endangered but, by God's grace, also preserved in the events connected with the Liberation in the Dutch churches during the 1940s.

Throughout this book it is clear that it is a great joy for the author to serve his God and Saviour, as well as God's covenant community, the Church, by following in the footsteps of one of his earthly mentors, Dr. Klaas Schilder. Like Dr. Schilder, he has laboured in obedience to the prayer of the Lord Jesus Christ in John 17: "That they all may be one!"

Subject: History / Doctrine   Age: 13-99
ISBN 0-921100-90-6   Can.$14.95 U.S.$12.90

The Covenantal Gospel by C. Van der Waal

G. Van Rongen in *Una Sancta*: . . . We would like to conclude this review with a quotation from the last lines of this — recommended! — book. They are the following: The Gospel is covenantal in every respect. If things go wrong in the churches, ask whether the covenant is indeed preached and understood. If missionary work is superficial, ask whether the covenant is taken into account. . . If sects and movements multiply, undoubtedly they speak of the covenant in a strange way, or ignore it deliberately. . . It must be proclaimed. Evangelical = Covenantal.

Subject: Bible   **Age: 16-99**
ISBN 0-921100-19-1   **Can.$17.95 U.S.$16.20**

Essays in Reformed Doctrine by J. Faber

Cecil Tuininga in *Christian Renewal*: This book is easy reading as far as the English goes. It can, I judge, be read by all with great profit. . . I found the first chapter on *The Significance of Dogmatology for the Training of the Ministry* excellent. The six essays on the Church I found very informative and worthwhile. . . What makes this book so valuable is that Dr. Faber deals with all the aspects of the Reformed faith from a strictly biblical and confessional viewpoint.

Subject: Theology / History   **Age: 18-99**
ISBN 0-921100-28-0   **Can.$19.95 U.S.$17.90**

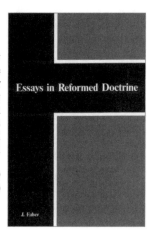

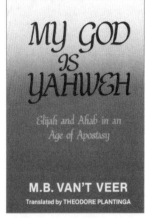

My God is Yahweh by M.B. Van't Veer
Elijah and Ahab in an Age of Apostasy

The time in which Ahab and Elijah lived and opposed each other was of special importance for the progress of God's Kingdom during the old dispensation. It was a vital stage in the history of divine revelation.

Subject: 1 Kings 16-19   **Age: 16-99**
ISBN 0-88815-035-0   **Can.$14.95 U.S.$12.95**

American Secession Theologians on Covenant and Baptism by Jelle Faber & *Extra-Scriptural Binding — A New Danger* by Klaas Schilder

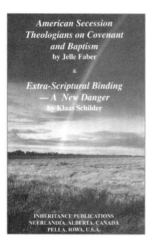

Jelle Tuininga in *Christian Renewal*: . . . The main purpose of Schilder was to dissuade and discourage Hoeksema (and the Prot. Ref. Churches) from adopting the so-called Brief Declaration. Schilder saw this, correctly I believe, as an "extra Scriptural binding" which would only lead to separate church federations instead of unity. . . I am happy that the publisher has made these essays available in English to a larger audience. The more so, because they deal with important issues which are now coming to the surface again. We must be informed on such salient points.
Subject: Church History / Theology   Age: 16-99
ISBN 0-921100-46-9   Can.$13.95 U.S.$11.90

Covenant and Election
by Dr. J. Van Genderen
All the commands and prohibitions of the Decalogue flow out of the covenant relation: "I am the LORD your God." That is the prologue to the entire law (Calvin). God thereby declares that He is the God of the Church. In light of these words the Reformer of Geneva expounds both the Ten Commandments as well as the summary of the law. For Calvin the law is the law of the covenant of grace. It is a confirmation of the covenant made with Abraham. Even though the law serves to bring out transgressions (Galatians 3:19) it is clothed with the covenant of grace (the covenant of God's gracious acceptance).   — from the book
Subject: Covenant Theology   Age: 16-99
ISBN 0-921100-60-4   Can.$11.95 U.S.$10.90

Always Obedient
Essays on the Teachings of
Dr. Klaas Schilder
Edited by J. Geertsema
"It is a delight to be Reformed," wrote Dutch theologian Klaas Schilder (1890-1952), a man whose life and work demonstrated unwavering loyalty to biblical authority. While parting with Abraham Kuyper on some issues, Schilder shared Kuyper's conviction that "there is not an inch of human life about which Christ, who is Sovereign over all, does not proclaim, 'Mine.' "
Subject: Theology   Age: 16-99
ISBN 0-87552-239-4   Can.$15.95 U.S.$10.99

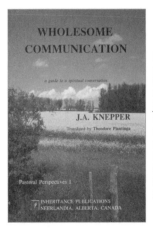

Wholesome Communication by J.A. Knepper
A Guide to a Spiritual Conversation
Pastoral Perspectives 1

K.V. Warren in *Vox Reformata*: Here is plenty of practical and down to earth advice as regards the ins and outs of conversation in general: non-verbal communications and its importance, posture, value judgments, leading and structuring a conversation, etc. G. Duncan Lowe in Covenanter Witness: This book deserves to be read throughout the Church. It is a manual of practical godliness within a clearly important area, and it is written by a man of experience and sensitivity who continually reflects upon God's Word.

Subject: Pastoral Care   Age: 16-99
ISBN 0-921100-13-2   Can.$9.95 U.S.$8.90

Thou Holdest My Right Hand by D. Los
Pastoral Perspectives 2

Johan D. Tangelder in *Christian Renewal*: A much needed book, which should be in every church library, and mandatory for all involved in ministry to the sick and dying.

Subject: Pastoral care of the dying   Age: 16-99
ISBN 0-921100-45-0   Can.$9.95 U.S.$8.90

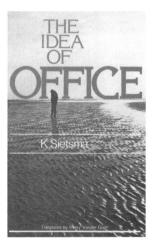

The Idea of Office by K. Sietsma

Henry Vander Kam in *Mid-America Journal of Theology*: The importance of this book is far greater than its small size . . . The author also deals with the office of all believers. He does so in the sense in which the Bible instructs us in this matter and as it was emphasized again by the reformers.

Subject: Christian Living   Age: 15-99
ISBN 0-88815-065-2   Can.$6.95 U.S.$5.90

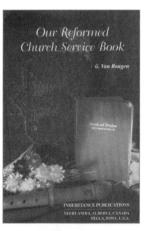

Our Reformed Church Service Book by G. Van Rongen

The author deals with the history of the *Book of Praise*, *Anglo-Genevan Psalter* and with the history of Reformed Psalters and liturgies from the early church till today.

Subject: Liturgy / Psalter   Age: 16-99
ISBN 0-921100-52-3   Can.$15.95 U.S.$13.90

The Self-Justification of God in the Life of Job **by Kornelis Sietsma**

Clarence Bouwman in *Una Sancta*: A year before World War II broke out, a minister of the Word preached seven sermons covering the book of Job, about how people struggle with understanding evil and what God's answer was to that struggle. Not so many years later this preacher, Rev Kornelis Sietsma, died in the concentration camp at Dachau. Meanwhile, the seven sermons he'd preached before the War had been published and so became a source of comfort and encouragement for the believers of the Netherlands in the dark days of suffering we know as World War Two.

Subject: Book of Job   **Age: 16-99**
ISBN0-921100-24-8   **Can.$10.95 U.S.$8.90**

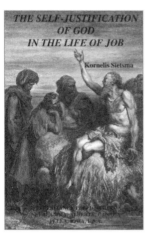

Hosea: Love's Complaint
by Herman Veldkamp

Jealousy, adultery, pain — these are the themes that dominate the prophecy of Hosea. Against the background of his deteriorating marriage Hosea addresses an urgent message to all of God's people begging them to listen to the complaint raised by the Lord's wounded love. Herman Veldkamp skilfully illuminates the prophet's hard hitting accusations.
Ideal for Bible Study societies.
(Six or more copies: 15% discount)

Subject: Book of Hosea   **Age: 16-99**
ISBN 0-88815-031-8   **Can.$9.95 U.S.$8.90**

The Farmer from Tekoa (Amos)
by Herman Veldkamp

Written in a very attractive style, this commentary [on the book of Amos] can be enjoyed by young people and adults.
— *The Presbyterian Journal*
Not only ministers, teachers, and students but indeed every serious-minded reader will find in this book tremendous helpful, brilliantly beautiful guidelines to understanding the prophetic messages of Amos.
— *The Banner*
(Six or more copies: 15% discount)

Subject: Book of Amos   **Age: 16-99**
ISBN 0-88815-000-8   **Can.$9.95 U.S.$8.90**

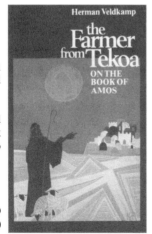

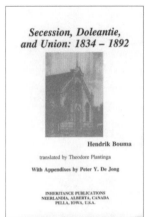

Secession, Doleantie, and Union 1834 - 1892 by Hendrik Bouma

. . . Bouma the story-teller charms us with a moving story about ecumenicity's outward, public side. . . In good Dutch Reformed style, Rev. Bouma wants things out in the open.
— From the *Introduction* by Nelson D. Kloosterman

Subject: Church History   **Age: 14-99**
ISBN 0-921100-36-1   **Can.$15.95 U.S.$13.90**

The Practice of Political Spirituality
by McKendree R. Langley
Episodes from the public career of Abraham Kuyper, 1879-1918

"In an age in which Christians sense a growing warfare with secular humanism, McKendree R. Langley's thorough study of Abraham Kuyper's largely successful application of Christian political ideas to Dutch life is extraordinarily valuable." — Joel Nederhood.

Time: 1879-1918   **Age: 16-99**
ISBN 0-88815-070-9   **Can.$9.95 U.S.$8.90**

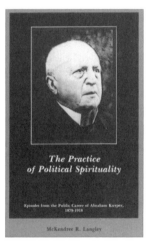

The Church in the Twentieth Century
by L. Praamsma

The Church in the world — that's the central theme of this stimulating survey of the fortunes of God's people in the twentieth century. Dr. Praamsma shows that our world is in turmoil; he highlights the warfare, upheaval, revolution, political confusion, and moral degeneration. The Church stands in the midst of this turmoil with a message of hope and redemption.

Time: 1900-1975   **Age: 13-99**
ISBN 0-88815-041-5   **Can.$9.95 U.S.$8.90**

R.B. A Prophet in the Land
by Edward Heerema

A biography of Rienk Bouke Kuiper, Preacher - Theologian - Churchman. P.Y. De Jong: This book had to appear. It is well written. It makes R.B. come alive. It reminds the reader of the tremendous impact which his life and labors have made on the Reformed community.

Subject: Biography   **Age: 14-99**
ISBN 0-88815-054-7   **Can.$9.95 U.S.$8.90**

A Theatre in Dachau by Hermanus Knoop

Rev. Jerome Julien in *The Outlook*, Those dreadful years of Nazi oppression in the Netherlands are catalogued here in an amazing way. Not only Jews, but faithful ministers of God's Word were touched, too. And from the caldron of torture the Lord received some of His servants to Himself: Revs. Kapteyn, Sietsma, and Tunderman. Others came through it, refined in God's crucible. . . The beauty of this book is found in the constant Christian testimony found in it. It is more than an account of atrocity; it is his personal reactions as a firmly founded believer to whom the Holy Spirit continued to apply God's marvellous Word. Every believer should read this little volume. This reviewer could hardly put it down because it is so moving.

Time: 1940-1943   Age: 14-99
ISBN 0-921100-20-5   Can.$14.95 U.S.$12.90

Johannes C. Sikkel: A Pioneer in Social Reform by R.H. Bremmer

The prophetical character of Sikkel's work lies, in the first place, in his Scriptural evaluation of the socialistic ideal of society. He discerned its anti-Christian character, which aimed to make the state all powerful. This criticism remains valid over against the neo-Marxists of today. In the second place, Sikkel's prophetical spirit becomes evident in his struggle for a vision of a society in which the antithesis between capital and labour is taken away through the establishment of enterprise as an organic community. The Christian commandment to love one's neighbour is Sikkel's driving force here. This love for one's neighbour demands that social warfare be settled and peace be restored by means of consultation between

capital and labour. In the third place, Sikkel's zeal for a Scriptural appreciation of labour as something which belongs to man's task as God's image bearer is of great importance. Labour is not, in the first place, a matter of wages but of fulfilling one's God-given task. The question of wages should be viewed from that perspective. To use Sikkel's words, "We Christians have the calling to proceed, to explore the way, if possible to clear the way, and in love to bring to our fellowmen the witness to the way of God. We Christians must believe that God lives, and that His grace is able to triumph over the spirit of evil. And in faith and with zeal, we must prayerfully look to the victory."

Time: 1856-1920   Age: 14-99
ISBN 0-921100-89-2   Can.$6.95 U.S.$5.90

Seeking Our Brothers in the Light: A Plea for Reformed Ecumenicity
Edited by Theodore Plantinga

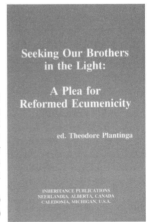

Al Bezuyen in *Revival*: The book should well serve office bearers and lay people interested in closer contact with the liberated Churches. The work is not exhaustive but rather functions as a spring board from which further study can find a solid beginning and seeks to clear the water that must be entered if ecumenical relations are to take place between the CRC and American / Canadian Reformed Churches.

Subject: Ecclesiastical Unity / History   Age: 15-99
ISBN 0-921100-48-5   Can.$5.00 U.S.$4.50

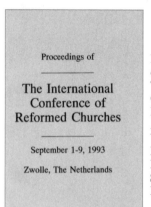

Proceedings of The International Conference of Reformed Churches September 1-9, 1993 Zwolle, The Netherlands

Included are the conference papers which were delivered for the general public in the evening sessions: The Wrath of God as an Essential Part of Mission - C.J. Haak; Prophecy Today? - Norris Wilson; Catechism Preaching - N.H. Gootjes; Christology and Mission - Alisdair I. Macleod; Recent Criticisms of the Westminster Confession of Faith - R.S. Ward; Redemptive Historical Preaching - H.M. Ohmann; Remarks on Church and Tolerance - J. Kamphuis.

Subject: Theology / Ethics Age: 16-99
ISBN 0-921100-49-3 Can.$9.95 U.S.$8.90

Proceedings *of The International Conference of Reformed Churches October 15-23, 1997 Seoul, Korea*

Biblical Principles for the Relation between Church and State - R. C. Beckett; The Principles of Reformed Missions - Mark T. Bube; Challenges of the Charismatic Movement to the Reformed Tradition - Richard B. Gaffin, Jr.; Women in Office: especially about "deaconesses" - Soon Gil Hur; The Ministry of the Word amongst Asian Religious People (Hindus, Buddhists, Jains, and Zoroastrians) - David John.

Subject: Theology / Ethics Age: 16-99
ISBN 0-921100-73-6 Can.$9.95 U.S.$8.90

Proceedings of the International Conference of Reformed Churches June 20-27, 2001 Philadelphia, U.S.A.

Included are the following papers: Biblical Principles of the Unity of the Church — A Reformed (Continental) Perspective - J. DeJong; The Unity of the Church in the Westminster Tradition - W.D.J. McKay; Hermeneutics and the Bible - J. van Bruggen; Work Among the Jewish People: Historical Perspectives and the Contemporary Challenge - J.S. Ross; The Regulative Principle of Worship - G.I. Williamson; The work of the Holy Spirit in the Believer: Illustrated by the Spirit's office of leading the believer from regeneration to glorification - C. Pronk.

Subject: Theology / Ethics Age: 16-99
ISBN 0-921100-16-7 Can.$11.95 U.S.$9.90

Also available: *Proceedings of The International Conference of Reformed Churches June 19-28, 1989 Langley, B.C. Canada*

Included are the conference papers which were delivered for the general public in the evening sessions: Nehemiah the Rebuilder - C. Graham; Baptism with the Holy Spirit - J. van Bruggen; Christology - D. Macleod; Apartheid - J. Douma; The Tangun Shrine Worship and Radical Christian Movement in Korea - Ho Jin Jun; The Elder as Preserver and Nurturer of Life in the Covenant - C. Van Dam.

Subject: Theology / Ethics Age: 16-99
Cat. Nr. ICRC 1989 Can.$9.95 U.S.$8.90

What the Spirit Says to the Churches
by Jerome M. Julien

Jelle Tuininga in *Christian Renewal*: The sermons are easy to read and to understand. . . the book is recommended, and would make a welcome gift.

Subject: Revelation 2 & 3   **Age: 12-99**
ISBN 0-921100-76-0   **Can.$9.95 U.S.$8.90**

Hal Lindsey and Biblical Prophecy
by C. Van der Waal

Hal Lindsey uses Biblical prophecy to open a supermarket, writes the author, a supermarket in which he sells inside information about the near future, especially World War III. The source of his information are the books of Daniel, Revelation, Ezekiel, and Matthew 24. Come, buy and read!

Dr. Van der Waal not only analyzes Lindsey's weaknesses and mistakes, he also lays down basic guidelines for reading Biblical prophecy - especially the book of Revelation.

Subject: Book of Revelation   **Age: 16-99**
ISBN 0-921100-31-0   **Can.$9.95 U.S.$8.90**

Is the Bible a Jigsaw Puzzle . . .
by T. Boersma

An Evaluation of Hal Lindsey's Writings. Is Lindsey's "jigsaw puzzle" approach the proper way to read Scripture? Was the Bible written to foretell the events of our decade?

Subject: Book of Revelation   **Age: 16-99**
ISBN 0-88815-019-9   **Can.$7.95 U.S.$6.90**

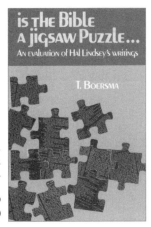

The Romance of Protestantism
by Deborah Alcock

The Romance of Protestantism addresses one of the most damaging and (historically) effective slanders against the Reformed faith, which is that it is cold and doctrinaire. What a delight to find a book which documents the true warmth of the Protestant soul. I recommend this book highly.
— Douglas Wilson, editor of *Credenda/Agenda*

Time: 1390-1800 **Age: 12-99**
ISBN 0-921100-88-4 **Can.$11.95 U.S.$9.90**

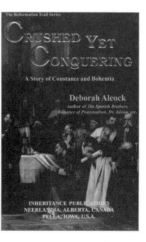

Crushed Yet Conquering
by Deborah Alcock

A gripping story filled with accurate historical facts about John Huss and the Hussite wars. Hardly any historical novel can be more captivating and edifying than this book. Even if Deborah Alcock was not the greatest of nineteenth century authors, certainly she is our most favourite.
— Roelof & Theresa Janssen

Time: 1414-1436 **Age: 11-99**
ISBN 1-894666-01-1 **Can.$19.95 U.S.$14.90**

A Sign of Faithfulness by H. Westerink

H. Westerink's book on baptism is a jewel. One seldom comes across a book that simultaneously matches such simplicity to profundity, and vice versa. The author excels at clarifying the marvellous continuity (and discontinuity) between the old and new covenant with respect to the question of baptism — infant baptism in particular. — J. Mark Beach

Subject: Covenant / Baptism **Age: 12-99**
ISBN 0-921100-00-0 **Can.$9.95 U.S.$8.90**

Abraham's Sacrifice
by
Cor Van Rijswijk

Abraham was rich. He had many cows and sheep, donkeys and camels. He also had lots of gold and silver. The Lord had given him all these animals and things.

This book is part of *The Word of the King Series*. The purpose of this series is to present Bible stories in such a fashion that young children can read them. Read them to your four or five-year-old, and let your six or seven-year-old use them as readers.

Time: Abraham **Age: 4-8**
ISBN 1-984666-21-6 **Can.$8.95 U.S.$7.90**